_____Man
Controlled

MAN
CONTROLLED

Readings in the Psychology of Behavior Control

Edited by
Marvin Karlins
and Lewis M. Andrews

THE FREE PRESS, NEW YORK
COLLIER-MACMILLAN LIMITED, LONDON

Fp

The Free Press
A Division of The Macmillan Company
866 Third Avenue, New York, New York 10022

Collier-Macmillan Canada Ltd., Toronto, Ontario

Library of Congress Catalog Card Number: 76-156841

printing number
1 2 3 4 5 6 7 8 9 10

For Annette, Shel, Jill,
Michelle, and Nancy.
M. K.

For my parents.
L. M. A.

Contents

Preface

The contemporary student demands a *relevant* education—a learning experience that is pertinent to his personal needs and social conscience. The subject matter of this book, the control of human behavior, meets the test of relevance—not only for the student but for every person. It is relevant because we are all practitioners and products of behavior control; because, in the final analysis, the manipulation of human conduct is intimately bound up with the present condition and future direction of mankind.

Ours is not the first book on behavior control, but hopefully it is the most comprehensive. Our goal in editing the volume will be achieved if we can give the reader a feeling for the pervasiveness of behavior control in his everyday life; if we can provide him with an appreciation of the myriad ways in which his day-to-day conduct can be regulated. To do this we will be examining not one or two, but all the major ways human behavior is controlled—some as ancient as human society, some as modern as radio-controlled electrical stimulation of the human brain.

In our efforts to compile a relevant set of readings we have taken the following steps to try to make this book more useful and meaningful to student and teacher alike:

(1) *Editorial comment introduces each article and each section in the book.*

(2) In all but two of the text selections, human (rather than animal) behavior is studied. In choosing mainly those works utilizing human subjects we were quite cognizant of the important role animals play in our understanding of behavior control. Certainly some of our most vital discoveries about regulating human conduct have and will come from work with lower organisms. Our decision to limit animal studies in the volume was not based, then, on a lack of appreciation for "rat research" but rather on the belief that a book about human behavior control should be grounded in studies utilizing the human organism as the object of investigation.

(3) Most of the text selections have been published in the past decade. In the rapidly advancing field of behavior control research—where today's discovery is tomorrow's footnote—knowledge of current scholarship is imperative. Discussion of "classic" studies will be reserved for editorial comment designed to place contemporary investigations in their proper historical perspective.

(4) The text is distinguished by its breadth of coverage. Unlike other books on behavior control which discuss *only* behavior modification *or* hypnosis *or* genetic engineering, etc., this volume introduces the reader to *all* the important forms of behavior regulation.

(5) We have included a list of further readings at the end of the text for those students who want additional literature sources on behavior control.

(6) Finally, we have tried to select articles which are well-written and interesting. The study of human behavior control can be a tremendously exciting undertaking. We have tried to convey that excitement to the reader through the text material we have selected.

Marvin Karlins
Lewis M. Andrews

ACKNOWLEDGMENT

The photographs herein identified in José M. R. Delgado's essay on brain stimulation (pp. 40ff.) as Figures 1 and 2 previously appeared in Delgado, J. M. R., "Free Behavior and Brain Stimulation," in Pfeiffer & Smythies (eds.), *International Review of Neurobiology* (New York: Academic Press, 1964). The Delgado Figure 3 photographs previously appeared in Delgado, J. M. R., "Aggression and Defense under Cerebral Radio Control," in Clemente & Lindsley (eds.), *Aggression and Defense: Neural Mechanisms and Social Patterns*, UCLA Forum in Medical Sciences, Vol. 5, No. 7 (Berkeley: University of California Press, 1967), pp. 171–193.

part 1:

An introduction to the study of behavior control

José Delgado is a man who does some very interesting things with electricity. Once he used "electric power" to fix a bullfight—a wise move, considering he was in the ring at the time and, as a Yale professor of medicine, not exactly an accomplished matador. Why did Delgado undertake such a Plimptonesque assignment? To demonstrate the behavior control potential of a scientific procedure known as ESB (electrical stimulation of the brain). Such a demonstration was made possible by "doctoring" the bull before it entered the ring: surgically implanting into its brain electrodes which were capable of delivering minute electrical pulses when activated by remote control radio signals. Once this was accomplished Delgado could engage his adversary without fear. When the bull began his charge, the Yale surgeon simply pressed a button on his radio transmitter and watched as the bull, properly stimulated, halted abruptly and lost interest in the flashing red cape.

Delgado has not limited his research to lower animals. He has also exposed the human brain to the ubiquitous electrical probe. Reading his latest book, *Physical Control of the Mind* (1969), one gets a feeling for the power and promise of brain stimulation as an instrument for behavior control. In the book, Delgado claims that brain implants in man have ". . . blocked the thinking process, inhibited speech and movement, or in other cases [have] evoked pleasure, laughter, friendliness, verbal output, hostility, fear, hallucinations, and memories." He draws on his own work

1

to support such a claim, work reported on pages 40 to 68 of this volume.

Some of Delgado's research reports read like science fiction scenarios. In one set of experiments, for example, he was able to elicit pleasurable sensations in three epilepsy patients by electrically stimulating their brains. The experience must have been rewarding. One patient, normally reserved and poised, ". . . openly expressed her fondness for the therapist (who was new to her), kissed his hands, and talked about her immense gratitude for what was being done for her" (Delgado, 1969). A second patient was not to be outdone; during the stimulation she expressed her desire to marry the therapist!

Delgado's exploits have not gone unnoticed. His research, for example, forms the basis for not one, but *two New York Times* editorials. To really appreciate the impact of his work, one must read these editorials. It is here that one gets a feeling for the importance of Delgado and an insight into the awesome implications of his research. We have reprinted the most recent editorial (September 19, 1970).

> If the late George Orwell were writing a sequel to "1984" today, he would probably reject as archaic the propaganda techniques for controlling people's minds described in his famous anti-Utopian classic. Today, for example, he might envisage a society in which a newborn baby's first experience would be neurosurgery, an operation in which the child's brain was fitted with miniaturized radio devices connected to every major center controlling reason and emotion.
>
> Children in such a society might be raised as flesh-and-blood electrical toys, whose ideas and behavior were directed by computer signals. Any aberrant or heretical ideas would be transmitted to the computer, which would be programmed to take appropriate action to restore control.
>
> If this is still fantasy, it is not so fantastic as it was before Dr. José M. R. Delgado of Yale reported his latest work. By fitting radio equipment into a chimpanzee's brain, he has developed a technique which permits a computer to make a specific change in the test animal's brain waves.
>
> That represents at least a first step down the road toward the nightmare vision of a brain-controlled population. Over the past decade Dr. Delgado has reported using electrical stimulation to stop a charging bull, to make a female monkey reject her children and to perform other similar feats. Dr. Delgado himself some years ago said that experimental evidence seems to "support the distasteful conclusion that motion, emotion and behavior can be directed by electrical forces and that humans can be controlled like robots by push-buttons."

Dr. Delgado's work is aimed at finding new techniques to help those striken with mental illness, epilepsy and such afflictions, not to create some future super-totalitarian state. Fortunately, human ignorance about the brain remains so vast that there is no imminent prospect that the techniques being worked on at Yale could have Orwellian significance. Nevertheless, the horrifying prospect arises that in the 21st century the lexicographers may have to drop the verb "to brainwash" and replace it with "to brainwave."

Professor Delgado is not the only investigator working with human brain stimulation, and human brain stimulation is not the only form of behavior control being scientifically investigated. We have used Delgado and his research to make a point: through new developments in the science of behavior control, man stands, for the first time, on the verge of regulating his own psychosocial evolution. And, say some, his next step will not be long in coming.

What are some of these new developments in the science of behavior control? We present them on pages 15 to 89. Brain stimulation is one. Behavior modification is another. So are advances in genetic engineering and psychopharmacology.

Although scientific methods for controlling behavior are becoming increasingly important, they are not the only methods by which human conduct is regulated. Other factors play a significant role in determining a person's actions—such as his peer group, his cultural background, and his heredity. Someday all of man's behavior may be manipulated by scientific procedures—but until that time, authors of books on behavior control are left with the task of reviewing the other variables that determine human conduct. The readings on pages 159 to 188 and 191 to 235 serve such a purpose. Taken in conjunction with pages 151 to 156, they will, hopefully, give the reader an appreciation of the forces regulating his behavior and help him judge for himself just how far man has come in his quest to control his own destiny.

Living with the Faustian power

Lewis M. Andrews and Marvin Karlins

Social science today is as much feared as a hidden persuader or manipulator of man as a generation ago it was admired as a liberator.

DAVID RIESMAN

INTRODUCTION Many people have lurid ideas about behavior control, particularly about the scientific regulation of human conduct. Some are frightened by investigators who try to control a person's actions; others think such efforts are evil. Still others believe that a clique of unscrupulous politicians might employ scientific procedures to enslave a nation. The following selection discusses some of the issues involved in behavior manipulation and points up three unwarranted assumptions many Americans make about it.

The fear of powerful new knowledge is a human reflex of long standing. It is reflected in the myths of Prometheus, Icarius, Dr. Faustus, and the tree of knowledge in the Garden of Eden. It is not surprising, then, that famed political scientist Herman Kahn should refer to the technology of behavior control as a "Faustian power." Nor is it surprising that such power should be regarded as evil. "Those who have explicitly avowed an interest in control have been roughly treated by history," notes psychologist B. F. Skinner. "Machiavelli is the great prototype. As Macaulay said of him, 'Out of his surname they coined an epithet for a knave and out of his Christian name a synonym for the devil'" (Rogers & Skinner, 1956).

Lewis M. Andrews and Marvin Karlins, *Requiem for Democracy?*, copyright 1971. Reprinted by permission of Holt, Rinehart & Winston, New York.

In contemporary America the fear of new knowledge is reinforced by the myth of the omnipotent scientist—the person endowed with awesome powers created in superlaboratories. That such people do not exist hardly seems to matter. The public persists in speculating that men armed with scientific know-how might be able to make anyone do anything.

The citizen can hardly be blamed for his unrest. His fear of scientific behavior control has been nurtured on a diet of exaggerations and half-truths from overzealous reporters, inflammatory pseudoscience writers, imaginative novelists, flamboyant scientists, and government alarmists. Why shouldn't he be uneasy? He hears vague references to brainwashing, truth serums, and hypnosis. He reads novels like *1984* and *Brave New World,* which describe awesome behavior control procedures such as socialization by aversive conditioning, chemical "stunting" of normal brain growth, mass use of lobotomy operations, and the attachment of human brains to computers by micro-surgery. If he prefers nonfiction, *The Hidden Persuaders, Battle for the Mind, The Rape of the Mind,* and *The Brain Watchers* treat him to some unsettling prophecies (Karlins & Abelson, 1970). The "danger" of behavior control is constantly exploited on television in such science-fiction operas as *Outer Limits, The Invaders, Man from U.N.C.L.E.,* and *Mission Impossible.* And Mary Shelley's *Frankenstein,* revived every few years by Hollywood, is a constant reminder to movie audiences of the "evil" inherent in behavior engineering.

Now it is certainly true that the technology of behavior control should not be taken lightly. We will argue that it has profound implications for society. But some of the current fears concerning the scientific control of behavior have little or no factual basis. In order to face the real problems of the Faustian power, we must dispel three *unwarranted* assumptions many Americans hold about behavior control.

1. *Man would be free in the absence of scientific behavior control.* In a famous speech before the American Psychological Association in 1956, the late Dr. J. Robert Oppenheimer warned that "the psychologist can hardly do anything without realizing that for him the acquisition of knowledge opens up the most terrifying prospects of controlling what people do and how they think and how they behave and how they feel." Implicit in Oppenheimer's statement is the idea that in the absence of behavioral science man is somehow "free." What follows from this is the fear that most forms of scientific behavior control are intrinsically evil because they deprive man of his "freedom."

We cannot deal rationally with the behavioral sciences until we realize that control per se is not even an issue. From the scientist's viewpoint, all human actions follow laws and patterns, just as physical events do, and are, in that sense, controlled. Behavior control techniques do not impose a "scientific straitjacket" on human behavior; they merely replace the so-called "normal" influences of nature and society, which may include arbitrary parents, incompetent teachers, unrealistic TV programs and chemically polluted food. As Nobel Laureate Joshua Lederberg has argued, abolishing the study and manipulation of human behavior would not alter the fact that man responds in consistent ways to his environment. The real question is not "Should man be controlled?" but "How should he be controlled?" By the erratic forces of nature, or by man himself?

The world is, in a sense, one large "Skinner box," or behavior control laboratory. The contents of a man's environment—his parents and friends, his house and clothing, his food and medicines, his tools and appliances—are the mechanisms by which his behavior is modified and directed. Skinner has frequently pointed out how people living together in groups consciously and unconsciously control each other's actions. When an individual behaves in a fashion approved by the group, he receives admiration, approval, affection, and many other reinforcements that increase the likelihood that he will continue to behave in the same fashion. Similarly, when he behaves in a disapproved manner, rewards are withdrawn or punishment is applied. Dissenters and nonconformists are not "free" of control; they have simply internalized a divergent program of attitudes and responses as a consequence of peculiar childhood and adolescent conditioning experiences. The relationship between early experience and student radicalism, for example, is carefully documented in Yale psychologist Kenneth Keniston's highly acclaimed study, *The Young Radicals.*

The knowledge that all behavior is controlled by scientifically determined laws is hard to accept. As Dostoevsky put it:

> Out of sheer ingratitude man will play you a dirty trick, just to prove that men are still men and not the keys of a piano. . . . And even if you could prove that man is only a piano key, he would still do something out of sheer perversity—he would create destruction and chaos—just to gain his point. . . . And if all of this could in turn be analyzed and prevented by prediction that it would occur, then man would go absolutely mad to prove his point [As quoted in Skinner, 1955–1956].

Psychologist Abraham Maslow (1966) has also commented on man's resentment of the notion that he is predictable. He cites the case of "a ten-year-old girl, known for always being a good citizen, law-abiding and dutiful [who] unexpectedly disrupted classroom discipline by passing out French fried potatoes instead of notebooks because, as she later said, everyone just took her good behavior for granted." As the distinguished scholar Ludwig Immergluck (1964) has pointed out, the notion that man is "a free agent propelled by self-initiated inner forces that defy, by their very nature, prediction or scientifically ordered description" seems to be a necessary illusion. But it *is* an illusion. Behavioral science does not create special biological and psychological laws in order to control man; it deals with patterns that already exist in nature.

2. *The scientific control of behavior is evil.* Once we realize that all behavior is controlled, it follows that the technology of behavior control is not good or bad, but neutral. Saying that behavioral control is evil is like condemning atomic physics. An atomic reaction can light a city or burn it. The problem is not the technology, but how man chooses to use it. There is a certain irony in the science of behavior control: as it develops the power to free men's minds from worry (for example, through therapy), it also gains the means to enslave his thoughts. Like the atom, the science of behavior control is neutral. Man will determine whether research findings will be used to liberate or to subjugate the human spirit, to serve or to destroy, to cure or to infect.

Since the popular arts have given so much attention to deleterious applications of behavioral science, we wish to stress its positive potential. Doctors have practiced behavioral control on a limited scale for centuries, using medicines to remedy diseases and bodily malfunctions. It is doubtful that a person cured of a once-fatal disease such as polio would complain that his freedom to die had been violated! Biomedical researchers are now working on ways to cure heart disease, cancer, and genetically induced defects, such as dwarfism, hemophilia, and assorted allergies. Psychologists are actively seeking ways to improve man's mental health, memory, and creative potential—all necessary attributes if man wishes to survive in his demanding, rapidly changing world.

Experiments at the University of Chicago and the Langley Neuropsychiatric Institute are aimed directly at employing behavioral science to free man from external and internal forces. Student subjects are trained to exercise conscious control over the production of alpha waves —waves measured by the EEG (electroencephalogram) that are associated with states of tranquility. Psychologist Joseph Kamiya (1968) suggests that if different subjective states—anxiety, misery, euphoria, and tranquility— can be mapped out and linked with specific brain states as measured by the EEG, people could be trained to control their moods at will. People in full control of their internal conscious states would be well prepared to resist coercion. Even Carl Rogers, who at times has been cynical about the benefits of a human control technology, concedes that "the behavioral sciences could move toward the release of potentialities and capacities. I think that there is enough work already done to indicate that one can set up conditions which release behavior that is more variable, more spon-

taneous, more creative, and hence in its specifics, more unpredictable"
(Rogers, 1961).

Those who equate behavior control with evil frequently refer to
Aldous Huxley's *Brave New World* to substantiate their arguments. On
the issue of control, Huxley is frequently misinterpreted. It is instructive
to compare *Brave New World* with *Island,* one of Huxley's later novels.
Both describe programmed societies, but with different results. In *Brave
New World,* people use technology to distract and enslave themselves.
In *Island* the same technology is employed to advance human awareness
and to broaden the scope of human action.

We do not overlook the possibility that behavior control is dangerous
in an accidental sense. If we can draw an analogy to ecology, we must recognize that the human animal is a delicate eco-system and that any attempt to change his behavior in a systematic way should be carefully
controlled for possible side effects. But the caution necessary in experiments with humans does not lead to the conclusion that control per se
is bad. If it did, medicine would still be in the hands of tribal witch
doctors.

3. *Only scientists or politicians can use behavior control technology
to regulate human conduct.* There is always the danger, of course, that unscrupulous men in science or government might try to employ behavior
control technology on a mass scale to impose their will on the public.
Today such a possibility is remote simply because regulatory procedures
are not yet powerful enough to sway a nation full of unwilling minds
without the active involvement of millions of scientific or political con-
spirators.

*At this point in the developing science of behavior control, the real
potential for irresponsible use of the Faustian power resides not with a
tyrannical government or an elite corps of scientists, but rather with individuals who employ behavior control technology on a personal or interpersonal basis.* (This is the reason psychologists are licensed.) It is at this
"local" level that regulatory procedures difficult to implement on a mass
scale become effective.

An example of interpersonal abuse is the case of two students who
decided to change an athlete roommate, by conditioning, into an art
lover. They hung various pictures on the walls and, knowing their friend
liked attention, deprived him of it. They ignored him completely, unless
he happened to notice a picture. Within a week the roommate was talking about the pictures all the time. The conversion was complete when
he got up one morning and said, "Hey, fellows, how about going to the
museum?" (Wald, 1965).

Many doctors, noting the widespread use of tranquilizers and anti-
depressants, have warned that people may unknowingly lock themselves

into self-imposed drug prisons. In a frightening article in the *Atlantic Monthly* (1966), journalist Bruce Jackson describes the refreshments at a middle-class pill party:

> Next to the candy dish filled with Dexedrine, Dexamyl, Eskatrol, Desbutal, and a few other products I haven't yet learned to identify, near the five pound box of Dexedrine tablets someone had brought, were two bottles. One was filled with Dexedrine Elixir, the other with Dexamyl Elixir.

Those who attend such parties are "well educated (largely college graduates), are older (25 to 40), and middle class (with a range of occupations: writers, artists, lawyers, TV executives, journalists, political aides, housewives)." The mere existence of drugs does not rob an individual of his autonomy, but it does give him the option of surrendering it. If, then, he evolves into a contented cow, it will not be because he is manipulated by a clique of omnipotent rulers. It will be because he has decided that there is nothing more worthwhile than "grazine."

NO ESCAPE FROM FREEDOM

The problem posed by behavior control is not external tyranny. On the contrary, the real problem is the threat of freedom. If we take the deterministic stance and agree with neurophysiologist Ralph W. Gerard that "there can be no twisted thought without a twisted molecule," and if we recognize that a perfected behavior control technology is within our grasp, then for the first time in history we are truly responsible for our destiny. Or as Julian Huxley put it, man is now, in effect, "managing director of the business of evolution" with no possibility of losing the job (Huxley, 1957). Whether he chooses to approach the problem or to let things drift, he makes a choice. Ironically, the deterministic science of man has burdened him with the hardest problem of all: freedom. In short, there are no more excuses for human misery. If man has the knowledge to create Julian Huxley's "fulfillment society," he can only blame himself if he produces anything less.

If the notion that determinism is liberating seems a paradox, we must recognize the extent to which tyrants have abused the concept of freedom in order to exact rigid social compliance from others. If man has free will, the tyrant argues, then he is responsible—that is, punishable—for not complying with the dictates of the social elite. Indeed, "freedom" is often a tool of repressive societies, both religious and secular. The early Christian leaders, for example, had to postulate human free will within the context of divine determinism in order to maintain control over the laity. Saint Augustine records his difficulty in disciplining a group of libertine monks whose claim to innocence was that their actions were "fated by an omnipotent God." The Russians have recently faced the same problem. Immediately after the Russian Revolution, the Soviets rejected introspectionist psychologies because they smacked of free will, which contradicated Marxist determinism. By the 1940s, however, the Soviets found it necessary to incorporate the concept of freedom in their psychology to justify increasing authoritarian suppression. Freedom was defined as "the recognition of necessity" by consciousness. This doctrine, in addition to resolving Marxism with voluntarism, served political purposes:

> By postulating that conscious man is free from the determination of the immediate situation, it makes him responsible for his immediate behavior. By stating that consciousness is the understanding of relationships and that "freedom is the recognition of necessity," it offers a rationale for the subjugation of the individual to the demands of society [Bauer, 1952].

History is rife with examples of tyrannical forces relying on the assumption of free will. As Skinner has observed, "The state is frequently defined in terms of power to punish, and jurisprudence leans heavily upon the associated notion of personal responsibility" (Skinner, 1955–1956).

In 1941, Erich Fromm wrote an influential book entitled *Escape from Freedom*. Its theme is familiar to any student of social science: "Modern man, freed from the bonds of traditional societies, has security, but is restrained by his desire to escape from freedom. Freedom, though it has brought him independence and rationality, has made him isolated and, thereby, anxious and powerless" (Fromm, 1941). The technology of behavior control has made escape impossible. Whatever man does, even if he burns all the behavioral science textbooks, he is choosing his ultimate destiny. Man fears the behavioral sciences, not only because they threaten to enslave him, but because—even more frightening—they threaten to free him. As Ernest Becker (1968) writes in *The Structure of Evil*, "The question that our civilization is now asked to face is whether we are ready to make man the master of his social games, rather than their unwitting servant."

REFERENCES

BAUER, R. *The new man in Soviet psychology.* Cambridge, Mass.: Harvard University Press, 1952.

BECKER, E. *The structure of evil.* New York: Braziller, 1968.

FROMM, E. *Escape from freedom.* New York: Holt, Rinehart & Winston, 1941.

HUXLEY, A. *Brave new world*. New York: Doubleday, 1932.

HUXLEY, A. *Island*. New York: Harper & Row, 1962.

HUXLEY, J. *New bottles for new wine*. New York: Harper & Row, 1957.

IMMERGLUCK, L. Determinism-freedom in contemporary psychology: An ancient problem revisited. *American Psychologist*, 19, 1964, 270–281.

JACKSON, B. White-collar pill party. *Atlantic Monthly*, August, 1966, 35–40.

KAHN, H., & WIENER, A. *The year 2000*. New York: Macmillan, 1967.

KAMIYA, J. Conscious control of brain waves. *Psychology Today*, 11, 1968, 57–60.

KARLINS, M., & ABELSON, H. *Persuasion*. New York: Springer, 1970.

KENISTON, K. *The young radicals*. New York: Harcourt, 1968.

LEDERBERG, J. Experimental genetics and human evolution. *Bulletin of the Atomic Scientists*, 22, 1966, 4–11.

MASLOW, A. *The psychology of science*. New York: Harper & Row, 1966.

OPPENHEIMER, J. R. Analogy in science. *American Psychologist*, 11, 1956, 127–135.

ROGERS, C. Cultural evolution as viewed by psychologists. *Daedalus*, 90, 1961, 574–575.

ROGERS, C., & SKINNER, B. Some issues concerning the control of human behavior: A symposium. *Science, 124*, 1956, 1057–1066.

SKINNER, B. Freedom and the control of men. *The American Scholar*, 25, 1955–1956, 47–65.

WALD, G. Determinancy, individuality, and the problem of free will. In J. Platt (Ed.), *New views of the nature of man*. Chicago: University of Chicago Press, 1965. Pp. 16–46.

part 2:

A look at some promising and not-so-promising procedures for controlling behavior

Ever since Eve's efforts were fruitful in the Garden of Eden, mortals have busied themselves creating methods to control each other's behavior. Some of these methods are well known, like brainwashing and hypnosis, others not so well known, like brain stimulation and genetic engineering. Some are relatively effective procedures for controlling behavior, others not so effective. As he reads on in this chapter, the student might be surprised to learn that the best known techniques of manipulation are *not* always the most powerful or promising approaches to regulating human conduct.

In this chapter we will examine behavior control methods that have attracted the attention of the scientific community. Scientists have raised some interesting questions and provided some interesting answers concerning the efficacy and potential of various behavior control procedures. We have listed a few of these questions below. Can you guess at the answers before you read further?

1. Can behavior modification be utilized to change a person's sexual behavior?

2. What are the implications of genetic engineering work for the control of human behavior?

3. What might happen if intelligence-controlling drugs were developed and put on the market?

4. What happens to man when the depths of his brain are stimulated by an electric probe?

5. Does advertising make a difference in consumer buying behavior?

6. Why study architecture in a book on behavior control?

7. Brainwashing: what really happened in North Korean prison camps?

8. Can hypnosis be utilized as a method of interrogation?

9. How much truth is there to truth serums?

Elimination of a sadistic fantasy by a client-controlled counterconditioning technique: a case study

Gerald C. Davison

INTRODUCTION   Under the direction of the trained professional, behavior control procedures can be used to help individuals overcome their personal problems and live happier, more meaningful lives. Nowhere is this more evident than in the practice of behavior modification—*a form of psychotherapy where the clinician systematically regulates human conduct through the use of rewards and/or punishments.*

Although behavior modification is a relatively new method of therapy, it has already shown promise in treating a wide variety of behavior problems (e.g., Brawley et al., 1969; Goorney, 1968; Hamblin et al., 1969; Lent, 1968). One such problem, a sexual aberration in a college student, is described and treated in the following case study.*

The modification of deviant sexual behavior has been approached largely through the contiguous pairing of a primary aversive stimulus with a stimulus eliciting an undesirable response (the "symptom"), the goal being to endow the inappropriate stimulus with negative properties, or at least to eliminate the unwanted positive attributes. Many such cases have been reviewed by Bandura (in press), Feldman (1966), Grossberg (1964), Kalish (1965), Rachman (1961), and Ullmann and Krasner (1965). Therapy of fetishism, homosexuality, and transvestism

* Complete bibliographic citations will be found in "Further readings," which begins on page 275.

has tended to follow this counterconditioning model (e.g., Blakemore, Thorpe, Barker, Conway, & Lavin, 1963; Davies & Morgenstern, 1960; Freund, 1960; Lavin, Thorpe, Barker, Blakemore, & Conway, 1961; Raymond, 1956; Thorpe, Schmidt, Brown, & Castell, 1964). In addition, several workers have introduced complementary procedures in attempts to endow suitable social stimuli with the positive attributes necessary to make less likely a reversion to the inappropriate goal-object. Thus, for example, Freund (1960) gave his male homosexuals not only aversion conditioning trials to pictures of men, but also exposures to pictures of nude women after injection of male hormones. Similar procedures have been employed by Thorpe, Schmidt, and Castell (1963) and Feldman and Mac-Culloch (1965).

Of particular relevance to the present study is the work of Thorpe et al. (1963). These writers report therapeutic benefit following presumably counterconditioning sessions during which efforts were made to pair female pictures with orgasm from masturbation. It was assumed that this intensely pleasurable sexual response counterconditioned the aversion to females which appeared to play a crucial role in the behavior of the homosexuals. These authors recognized the importance of a person's fantasy life to his overt behavioral adjustment, and they assumed that beneficial generalization would occur from pictorial to the real-life situation, similar to the assumptions made for systematic desensitization (Davison, in press; Wolpe, 1958). Although the therapeutic outcomes reported by Thorpe and his co-workers are equivocal in respect to actual sexual behavior, the procedures did have considerable effect on fantasies.

The possibility of extending this kind of work to an out-patient setting presented itself to the author during the course of his private practice. Various modifications of procedures used by Thorpe et al. (1963) were employed, apparently to good effect. In addition, other important issues became evident in the course of therapy, which required fewer than 5 consulting-room hours over a span of 10 wk., and it is for these heuristic reasons that the following is reported.

CASE STUDY

The client was a 21-yr.-old unmarried white male college senior majoring in history. The university counseling center had received an anxious letter from his parents, requesting help for their son in treating his introversion, procrastination, and "masochism." After working with the student for a few weeks on his tendency to wait until the last minute in his academic work, the psychologist at the center referred him to the author for help with his sexual difficulties.

Mr. M's statement of the problem was: "I'm a sadist." There followed a rather troubled account of a complete absence of "normal" sexual fantasies and activities since age 11. Masturbating about five times a week, the client's fantasies had been exclusively sadistic ones, specifically, inflicting tortures on women. He declared emphatically that he had never been sexually aroused by any other kind of image. Although generally uninterested in dating girls, he felt no aversion to them; on the contrary, he sometimes felt a "warm glow" when near them, but did not describe this at all in sexual terms. Because of his extreme concern over the content of his fantasies, however, he had dated very little and expressed no interest in the co-eds at the college. He recalled having kissed only two girls in his life, with no sexual arousal accompanying these fleeting episodes. He had never engaged in any homosexual activities or fantasies. Although expressing no guilt about his problem, he was very much worried about it inasmuch as he felt it impossible to ever contemplate marriage. This concern had recently been markedly increased upon reading an account of a Freudian interpretation of "sado-masochism." He was especially perturbed about the poor prognosis for this "illness."

Because his concern over the gravity and implications of his problem seemed at least as disruptive as the problem itself, the therapist spent most of the first session raising arguments against a disease interpretation of unusual behavior. Psychoanalytic notions were critically reviewed, and attention was directed especially to the untestability of many Freudian concepts (Levy, 1963). Instances in the therapist's own clinical work were cited to illustrate the liberating effects observed in many people when they interpret their maladaptive behavior as determined by "normal" psychological processes rather than by insidious disease processes (cf. Davison, 1966; Glasser, 1965; Maher, 1966; Mainord, 1962). Mr. M. frequently expressed relief at these ideas, and the therapist, indeed, took full advantage of his prestigious position to reinforce these notions.

Table 1—"Target" and "Back-Up" Sexual Stimuli for Client-Controlled Masturbation Sessions

Week	Target stimulus	Back-up stimulus
1	Playboy, real stimulus	Sadistic fantasy
2	Bathing-suit, real stimulus	Playboy, real stimulus
	Playboy, imaginal stimulus	Sadistic fantasy
3	Same as Week 2	Same as Week 2
4	Bathing suit, real stimulus	Playboy, real stimulus
	Playboy, imaginal stimulus	None

At the end of the session, the counterconditioning orientation which would be followed was explained (Davison, in press; Guthrie, 1935;

Wolpe, 1958), as well as the specific activities which he was to engage in during the coming week. When assured of privacy in his dormitory room (primarily on the weekend), he was first to obtain an erection by whatever means possible—undoubtedly with a sadistic fantasy, as he indicated. He was then to begin to masturbate while looking at a picture of a sexy, nude woman (the "target" sexual stimulus); *Playboy* magazine was suggested to him as a good source. If he began losing the erection, he was to switch back to his sadistic fantasy until he could begin masturbating effectively again. Concentrating again on the *Playboy* picture, he was to continue masturbating, using the fantasy only to regain erection. As orgasm was approaching, he was at all costs to focus on the *Playboy* picture, even if sadistic fantasies began to intrude. It was impressed on him that gains would ensue only when sexual arousal was associated with the picture, and that he need not worry about indulging in sadistic fantasies at this point. The client appeared enthusiastic and hopeful as he left the office. (Table 1 summarizes the client-controlled masturbation assignments following this and succeeding consulting-room sessions.)

At the second session he reported success with the assignment: he had been able to masturbate effectively and enjoyably three times over the weekend to a particular picture from *Playboy* without once having to use a sadistic fantasy; however, it did take significantly longer to climax with the *Playboy* photograph than with the usual kind of sadistic fantasy. During the rest of the week, when he had not had enough privacy for real-life visual stimulation, he had "broken down" a few times and used his sadistic fantasies.

Much of this session was then spent in talking to him about some of the social-sexual games which most males play in our culture, especially the "mental undressing" of attractive women. The purpose was to engage him in the kind of "stud" conversation which he had never experienced and which, it was felt, would help to change his orientation toward girls. The therapist reassured him that the first direct contacts with girls are sometimes disappointing; he had to admit, however, that his extreme sensitivity about the sadistic fantasies had severely limited his experience.

During the coming week he was, first of all, to ask out on a coffee date any girl whom he felt he *might* find attractive, even for a sadistic fantasy. He was also to spend some time between classes just looking at some of the co-eds and noting some of their more remarkable attributes. Finally, his masturbation sessions were to be structured as follows: The real-life pictorial stimuli were to be girls either in bathing suits or lingerie, used in the same way as the *Playboy* picture the preceding week; this latter stimulus was to be used as "back-up" stimulus, replacing the sadistic fantasies in the event that he was losing his erection. Attention was also to be directed to imaginal sexual stimuli, and when masturbating in this way he was to use the *Playboy* image, with a sadistic fantasy as back-up.

The third session lasted half an hour. He had procrastinated so long in asking for a date that the girls he contacted had already made other plans; the therapist expressed his disappointment quite openly and urged him even more strongly to follow through with this task. He had managed to spend some time looking at girls but did not note significant sexual arousal, except when a sadistic fantasy crept in occasionally. He had masturbated only once to real-life stimuli, using some bathing-suit pictures from a weekly national news magazine; this was successful, though it took longer even than when the *Playboy* material was used previously. When masturbating to imaginal sexual stimuli, he had relied almost exclusively on his sadistic fantasies rather than utilizing the *Playboy* picture in imagination as he had in real life 1 wk. earlier.

His reluctance to give up the sadistic fantasies prompted the use of the following procedure, the idea for which had been obtained from Lazarus (1958). With his eyes closed, he was instructed to imagine a typical sadistic scene, a pretty girl tied to stakes on the ground and struggling tearfully to extricate herself. While looking at the girl, he was told to imagine someone bringing a branding iron toward his eyes, ultimately searing his eyebrows. A second image was attempted when this proved abortive, namely, being kicked in the groin by a ferocious-looking karate expert. When he reported himself indifferent to this image as well, the therapist depicted to him a large bowl of "soup," composed of steaming urine with reeking fecal boli bobbing around on top. His grimaces, contortions, and groans indicated that an effective image had been found, and the following 5 min. were spent portraying his drinking from the bowl, with accompanying nausea, at all times while peering over the floating debris at the struggling girl. After opening his eyes at the end of the imaginal ordeal, he reported spontaneously that he felt quite nauseated, and some time was spent in casual conversation in order to dispel the mood.

His assignments for masturbation during the coming week entailed increasing the frequency of his real-life masturbatory exposures to bathing-suit pictures, along with concerted efforts to use the *Playboy* stimuli in imagination as he had in real life 2 wk. earlier, resorting to sadistic fantasies if necessary.

The fourth session lasted only 15 min. He had managed to arrange a date for the coming weekend and found himself almost looking forward to it. Again, he had masturbated several times to a real-life picture of a bathing beauty. In fantasy he had managed to use the *Playboy* girl exclusively two out of five times, with no noticeable diminution in enjoyment.

He was to continue using the bathing-suit pictures while masturbating to real-life stimuli, but to avoid sadistic fantasies altogether, the idea being that any frustration engendered by this deprivation would simply add to his general sexual arousal and thereby make it all the easier to use the *Playboy* stimuli in imagination.

The fifth session, also lasting only 15 min., opened with Mr. M animatedly praising the efficacy of the therapy. He had masturbated several times, mostly to real-life bathing-suit pictures, with no problems and, most importantly, had found himself *unable* to obtain an erection to a sadistic fantasy. In fact, he even had difficulty conjuring up an image. He had also spent considerable time with two girls, finding himself at one point having to resist an urge to hug one of them—a totally new experience for him. He enthusiastically spoke of how different he felt about "normal dating," and a 1-mo. period without interviews was decided upon to let him follow his new inclinations.

The sixth session, 1 mo. later, revealed that his sadistic fantasies had not reappeared, and that he had been masturbating effectively to both real-life and imaginal appropriate sexual stimuli. He had not, however, been dating, and some time was spent stressing the importance of seeking "normal" sexual outlets. He felt strongly, however, that the sexual problem had been successfully handled and requested that his procrastination problem be taken up. Two sessions were subsequently devoted to following the same general strategy that had been adopted, with some success, by the college counselor, that is, arranging for various rewards to be made contingent upon certain academic task-performances. Mr. M did report doing "an enormous amount of work" during 1 wk.—out of fear of having to admit to the therapist that he had been loafing. Practical considerations, however, made it clear that this handling of the problem, even if it should prove effective, was not as realistic as his facing the reality that there was no "magic pill" to eliminate his procrastination. Therapy, therefore, was terminated, with no sadistic fantasies having occurred for over 1 mo., and with the problem of procrastination left more or less untouched.

A follow-up of 1 mo. was obtained by telephone. Mr. M reported that there was still no sign of sadistic fantasies and that, indeed, he was no longer even thinking about the issue. He had still not "gotten around" to asking any girl out on a date, and the therapist urged him in no uncertain terms to tackle this aspect of his procrastination problem with the vigor that he had shown in regard to his studies (where significant improvement had been made). Extensive and persistent questioning failed to evoke any reported aversion to girls as the basis of his reluctance to ask them out.

DISCUSSION

As with every case study, one must necessarily speculate, to a large extent, on the "active ingredients." Hypotheses are not readily strengthened from such data. As a demonstration of various strategies, however, the present report does seem to be of heuristic value.

1. The first significant event in therapy was the author's general reaction to the client's statement of the problem, "I'm a sadist." After Mr. M had recounted the horror with which he had read about his mysterious "illness" in Freudian terms, the therapist countered with a logical attack that made the hour take on more the characteristics of a graduate seminar than a psychotherapy session, except perhaps for the warmth, support, and acceptance which were deliberately conveyed. A key factor in this initial phase was an attempt to change the client's general orientation to his problem. As this writer has usually found, the client had been regarding himself as "sick," qualitatively different from so-called "normals." Furthermore, the idea that much of his behavior was determined by forces working in devious ways in his "unconscious" was quite troubling, as was the poor prognosis. As reported in the case material, these issues were dealt with immediately, and significant relief was afforded the young man simply by reconstructing the problem for him in conditioning terms. It would, indeed, have been interesting and valuable to attempt some sort of assessment of improvement at this very point.

2. Inextricably intertwined with the foregoing was the outlining of a therapeutic strategy: his sadistic fantasies were to be attacked by procedures aimed at counterconditioning the maladaptive emotional reactions to specific kinds of stimuli. The client perceived the theoretical rationale as reasonable and was satisfied with the actual techniques which would be employed. Furthermore, being able to buttress the plan with both clinical and experimental data added to its credibility. It must be emphasized that whether the data cited, or the explanation offered, are valid is an irrelevant question in the present situation. The important point is that the client's enthusiastic participation was enlisted in a therapeutic regime which, by all counts, was to be highly unconventional.

3. A third conceivably relevant variable was the "older brother" type of relationship which the therapist established in talking with Mr. M about conventional sex. Clearly the client had missed this part of the average American male's upbringing and, as has been reported, much time was spent in deliberately provocative "locker-room talk," not as an end in itself, but rather as a means of exposing him to the kinds of heterosexual ideations which seemed to the author useful in promoting nonsadistic fantasies about girls.

4. It is likely that the two positive exposures to actual women contributed to therapeutic improvement. Mr. M, having been goaded into direct social contact with girls, was fortunately able to appreciate the enjoyment that can come from a satisfactory relationship with a woman, albeit on nonsexual terms. In addition, having felt a very strong urge to hug one of them, in a nonsadistic fashion, was reported by the client as a highly significant event and must surely have fostered some change in his concept of himself as a sexual misfit. Furthermore, aside from any alleged counterconditioning with respect to appropriate stimuli (see below), it is also suggested that a favorable change in self-concept developed as he saw himself able to respond sexually to imaginal and pictorial stimuli that had previously left him unaroused.

5. It is assumed that the most important variable in therapy was the masturbation sessions which the client carried out privately. As discussed by Thorpe et al. (1963), it was felt that more appropriate social-sexual behavior would probably follow upon a change in sexual fantasies; in the present case a focus on the fantasies seemed all the more reasonable in view of the fact that *they formed the basis of the referral.* According to the client, it was his fantasy life which had retarded his sexual development, and it was this that he was most worried about. It was assumed that generalization to real-life girls would be effected in a fashion similar to the generalization which has been reported for Wolpe's technique of systematic desensitization (Davison, in press; Lang & Lazovik, 1963; Lang, Lazovik, & Reynolds, 1965; Lazarus, 1961; Paul, 1966; Paul & Shannon, 1966; Rachman, 1966; Schubot, 1966; Wolpin & Raines, 1966; Zeisset, 1966). Of course, whether Mr. M would actually begin dating regularly, or at all, would seem to depend importantly on factors other than those dealt with in this brief therapy, for example, the client's physical attractiveness, his conversational and sexual techniques, the availability of women attractive to him, and so forth. The generalization spoken of here, then, is best restricted to the thoughts and feelings which he had about women and about the prospects of relating to them nonsadistically; the case-study data contain ample verification for this.

The actual procedure followed was unique in that control of the pairing was vested entirely in the client, as is done in the use of differential relaxation with in vivo exposures to aversive stimuli (Davison, 1965; Wolpe & Lazarus, 1966). The sadistic fantasies were used initially to enable Mr. M to obtain and maintain an erection. During this arousal, he looked at culture-appropriate sexual stimuli (a nude *Playboy* photo) and masturbated. The assumption is made (and must obviously be investigated experimentally) that the pairing of masturbatory arousal with the *Playboy* picture served to replace neutral emotional responses to the picture with intensely pleasurable sexual responses. In succeeding sessions the content of the new sexual stimuli was changed to less openly provocative female pictures (bathing-suit photographs), with the already established *Playboy* picture used as back-up. Then the stimuli were made solely imaginal in similar fashion. Obviously, if this procedure worked for counterconditioning reasons, the client exhibited considerable control over the content of his fantasies, switching back and forth as he had been directed. This control of imagery is a central issue in desensitization research as well (Davison, in press).

6. Probably very instrumental in changing the content of his fantasies was the intensive "imaginal aversive countercounditioning" (or "covert sensitization," viz, Cautela, 1966; Lazarus, 1958) conducted by the therapist, in which extreme feelings of disgust were generated by fantasy and then related to the sadistic image. One can fruitfully compare this technique with the "emotive imagery" procedure described by Lazarus and Abramovitz (1962), in which pleasant images were generated in fearful children and then related by the therapist to conditioned aversive stimuli. The procedure was resorted to in the present case because the client appeared unable to give up the sadistic fantasy solely on the basis of beginning to find the nonsadistic pictures and images effective in maintaining erection and leading to orgasm.

The assessment of therapeutic outcome poses some difficulty here, as indeed it does for any therapy. Explicitly rejected as criteria of "cure" are the client's "self-actualization," "mental health," "ego strength," or other vague notions. While the intention is not simply to beg the question, it does seem more appropriate for the present case report to restrict judgment to the problem as presented by the client, namely, the sadistic fantasies and the attendant worry and doubt about suitability for normal human intercourse.

The clinical data on change in fantasy are self-reports, supplemented by the therapist's inference of the client's credibility. The orderliness of response to therapy, along with the enthusiasm which accompanied the progress reports, serves to bolster the conclusion that Mr. M did, in fact, give up his sadistic fantasies of 10 years' standing in favor of the kinds of fantasies which he felt were a sine qua non for appropriate sociosexual behavior. Both preceding and accompanying these changes was the radical difference in outlook. Simply stated, Mr. M stopped worrying about himself as an "oddball," doomed to a solitary life, and did make some initial attempts to establish appropriate relationships with girls. That he has not yet done so (as of this writing) may, indeed, be due to a return of the original problem; however, this alternative seems less likely than that verbalized by the client, namely, that he has always had trouble doing what he knows he ought to do, and that, above all, being a so-called sexual deviate has ceased being an issue for him. Moreover, as mentioned above, variables other than the content of fantasies would seem to bear importantly on the matter of overt sexual behavior. Clearly, if usual dating habits were to be used as a criterion for outcome, the therapy must be considered a failure—although this would qualify many a young adult as "maladjusted" or "abnormal." Be that as it may, a relevant, well-established class of behaviors was modified, setting the stage for a social adjustment from which the client had initially seen himself utterly alienated.

Supplementary Follow-Up Data

A follow-up report was received by mail 16 mo. following termination. The client reported that, since the therapy had so readily eliminated the arousal from sadistic fantasies, and, most importantly, had altered his outlook for "normal" sexual behavior, he allowed himself, "premeditatedly," to return to the use of the sadistic fantasies 6 mo. after termination, ". . . resolving to enjoy my fantasies until June 1, and then to reform once more. This I did. One June 1 [1967], right on schedule, I bought an issue of *Playboy* and proceeded to give myself the treatment again. Once again, it worked like a charm. In two weeks, I was back in my reformed state, where I am now [August 1967]. I have no need for sadistic fantasies. . . . I have [also] been pursuing a vigorous (well, vigorous for *me*) program of dating. In this way, I have gotten to know a lot of girls of whose existence I was previously only peripherally aware. As you probably know, I was very shy with girls before; well, now I am not one-fifth as shy as I used to be. In fact, by my old standards, I have become a regular rake!"

A telephone call was made to obtain more specific information about his return to the sadistic fantasies. He reported that the return was "fairly immediate," with a concomitant withdrawal of interest in conventional sexual stimuli. His self-administered therapy in June 1967 followed the gradual pattern of the original therapy, although progress was much faster. The author advised him not to make any more "premeditated" returns, rather to consolidate his gains in dating and other conventional heterosexual activities and interests. The client indicated that this plan could and would be readily implemented.

Of the past 16 mo., then, the client has been free of the sadistic fantasies for 7 mo., the other 9 mo. involving what he terms a willful return for sexual stimulation while masturbating. Constant throughout this follow-up period has been the relief which he derived from finding himself able to respond sexually to conventional sexual stimuli. Additional gains are his dating activities, which, it will be recalled, were not in evidence while the writer was in direct contact with him.

Still aware of the limitations of these case-study data, it does seem noteworthy and possibly quite important that the client's self-initiated partial "relapse" took place in a step-wise fashion, that is, without a *gradual* reorientation to the sadistic fantasies: he reported himself almost immediately excited by them once he had made the decision to become so. This sudden shift raises questions as to whether "aversive counterconditioning" underlay the indifference to the fantasies which was effected during therapy. This surprising finding also underlines the probable importance of other-than-conditioning variables in the treatment.

REFERENCES

BANDURA, A. *Principles of behavior modification.* New York: Holt, Rinehart & Winston, in press.

BLAKEMORE, C. B., THORPE, J. G., BARKER, J. C., CONWAY, C. G., & LAVIN, N. I. The application of faradic aversion conditioning in a case of transvestism. *Behaviour Research and Therapy,* 1963, **1**, 29–34.

CAUTELA, J. R. Treatment of compulsive behavior by covert sensitization. *The Psychological Record,* 1966, **16**, 33–41.

DAVIES, B., & MORGENSTERN, F. A case of cysticercosis, temporal lobe epilepsy, and transvestism. *Journal of Neurological and Neurosurgical Psychiatry,* 1960, **23**, 247–249.

DAVISON, G. C. Relative contributions of differential relaxation and graded exposure to in vivo desensitization of a neurotic fear. *Proceedings of the 73rd annual convention of the American Psychological Association,* 1965, 209–210.

DAVISON, G. C. Differential relaxation and cognitive restructuring in therapy with a "paranoid schizophrenic" or "paranoid state." *Proceedings of the 74th annual convention of the American Psychological Association,* 1966, **2**, 177–178.

DAVISON, G. C. Systematic desensitization as a counterconditioning process. *Journal of Abnormal Psychology,* 1968, in press.

FELDMAN, M. P. Aversion therapy for sexual deviations: A critical review. *Psychological Bulletin,* 1966, **65**, 65–79.

FELDMAN, M. P., & MACCULLOCH, M. J. The application of anticipatory avoidance learning to the treatment of homosexuality: I. Theory, technique and preliminary results. *Behaviour Research and Therapy,* 1965, **2**, 165–183.

FREUND, K. Some problems in the treatment of homosexuality. In H. J. Eysenck (Ed.), *Behaviour therapy and the neurosis.* London: Pergamon, 1960. Pp. 312–326.

GLASSER, W. *Reality therapy: A new approach to psychiatry.* New York: Harper & Row, 1965.

GROSSBERG, J. M. Behavior therapy: A review. *Psychological Bulletin*, 1964, **62**, 73–88.

GUTHRIE, E. R. *The psychology of learning.* New York: Harper, 1935.

KALISH, H. I. Behavior therapy. In B. B. Wolman (Ed.), *Handbook of clinical psychology.* New York: McGraw-Hill, 1965. Pp. 1230–1253.

LANG, P. J., & LAZOVIK, A. D. Experimental desensitization of a phobia. *Journal of Abnormal and Social Psychology*, 1963, **66**, 519–525.

LANG, P. J., LAZOVIK, A. D., & REYNOLDS, D. J. Desensitization, suggestibility, and pseudotherapy. *Journal of Abnormal Psychology*, 1965, **70**, 395–402.

LAVIN, N. I., THORPE, J. G., BARKER, J. C., BLAKEMORE, C. B., & CONWAY, C. G. Behavior therapy in a case of transvestism. *Journal of Nervous and Mental Disease*, 1961, **133**, 346–353.

LAZARUS, A. A. New methods in psychotherapy: A case study. *South African Medical Journal*, 1958, **33**, 660–663.

LAZARUS, A. A. Group therapy of phobic disorders by systematic desensitization. *Journal of Abnormal and Social Psychology*, 1961, **63**, 504–510.

LAZARUS, A. A., & ABRAMOVITZ, A. The use of "emotive imagery" in the treatment of children's phobias. *Journal of Mental Science*, 1962, **108**, 191–195.

LEVY, L. H. *Psychological interpretation.* New York: Holt, Rinehart & Winston, 1963.

MAHER, B. A. *Principles of psychopathology: An experimental approach.* New York: McGraw-Hill, 1966.

MAINORD, W. A. A therapy. *Research Bulletin*, Mental Health Research Institute, Ft. Steilacom, Washington, 1962, **5**, 85–92.

PAUL, G. L. *Insight vs. desensitization in psychotherapy: An experiment in anxiety reduction.* Stanford: Stanford University Press, 1966.

PAUL, G. L., & SHANNON, D. T. Treatment of anxiety through systematic desensitization in therapy groups. *Journal of Abnormal Psychology*, 1966, **71**, 124–135.

RACHMAN, S. Sexual disorders and behaviour therapy. *American Journal of Psychiatry*, 1961, **118**, 235–240.

RACHMAN, S. Studies in desensitization—III: Speed of generalization. *Behaviour Research and Therapy*, 1966, **4**, 7–15.

RAYMOND, M. J. Case of fetishism treated by aversion therapy. *British Medical Journal*, 1956, **2**, 854–857.

SCHUBOT, E. The influence of hypnotic and muscular relaxation in systematic desensitization of phobias. Unpublished doctoral dissertation, Stanford University, 1966.

THORPE, J. G., SCHMIDT, E., BROWN, P. T., & CASTELL, D. Aversion-relief therapy: A new method for general application. *Behaviour Research and Therapy*, 1964, **2**, 71–82.

THORPE, J. G., SCHMIDT, E., & CASTELL, D. A comparison of positive and negative (aversive) conditioning in the treatment of homosexuality. *Behaviour Research and Therapy*, 1963, **1**, 357–362.

ULLMANN, L., & KRASNER, L. P. (Eds.) *Case studies in behavior modification.* New York: Holt, Rinehart & Winston, 1965.

WOLPE, J. *Psychotherapy by reciprocal inhibition.* Stanford: Stanford University Press, 1958.

WOLPE, J., & LAZARUS, A. A. *Behavior therapy techniques.* New York: Pergamon, 1966.

WOLPIN, M., & RAINES, J. Visual imagery, expected roles and extinction as possible factors in reducing fear and avoidance behavior. *Behaviour Research and Therapy,* 1966, 4, 25–37.

ZEISSET, R. M. Desensitization and relaxation in the modification of psychiatric patients' interview behavior. Unpublished doctoral dissertation, University of Illinois, 1966.

Preliminary report on the application of contingent reinforcement procedures (token economy) on a "chronic" psychiatric ward

John M. Atthowe, Jr. and Leonard Krasner

INTRODUCTION Behavior modification procedures can be utilized effectively with groups as well as individuals, as the following study should readily indicate. Atthowe and Krasner employ a "token economy" to regulate the behaviors of an entire ward of patients undergoing psychiatric treatment. Their pioneering venture, which demonstrates the power of reinforcement in modifying human behavior, has been extended in recent years. Today behavior modification is being employed with increasing frequency and success in treating the mentally ill and retarded.

Although investigators may disagree as to what specific strategies or tactics to pursue, they would agree that current treatment programs in mental hospitals are in need of vast improvement. Release rates for patients hospitalized 5 or more years have not materially changed in this century (Kramer, Goldstein, Israel, & Johnson, 1956). After 5 yr. of hospitalization, the likelihood of release is approximately 6% (Kramer et al., 1956; Morgan & Johnson, 1957; Odegard, 1961), and, as patients grow older and their length of hospitalization increases, the possibility of discharge approaches zero. Even for those chronic patients who do leave the hospital, more than two out of every three return within 6 mo. (Fairweather, Simon, Gebhard, Weingarten, Holland, Sanders,

Atthowe, J., & Krasner, L. Preliminary report on the application of contingent reinforcement procedures (token economy) on a "chronic" psychiatric ward. *Journal of Abnormal Psychology*, 1968, 73, 37–43. Copyright 1968 by the American Psychological Association, and reproduced by permission.

Stone, & Reahl, 1960). There is certainly need for new programs of dem-onstrated efficiency in modifying the behavior of long-term hospitalized patients.

In September 1963 a research program in behavior modification was begun which was intimately woven into the hospital's ongoing service and training programs. The objective was to create and maintain a sys-tematic ward program within the ongoing social system of the hospital. The program reported here involves the life of the entire ward, patients, and staff, plus others who come in contact with the patients. The pur-pose of the program was to change the chronic patients' aberrant be-havior, especially that behavior judged to be apathetic, overly dependent, detrimental, or annoying to others. The goal was to foster more responsi-ble, active, and interested individuals who would be able to perform the routine activities associated with self-care, to make responsible decisions, and to delay immediate reinforcement in order to plan for the future.

THE WARD POPULATION

An 86-bed closed ward in the custodial section of the Veterans Ad-ministration Hospital in Palo Alto was selected. The median age of the patients was 57 yr. and more than one-third were over 65. Their overall length of hospitalization varied from 3 to 48 yr. with a median length of hospitalization of 22 yr. Most of the patients had previously been labeled as chronic schizophrenics; the remainder were classified as having some organic involvement.

The patients fell into three general performance classes. The largest group, approximately 60% of the ward, required constant supervision. Whenever they left the ward, an aide had to accompany them. The sec-ond group, about 25%, had ground privileges and were able to leave the ward unescorted. The third group, 15% of the patients, required only minimal supervision and could probably function in a boarding home under proper conditions if the fear of leaving the hospital could be over-come.

In order to insure a stable research sample for the 2 yr. of the project, 60 patients were selected to remain on the ward for the duration of the study. The patients selected were older and had, for the most part, ob-vious and annoying behavioral deficits. This "core" sample served as the experimental population in studying the long-term effectiveness of the research program, the token economy.

THE TOKEN ECONOMY

Based on the work of Ayllon and his associates (Ayllon, 1963; Ayllon & Azrin, 1965; Ayllon & Houghton, 1962; Ayllon & Michael, 1959) and the principle of reinforcement as espoused by Skinner (1938, 1953), we have tried to incorporate every important phase of ward and hospital life within a systematic contingency program. The attainment of the "good things in life" was made contingent upon the patient's performance.

If a patient adequately cared for his personal needs, attended his scheduled activities, helped on the ward, interacted with other patients, or showed increased responsibility in any way, he was rewarded. The problem was to find rewards that were valued by everyone. Tokens, which could in turn be exchanged for the things a patient regards as important or necessary, were introduced. As stated in the manual distributed to patients (Atthowe, 1964):

> The token program is an incentive program in which each person can do as much or as little as he wants as long as he abides by the general rules of the hospital, *but,* in order to gain certain ends or do certain things, he must have tokens. . . . The more you do the more tokens you get [p. 2].

Cigarettes, money, passes, watching television, etc., were some of the more obvious reinforcers, but some of the most effective reinforcers were idiosyncratic, such as sitting on the ward or feeding kittens. For some patients, hoarding tokens became highly valued. This latter practice necessitated changing the tokens every 30 days. In addition, the tokens a patient still had left at the end of each month were devaluated 25%, hence the greater incentive for the patient to spend them quickly. The more tokens a patient earned or spent, the less likely he would be to remain apathetic.

In general, each patient was reinforced immediately after the completion of some "therapeutic" activity, but those patients who attended scheduled activities by themselves were paid their tokens only once a week on a regularly scheduled pay day. Consequently, the more independent and responsible patient had to learn "to punch a time card" and to receive his "pay" at a specified future date. He then had to "budget" his tokens so they covered his wants for the next 7 days.

In addition, a small group of 12 patients was in a position of receiving what might be considered as the ultimate in reinforcement. They were allowed to become independent of the token system. These patients carried a "carte blanche" which entitled them to all the privileges within the token economy plus a few added privileges and a greater status. For this special status, the patient had to work 25 hr. per week in special vocational assignments. In order to become a member of the "elite group," patients had to accumulate 120 tokens which entailed a considerable delay in gratification.

The token economy was developed to cover all phases of a patient's life. This extension of contingencies to all of the patient's routine activities should bring about a greater generality and permanence of the behavior modified. One criticism of conditioning therapies has been that the behavior changed is specific with little evidence of carry-over to other situations. In this project plans were incorporated to program transfer of training as well as behavior change, per se. As a major step in this direction, token reinforcements were associated with social approval.

The attainment of goals which bring about greater independence should also result in strong sustaining reinforcement in and of itself. The aim of this study was to support more effective behavior and to weaken ineffective behavior by withdrawal of approval and attention and, if necessary, by penalties. Penalties comprised "fines" of specified numbers of tokens levied for especially undesirable behavior or for *not* paying the tokens required by the system. The fines can be seen as actually representing a high token payment to do something socially undesirable, for example, three tokens for cursing someone.

METHOD

The research program was initiated in September of 1963 when the senior author joined the ward as the ward psychologist and program administrator. The remainder of 1963 was a period of observation, pilot studies, and planning. Steps were taken to establish a research clinic and to modify the traditional service orientation of the nursing staff. In January 1964, the base-line measures were begun. The base-line or operant period lasted approximately 6 mo. and was followed by 3 mo. in which the patients were gradually prepared to participate in the token economy. In October 1964, the token economy was established and, at the time of writing, is still in operation. This report represents results based on the completion of the first year of the program.

The general design of the study was as follows: A 6-mo. base-line period, a 3-mo. shaping period, and an 11-mo. experimental period. During the base-line period, the frequency of particular behaviors was recorded daily, and ratings were carried out periodically. The shaping period was largely devoted to those patients requiring continual supervision. At first, the availability of canteen booklets, which served as money in the hospital canteen, was made contingent upon the amount of scheduled activities a patient attended. It soon became clear that almost one-half of the patients were not interested in money or canteen books. They did not know how to use the booklets, and they never bought things for themselves. Consequently, for 6 wk. patients were taken to the canteen and urged or "cajoled" into buying items which seemed to interest them (e.g., coffee, ice cream, pencils, handkerchiefs, etc.). Then all contingencies were temporarily abandoned, and patients were further encouraged to utilize the canteen books. Next, tokens were introduced but on a noncontingent basis. No one was allowed to purchase items in the ward canteen without first presenting tokens. Patients were instructed to pick up tokens from an office directly across the hall from the ward canteen and exchange them for the items they desired. After 2 wk. the tokens were made contingent upon performance and the experimental phase of the study began.

Within a reinforcement approach, the principles of successive approximation in gradually shaping the desired patient behavior were utilized. Once the tokens were introduced, shaping procedures were reduced. It would be impossible to hold reinforcement and shaping procedures constant throughout the experimental period or to match our ward or our patients with another ward or comparable group of patients. Consequently, a classical statistical design does not suit our paradigm. It is much more feasible, in addition to reducing sampling errors, to use the patients as their own controls. Therefore, we first established a base line over an extended period of time. Any changes in behavior from that defined by the base line must be taken into account. The effects of any type of experimental intervention become immediately obvious. We do not have to rely solely on the inferences teased out of statistical analyses.

Other than an automatic timer for the television set, the only major piece of equipment was the tokens. After a considerable search, a durable and physically safe token was constructed. This token was a $1\frac{3}{4} \times 3\frac{1}{2}$ in. plastic, nonlaminated, file card which came in seven colors varying from a bright red to a light tan. Different exchange values were assigned to the different colors. The token had the appearance of the usual credit card so prevalent in our society.

Whenever possible, the giving of the tokens was accompanied by some expression of social approval such as smiling, "good," "fine job," and a verbal description of the contingencies involved, for example, "Here's a token because of the good job of shaving you did this morning."

RESULTS

There has been a significant increase in those behaviors indicating responsibility and activity. Figure 1 shows the improvement in the frequency of attendance at group activities. During the base-line period, the average hourly rate of attendance per week was 5.85 hr. per patient. With the introduction of tokens, this rate increased to 8.4 the first month and averaged 8.5 during the experimental period, except for a period of 3 mo. when the reinforcing value of the tokens was increased from one to two tokens per hour of attendance. Increasing the reinforcing value of

John M. Atthowe, Jr., and Leonard Krasner   33

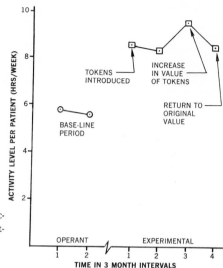

Fig. 1. Attendance at group activities. (Art adapted from Atthowe and Krasner.)

the tokens increased the contingent behavior accordingly. With an increase in the amount of reinforcement, activity increased from 8.4 hr. per week in the month before to 9.2 the first month under the new schedule. This gain was maintained throughout the period of greater reinforcement and for 1 mo. thereafter.

Thirty-two patients of the core sample comprised the group-activity sample. Nine patients were discharged or transferred during the project, and the remaining patients were on individual assignments and did not enter into these computations. Of the 32 patients, 18 increased their weekly attendance by at least 2 hr., while only 4 decreased their attendance by this amount. The probability that this is a significant difference is .004, using a sign test and a two-tailed estimate. Of those patients going to group activities, 18% changed to the more token-producing and more responsible individual assignments within 4 mo. of the onset of the token economy.

A widening of interest and a lessening of apathy were shown by a marked increase in the number of patients going on passes, drawing weekly cash, and utilizing the ward canteen. Of the core sample of 60 patients, 80% had never been off the hospital grounds on their own for a period of 8 hr. since their hospitalization. During the experimental period, 19% went on overnight or longer passes, 17% went on day passes, and 12% went out on accompanied passes for the first time. In other words, approximately one-half of those who had been too apathetic to leave the hospital grounds increased their interest and commitment in the world outside. Furthermore, 13% of the core sample left on one or more trial visits of at least 30 days during the token program, although 6 out of every 10 returned to the hospital.

For the entire ward, the lessening of apathy was dramatic. The number of patients going on passes and drawing weekly cash tripled. Twenty-four patients were discharged and 8 were transferred to more active and discharge-oriented ward programs as compared to 11 discharges and no such transfers in the preceding 11-mo. period. Of the 24 patients released, 11 returned to the hospital within 9 mo.

Independence and greater self-sufficiency were shown by an increase in the number of patients receiving tokens for shaving and appearing neatly dressed. Fewer patients missed their showers, and bed-wetting markedly diminished.

At the beginning of the study, there were 12 bed-wetters, 4 of whom were classified as "frequent" wetters and 2 were classified as "infrequent." All bed-wetters were awakened and taken to the bathroom at 11 PM, 12:30 PM, 2 AM, and 4 AM regularly. As the program progressed, patients who did not wet during the night were paid tokens the following morning. In addition, they were only awakened at 11 PM the next night. After a week of no bed-wetting, patients were taken off the schedule altogether. At the end of the experimental period no one was wetting regularly and, for all practical purposes, there were no bed-wetters on the ward. The aversive schedule of being awakened during the night together with the receiving of tokens for a successful non-bed-wetting night seemed to instigate getting up on one's own and going to the bathroom, even in markedly deteriorated patients.

Another ward problem which had required extra aide coverage in the mornings was the lack of "cooperativeness" in getting out of bed, making one's bed, and leaving the bed area by a specified time. Just before the system of specific contingency tokens was introduced, the number of infractions in each of these areas was recorded for 3 wk. This 3-wk. baseline period yielded an average of 75 "infractions" per week for the entire ward, varying from 71 to 77. A token given daily was then made contingent upon not having a recorded infraction in any of the three areas above. This token was given as the patients lined up to go to breakfast each morning. In the week following the establishment of the contingency, the frequency of infractions dropped to 30 and then to 18. The next week the number of infractions rose to 39 but then declined steadily to 5 per week by the end of 9 wk. (see Figure 2). During the last 6 mo., the frequency of infractions varied between 6 and 13, averaging 9 per week.

A significant increase was shown in measures of social interaction

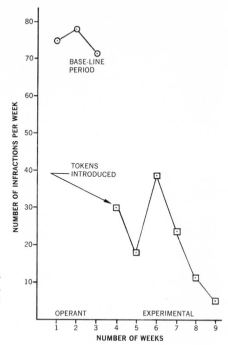

Fig. 2. Number of infractions in carrying out morning routines. (Art adapted from Atthowe and Krasner.)

and communication. A brief version of the Palo Alto Group Psychotherapy scale (Finney, 1954) was used to measure social responsiveness in weekly group meetings. The change in ratings by one group of raters 1 mo. before the introduction of tokens compared with those of a second group of raters 4 mo. later was significant at the .001 level. A simple sign test based upon a two-tailed probability estimate was used. Neither set of raters knew which of their patients was included within the core sample. The rater reliability of the scale is .90 (Finney, 1954). Evidence of enhanced social interaction was dramatically shown by the appearance of card games using tokens as money among some of the more "disturbed" patients and an increased frequency in playing pool together.

DISCUSSION AND CONCLUSION

A detailed description of the entire procedures and results is in preparation. However, we wish to point out in this paper the usefulness of a systematic contingency program with chronic patients. The program has been quite successful in combating institutional behavior. Prior to the introduction of tokens most patients rarely left the ward. The ward and its surrounding grounds were dominated by sleeping patients. Little interest was shown in ward activities or parties. Before the tokens were introduced, the ward was cleaned and the clothing room operated by patients from "better" wards. During the experimental period the ward was cleaned and the clothing room operated by the patients of this ward themselves. Now, no one stays on the ward without first earning tokens, and, in comparison to prior standards, the ward could be considered "jumping."

Over 90% of the patients have meaningfully participated in the program. All patients do take tokens, a few only infrequently. However, for about 10%, the tokens seem to be of little utility in effecting marked behavior change. With most patients, the changes in behavior have been quite dramatic; the changes in a few have been gradual and hardly noticeable. These instances of lack of responsiveness to the program seem to be evident in those patients who have previously been "catatonically" withdrawn and isolated. Although most of the patients in this category were favorably responsive to the program, what "failures" there were, did come from this type of patient. Our program has been directed toward all patients; consequently, individual shaping has been limited. We feel that the results would be more dramatic if we could have dealt individually with the specific behavior of every patient. On the other hand, a total ward token program is needed both to maintain any behavioral gains and to bring about greater generality and permanence. Although it was not our initial objective to discharge patients, we are pleased that the general lessening of apathy has brought about a greater discharge rate. But, even more important, the greater discharge rate would point to the generalized effects of a total token economy.

The greater demands on the patient necessitated by dealing with future events and delaying immediate gratifications which were built into the program have been of value in lessening patients' isolation and withdrawal. The program's most notable contribution to patient life is the lessening of staff control and putting the burden of responsibility, and thus more self-respect, on the patient himself. In the administration of a ward, the program provides behavioral steps by which the staff can judge the patient's readiness to assume more responsibility and thus to leave on pass or be discharged.

The program thus far has demonstrated that a systematic procedure of applying contingent reinforcement via a token economy appears effective in modifying specific patient behaviors. However, the evidence in the literature based on research in mental hospitals indicates that many programs, different in theoretical orientation and design, appear to be successful for a period of time with hospitalized patients. The question which arises is whether the success in modifying behavior is a function of the specific procedures utilized in a given program or a function of the more general social influence process (Krasner, 1962). If it is the latter, whether it be termed "placebo effect" or "Hawthorne effect," then the specific procedures may be irrelevant. All that would matter is the interest, enthusiasm, attention, and hopeful expectancies of the staff. Advocates of behavior-modification procedures (of which the token economy is illustrative) argue that change in behavior is a function of the specific reinforcement procedures used. The study which most nearly involves the approach described in this paper is that of Ayllon and Azrin (1965) whose procedures were basic to the development of our own program. Their study was designed to demonstrate the relationship between contingency reinforcement and change in patient behavior. To do this they withdrew the tokens on a systematic basis for specific behaviors and, after a period of time, reinstated them. They concluded, based upon six specific experiments within the overall design, that

> the reinforcement procedure was effective in maintaining desired performance. In each experiment, the performance fell to a near-zero level when the established response-reinforcement relation was discontinued. On the other hand, reintroduction of the reinforcement procedure restored performance almost immediately and maintained it at a high level for as long as the reinforcement procedure was in effect [Ayllon & Azrin, 1965, p. 381].

They found that performance of desirable behaviors decreased when the response-reinforcement relation was disrupted by: delivering tokens independently of the response while still allowing exchange of tokens for the reinforcers; or by discontinuing the token system by providing continuing access to the reinforcers; or by discontinuing the delivery of tokens for a previously reinforced response while simultaneously providing tokens for a different, alternative response.

In the first year of our program we did not test the specific effects of the tokens by withdrawing them. Rather, we approached this problem in two ways. First, we incorporated within the base-line period of 9 mo. a 3-mo. period in which tokens were received on a noncontingent basis. During this period patients received tokens with concomitant attention, interest, and general social reinforcement. This resulted in slight but nonsignificant change in general ward behavior. The results of the experimental period were then compared with the base line which included the nonspecific reinforcement. The results indicate that the more drastic changes in behavior were a function of the specific procedures involved. The other technique we used was to change the token value of certain specific activities. An increase in value (more tokens) was related to an increase in performance; return to the old value meant a decrement to the previous level of performance (see Figure 1).

We should also point out that the situation in the hospital is such that the token economy did not mean that there were more of the "good things in life" available to these patients because they were in a special program. The patients in the program had had access to these items, for example, extra food, beds, cigarettes, chairs, television, recreational activities, passes, before the program began, as had all patients in other wards, free of charge. Thus we cannot attribute change to the fact of more "good things" being available to these patients and not available to other patients.

Thus far, a contingent reinforcement program represented by a token economy has been successful in combating institutionalism, increasing initiative, responsibility, and social interaction, and in putting the control of patient behavior in the hands of the patient. The behavioral changes have generalized to other areas of performance. A token economy can be an important adjunct to any rehabilitation program for chronic or apathetic patients.

REFERENCES

ATTHOWE, J. M., JR. Ward 113 Program: Incentives and costs—a manual for patients. Palo Alto, Calif.: Veterans Administration Hospital, 1964.

AYLLON, T. Intensive treatment of psychotic behavior by stimulus satiation and food reinforcement. *Behaviour Research and Therapy,* 1963, 1, 53–61.

AYLLON, T., & AZRIN, N. H. The measurement and reinforcement of behavior of psychotics. *Journal of the Experimental Analysis of Behavior,* 1965, 8, 357–384.

AYLLON, T., & HOUGHTON, E. Control of the behavior of schizophrenic patients by food. *Journal of the Experimental Analysis of Behavior,* 1962, 5, 343–352.

AYLLON, T., & MICHAEL, J. The psychiatric nurse as a behavioral engineer. *Journal of the Experimental Analysis of Behavior,* 1959, 2, 323–334.

FAIRWEATHER, G. W., SIMON, R., GEBHARD, M. E., WEINGARTEN, E., HOLLAND, J. L., SANDERS, R., STONE, G. B., & REAHL, J. E. Relative effectiveness of psychotherapeutic programs: A multicriteria comparison of four programs for three different patient groups, *Psychological Monographs,* 1960, 74 (5, Whole No. 492).

FINNEY, B. C. A scale to measure interpersonal relationships in group psychotherapy. *Group Psychotherapy,* 1954, 7, 52–66.

KRAMER, M., GOLDSTEIN, H., ISRAEL, R. H., & JOHNSON, N. A. Application of life table methodology to the study of mental hospital populations. *Psychiatric Research Reports,* 1956, 5, 49–76.

KRASNER, L. The therapist as a social reinforcement machine. In H. H. Strupp & L. Luborsky (Eds.), *Research in psychotherapy.* Washington, D. C.: American Psychological Association, 1962. Pp. 61–94.

MORGAN, N. C., & JOHNSON, N. A. The chronic hospital patient. *American Journal of Psychiatry*, 1957, 113, 824–830.

ODEGARD, O. Current studies of incidence and prevalence of hospitalized mental patients in Scandinavia. In P. H. Hoch & J. Zubin (Eds.), *Comparative epidemology of the mental disorders.* New York: Grune & Stratton, 1961. Pp. 45–55.

SKINNER, B. F. *The behavior of organisms.* New York: Appleton-Century-Crofts, 1938.

SKINNER, B. F. *Science and human behavior.* New York: Macmillan, 1953.

Hell and Heaven within the brain: the systems for punishment and reward

José M. R. Delgado

INTRODUCTION   The study of brain stimulation has gained momentum ever since the early fifties, when James Olds implanted an electrode into a rat's brain and discovered the reinforcing properties of intercranial electrical stimuli (Olds & Milner, 1954). Andrews and Karlins (1971) state:

> *The most impressive aspect of brain stimulation is the fact that animals low on the phylogenetic scale (cats, rats) display rigid, stimulus-bound behavior in the face of it. When one witnesses an animal under the influence of chemical or electrical stimulation of the brain he cannot help being awed by how the organism's behavior can be turned "on" and "off" at the experimenter's will. Another impressive aspect of brain stimulation is what it can induce an animal to do or not to do. For example, brain stimulation has been used to make animals docile or savage, alert or lethargic, dominant or submissive, and obese or emaciated. With brain stimulation rats have been known to press a lever up to 7,000 times an hour to get an intercranial electric jolt; female animals have undertaken male sexual behavior (one female rat tried to mount her male partner unsuccessfully for eight weeks!); and male animals have developed an unquenchable sexual appetite (copulating with their partners as long as stimulation continued).*

Man too has been subjected to electrical brain stimulation. The results, though not as dramatic as those obtained with lower animals, are nonetheless fascinating. For example, some patients have reported pleas-

*urable sensations (Heath, 1963) and the recall of memories (Penfield, 1959)
while undergoing brain stimulation; others have experienced sexual
arousal (Delgado, 1969).*

*In the following selection a leading scientist discusses some of his
brain stimulation research on animals and humans. As we mentioned in
the first reading, do not be surprised if parts of the report read like a
science fiction novel. Sometimes the frontiers of scientific inquiry go beyond the borders of even a writer's imagination.*

When man evolved above other powerful animals, the
size and complexity of his brain increased, giving him superior intelligence along with more anguish, deeper sorrow, and greater sensitivity
than any other living creature. Man also learned to enjoy beauty, to dream
and to create, to love and to hate. In the education of children as well as
in the training of animals, punishment and reward constitute the most
powerful motivations for learning. In our hedonistic orientation of life
to minimize pain and seek pleasure, we often attribute these qualities to
the environment without realizing that sensations depend on a chain of
events which culminates in the activation of determined intracerebral
mechanisms. Physical damage, the loss of a beloved child, or apocalyptic
disaster cannot make us suffer if some of our cerebral structures have been
blocked by anesthesia. Pleasure is not in the skin being caressed or in a
full stomach, but somewhere inside the cranial vault.

At the same time pain and pleasure have important psychic and cultural components related to individual history. Men inhibited by some
extraordinary tribal or religious training to endure discomfort have been
tortured to death without showing signs of suffering. It is also known
that in the absence of physical injury, mental elaboration of information
may produce the worst kind of suffering. Social rejection, guilt feelings,
and other personal tragedies may produce greater autonomic, somatic,
and psychological manifestations than actual physical pain.

There is strong reluctance to accept that such personal and refined
interpretations of reality as being afraid and being in love are contingent
on the membrane depolarization of determined clusters of neurons, but
this is one aspect of emotional phenomena which should not be ignored.
After frontal lobotomy, cancer patients have reported that the pain persisted undiminished, but that their subjective suffering was radically
reduced, and they did not complain or request as much medication as
before surgery. Lobotomized patients reacted to noxious stimuli as much,

if not more, than before their operations, jumping at pinpricks and responding quickly to objective tests of excessive heat, but they showed decreased concern. It seems that in the frontal lobes there is a potentiating
mechanism for the evaluation of personal suffering, and after lobotomy
the initial sensation of pain is unmodified, while the reactive component
to that feeling is greatly diminished. This mechanism is rather specific
of the frontal lobes; bilateral destruction of the temporal lobes fails to
modify personal suffering.

Important questions to resolve are: Do some cerebral structures have
the specific role of analyzing determined types of sensations? Is the coding
of information at the receptor level essential for the activation of these
structures? Not too long ago, many scientists would have dismissed as
naive the already demonstrated fact that punishment and reward can be
induced at will by manipulating the controls of an electrical instrument
connected to the brain.

PERCEPTION OF SUFFERING

In textbooks and scientific papers, terms such as "pain receptors,"
"pain fibers," and "pain pathways" are frequently used, but it should be
clarified that peripheral nerves do not carry sensations. Neuronal pathways transmit only patterns of electrical activity with a message that must
be deciphered by the central nervous system, and in the absence of brain
there is no pain, even if some reflex motor reactions may still be present.
A decapitated frog cannot feel but will jump away with fairly good motor
coordination when pinched in the hind legs. During competitive sports
or on the battlefield, emotion and stress may temporarily block the feeling of pain in man, and often injuries are not immediately noticed. The
cerebral interpretation of sensory signals is so decisive that the same stimulus may be considered pleasant or unpleasant depending on circumstances. A strong electrical shock on the feet scares a dog and inhibits its
secretion of saliva. If, however, the same "painful" excitation is followed
for several days by administration of food, the animal accepts the shock,
wagging its tail happily and salivating in anticipation of the food reward. Some of these dogs have been trained to press a lever to trigger
the electric shock which preceded food. During sexual relations in man,
bites, scratches, and other potentially painful sensations are often interpreted as enjoyable, and some sexual deviates seek physical punishment
as a source of pleasure.

The paradox is that while skin and viscera have plentiful nerve end-
ings for sensory reception, the brain does not possess this type of innervation. In patients under local anesthesia, the cerebral tissue may be cut,
burned, pulled apart, or frozen without causing any discomfort. This

organ so insensitive to its own destruction is, however, the exquisite sensor of information received from the periphery. In higher animal species there is sensory differentiation involving specialized peripheral receptors which code external information into electrical impulses and internal analyzers which decode the circulating inputs in order to give rise to the perception of sensations.

Most sensory messages travel through peripheral nerves, dorsal roots, spinal cord, and medulla to the thalamic nuclei in the brain, but from there we lose their trail and do not know where the information is interpreted as painful or pleasurable, or how affective components are attributed to a sensation (212, 220).* Although anatomical investigations indicate that thalamic fibers project to the parietal "sensory" cortex, stimulation of this area does not produce pain in animals or man. No discomfort has been reported following electrical excitation of the surface or depth of the motor areas, frontal lobes, occipital lobes, cingulate gyrus, and many other structures, while pain, rage, and fear have been evoked by excitation of the central gray tegmentum, and a few other regions.

Animals share with man the expressive aspect of emotional manifestations. When a dog wags its tail, we suppose it is happy, and when a cat hisses and spits we assume that it is enraged, but these interpretations are anthropomorphic and in reality we do not know the feelings of any animal. Several authors have tried to correlate objective manifestations with sensations; for example, stimulation of the cornea of the eye provokes struggling, pupillary dilatation, and rise of blood pressure (87), but these responses are not necessarily related to awareness of feelings, as is clearly demonstrated by the defensive agility of the decapitated frog. Experimental investigation of the mechanisms of pain and pleasure is handicapped in animals by their lack of verbal communication, but fortunately we can investigate whether an animal likes or dislikes the perceived sensations by analyzing its instrumental responses. Rats, monkeys, and other species can learn to press a lever in order to receive a reward such as a food pellet or to avoid something unpleasant such as an electric shock to the skin. By the voluntary act of instrumental manipulation, an animal expresses whether or not the food, shock, or brain stimulation is desirable, allowing for the objective qualification of the sensation. In this way, many cerebral structures have been explored to identify their positive or negative reinforcing properties.

At present it is generally accepted that specific areas of the brain participate in the integration of pain sensations, but the mechanism is far from clear, and in our animal experiments we do not know if we are stimulating pathways or higher centers of integration. The concept of a

---

* These numbers refer to the References on pp. 66ff.–Eds.

straight conduction of pain messages from the periphery up to the central nervous system was too elemental. Incoming messages are probably processed at many levels with feedbacks which modify the sensitivity and the filtering of information at many stages including the peripheral receptor level. Brain excitation, therefore, may affect transmission as well as the elaboration of inputs and feedback modulation. Electrical stimuli do not carry any specific message because they are a monotonous repetition of similar pulses, and the fact that they constitute a suitable trigger for central perception of pain means that the reception of a patterned code is not required, but only the nonspecific activation of neuronal pools which are accessible to investigation. In addition to the importance of these studies for finding better therapies for the alleviation of pain, there is another aspect which has great social interest: the possible relations between pain perception and violence.

VIOLENCE WITHIN THE BRAIN

The chronicle of human civilization is the story of a cooperative venture consistently marred by self-destruction, and every advance has been accompanied by increased efficiency of violent behavior. Early man needed considerable physical strength and skill to defend himself or attack other men or beasts with stones, arrows, or swords, but the invention of explosives and subsequent development of firearms have made unskilled individuals more powerful than mythical warriors of the past. The technology for destruction has now placed at the disposal of man a vast arsenal of ingenious weapons which facilitate all forms of violence including crimes against property, assassinations, riots, and wars, threatening not only individual life and national stability but the very existence of civilization.

Ours is a tragically imbalanced industrial society which devotes most of its resources to the acquisition of destructive power and invests insignificant effort in the search which could provide the true weapons of self-defense: knowledge of the mechanisms responsible for violent behavior. They are necessarily related with intracerebral processes of neuronal activity, even if the triggering causality may reside in environmental circumstances. Violence is a product of cultural environment and is an extreme form of aggression, distinct from modes of self-expression required for survival and development under normal conditions. Man may react to unpleasant or painful stimuli with violence—he may retaliate even more vigorously than he is attacked—but only if he has been taught by his culture to react in this manner. A major role of education is to "build internal controls in human beings so that they can withstand external pressures and maintain internal equilibrium" (157). We should remember that it is normal for an animal to urinate when the bladder is full and to mount any available female during the mating season, but that these behaviors may be controlled in man through training. The distinctly human quality of cerebralization of behavior is possible through education.

Human aggression may be considered a behavioral response characterized by the exercise of force with the intent to inflict damage on persons or objects. The phenomenon may be analyzed in three components: *inputs,* determined by environmental circumstances perceived through sensory receptors and acting upon the individual; *throughputs,* which are the personal processing of these circumstances through the intracerebral mechanisms established by genetic endowment and previous experiences; and *outputs,* represented by the expressions of individual and social behavior which constitute the observable manifestations of aggression. Increasing awareness of the need to investigate these subjects has already resulted in the creation of specialized institutes, but surprisingly enough the most essential element in the whole process of violence is usually neglected. Attention is directed to economic, ideological, social, and political factors and to their consequences, which are expressed as individual and mass behavior, while the essential link in the central nervous system is often forgotten. It is, however, an incontrovertible fact that the environment is only the provider of sensory inputs which must be interpreted by the brain, and that any kind of behavior is the result of intracerebral activity.

It would be naive to investigate the reasons for a riot by recording the intracerebral electrical activity of the participants, but it would be equally wrong to ignore the fact that each participant has a brain and that determined neuronal groups are reacting to sensory inputs and are subsequently producing the behavioral expression of violence. Both neurophysiological and environmental factors must be evaluated, and today methodology is available for their combined study. Humanity behaves in general no more intelligently than animals would under the same circumstances, and this alarming reality is due largely to "that spiritual pride which prevents men from regarding themselves and their behavior as parts of nature and as subject to its universal laws" (148). Experimental investigation of the cerebral structures responsible for aggressive behavior is an essential counterpart of social studies, and this should be recognized by sociologists as well as biologists.

In animals, the first demonstration that offensive activity could be evoked by ESB was provided by Hess (105), and it has subsequently been confirmed by numerous investigators. Cats under electrical stimulation of the periventricular gray matter acted "as if threatened by a dog," responding with unsheathed claws and well-aimed blows. "The animal spits, snorts or growls. At the same time the hair on its back stands on end, and its tail becomes bushy. Its pupils widen sometimes to their maximum, and

its ears lie back or move back and forth to frighten the nonexisting enemy" (106). In these experiments it is important to know how the cat really feels. Is it aware of its own responses? Is the hostility purposefully oriented to do harm? Or is the entire phenomenon a pseudoaffective reaction, a false or sham rage containing the motor components of offensive

Fig. 1. At upper left, the control, two friendly cats. At lower left, electrical stimulation of the anterior hypothalamus evoked an aggressive expression not directed against the other cat which, however, reacts with a defensive attitude. Above, the normal cat attacks the stimulated animal which lowers its head, flattens its ears, and does not retaliate. This experiment is an example of false rage (53). (Photos courtesy of José M. R. Delgado.)

display without actual emotional participation? These issues have been debated over the years, but today it is clear that both sham and true rage can be elicited by ESB depending on the location of stimulation. Excitation of the anterior hypothalamus may induce a threatening display with hissing and growling which should be interpreted as false rage because the display was not directed against other animals. When other cats reacted by hissing and attacking the stimulated animal, it did not retaliate or escape and simply lowered its head and flattened its ears, and these brain stimulations could not be conditioned to sensory cues.

In contrast, true rage has been demonstrated in other experiments. . . . Stimulation of the lateral hypothalamus produced an aggressive display clearly directed toward a control animal which reacted properly in facing the threat. The stimulated animal started prowling around looking for fights with other subordinate animals, but avoided the most powerful cat in the group. It was evident that brain stimulation had created a state of increased aggressiveness, but it was also clear that the cat directed its hostility intelligently, choosing the enemy and the moment of attack, changing tactics, and adapting its movements to the motor reaction of its opponent. Brain stimulation determined the affective state of

Fig. 2. Electrical stimulation of the lateral hypothalamus evoked true rage which is characterized by aggressive display oriented toward another cat (above); attack with well-oriented claws directed against other cats (below); attack against gloved hands of investigators with whom relations had previously been

friendly (above); learning of instrumental responses, such as rotating a paddle wheel, in order to stop the brain stimulation (below). In this way the test cat expresses its dislike of being stimulated in a particular area (53). (Photos courtesy of José M. R. Delgado.)

hostility, but behavioral performance depended on the individual characteristics of the stimulated animal, including learned skills and previous experiences. Stimulations were usually tested for 5 to 10 seconds, but since it was important to know the fatigability of the effect, a longer experiment was performed, reducing the applied intensity to a level which did not evoke overt rage. The experimental subject was an affectionate cat which usually sought petting and purred while it was held in the experimenter's arms. Then it was introduced into the colony with five other cats and was radio stimulated continuously for two hours. During this period the animal sat motionless in a corner of the cage, uttering barely audible growls from time to time. If any other cat approached, the stimulated animal started hissing and threatening, and if the experimenter tried to pet it, the growls increased in intensity and the animal often spat and hissed. This hostile attitude disappeared as soon as the stimulation was over, and the cat became as friendly as before. These experiments demonstrated that brain excitation could modify reactions toward normal sensory stimuli and could modulate the quality of the responses in a way similar to modulation during spontaneous emotional states.

Monkeys are more interesting subjects than cats for the study of social interactions because of their more numerous and skillful spontaneous activities. It is well known that monkey colonies constitute autocratic societies in which one animal establishes itself as boss of the group, claiming a large portion of the territory, feeding first, and being avoided by the others, who usually express their submissiveness by grimacing, crouching, and offering sexual play. In several colonies we have observed that radio stimulation of specific points in the thalamus or central gray in the boss monkey increased his aggressiveness and induced well-directed attacks against other members of the group, whom he chased around and occasionally bit . . . (56). It was evident that his hostility was oriented purposefully and according to his previous experience because he usually attacked the other male who represented a challenge to his authority, and he always spared the little female who was his favorite partner.

A high-ranking monkey expresses rage by attacking submissive members of the colony, but what would be the consequences of stimulating the brain of lower-ranking animals? Could they be induced to challenge the authority of other monkeys, including perhaps even the boss, or would their social inhibitions block the electrically induced hostility? These questions were investigated in one colony by changing its composition to increase progressively the social rank of one member, a female named Lina, who in the first grouping of four animals ranked lowest, progressing to third rank in the second group and to second rank in the third group. Social dominance was evaluated during extended control periods using the criteria of number of spontaneous agonistic and sexual interactions, priority in food getting, and territoriality. On two successive mornings in each colony Lina was radio stimulated for 5 seconds once a minute for one hour in the nucleus posterolateralis of the thalamus. In all three colonies, those stimulations induced Lina to run across the cage, climb to the ceiling, lick, vocalize, and according to her social status, to attack other animals. In group 1, where Lina was submissive, she tried to attack another monkey only once, and she was threatened or attacked 24 times. In group 2 she became more aggressive (24 occurrences) and was attacked only 3 times, while in group 3 Lina attacked other monkeys 79 times and was not threatened at all. No changes in the number of agonistic acts were observed in any group before or after the stimulation hour, showing that alterations in Lina's aggressive behavior were determined by ESB.

In summary, intraspecies aggression has been evoked in cats and monkeys by electrical stimulation of several cerebral structures, and its expression is dependent on the social setting. Unlike purely motor effects including complex sequences which have no social significance, an artificially evoked aggressive act may be directed against a specific group member or may be entirely suppressed, according to the stimulated subject's social rank.

Many questions remain to be answered. Which cerebral areas are responsible for spontaneous aggressive behavior? By what mechanisms are environmental inputs interpreted as undesirable? How does cultural training influence the reactivity of specific cerebral areas? Can neurophysiological mechanisms of violence be re-educated, or are individual responses set for life after early imprinting? It is interesting that application of ESB modified the interpretation of the environment, changing the peaceful relations of a group of animals into sudden overt hostility. The same sensory inputs provided by the presence of other animals, which were neutral during control periods, were under ESB the cue for a ferocious and well-directed attack. Apparently brain stimulation introduced an emotional bias which altered interpretation of the surroundings.

While neurophysiological activity may be influenced or perhaps even set by genetic factors and past experience, the brain is the direct interpreter of environmental inputs and the determinant of behavioral responses. To understand the causes and plan remedies for intraspecific aggression in animals and man require knowledge of both sociology and neurophysiology. Electricity cannot determine the target for hostility or direct the sequences of aggressive behavior, which are both related to the past history of the stimulated subject and to his immediate adaptation to changing circumstances. Artificially triggered and spontaneously provoked aggression have many elements in common, suggesting that in both cases similar areas of the brain have been activated.

While individual and collective acts of violence may seem rather dis-

Fig. 3. Examples of threatening attitude and aggressive behavior produced by brain stimulation. Observe that the stimulated monkey chooses another one as a specific target, and this animal usually expresses submissiveness by grimacing,

tant from the electrical discharges of neurons, we should remember that personality is not in the environment but in the nervous tissue. Possible solutions to undesirable aggression obviously will not be found in the use of ESB. This is only a methodology for investigation of the problem and

crouching, or escaping. A toy tiger is also a suitable target for aggressive display. (Photos courtesy of José M. R. Delgado.)

acquisition of necessary information about the brain mechanisms involved. It is well known that medical treatment of cardiac patients is based on anatomical and physiological studies of the heart, and that without this information it would not have been possible to discover new drugs or to give effective medical advice. Similarly, without knowledge of the brain it will be difficult to correlate social causality with individual reactivity.

ANXIETY, FEAR, AND VIOLENCE EVOKED BY ESB IN MAN

Anxiety has been considered the alpha and omega of psychiatry. It is one of the central themes of existential philosophy, and it shades the normal—and abnormal—life of most human beings. Several emotional states may be classified under the headings of anxiety, including fear, fright, panic, and terror, which are variations of the same basic experience. One of the most complex mental disturbances, unreasonable or excessive anxiety, including phobias and compulsive obsessions, often does not respond to standard therapies, and in some instances it has been improved by electrocoagulation of discrete areas of the frontal pole. Grey Walter (234) has claimed an 85 per cent total social recovery in a group of sixty patients with anxiety and obsessions treated with carefully dosified coagulations made through electrodes implanted in the frontal lobes.

Without entering into semantic discussions, we may consider anxiety an emotional state of conscious or subconscious tension related to real or imaginary threats to psychological or physical individual integrity. A mild degree of anxiety may mobilize, while excessive degrees may paralyze somatic and mental activity. Beyond a certain limit, anxiety has unpleasant characteristics. In normal circumstances, it is produced, as is any other emotion, by sensory inputs from the environment and by recollections, both of which require mental elaboration of messages which may be influenced by humoral and neuronal factors. In addition, there is abundant evidence that anxiety and fear may be induced as either a primary or a secondary category of response by direct electrical stimulation of the brain. The perception or expectancy of pain can be frightening, and in some cases when ESB produced localized or generalized discomfort, patients have expressed concern about continuation of the exploratory procedures. In addition to the natural fear of possible further discomfort, there may have been a component of primary anxiety which would be difficult to evaluate.

Destruction of discrete parts of the thalamus produces relief from anxiety neurosis and obsessive-compulsive neurosis which is probably related to the interruption of tonic pathways to the frontal lobes. Stimulation of the thalamic nucleus, however, very seldom produces anxiety, and the reports of patients are limited to feelings of weakness, being different, dizziness, floating, and something like alcoholic intoxication (214).

Clearer demonstrations of direct induction of fear without any other accompanying sensations have been reported by several investigators. Lesions in the medial thalamus give effective pain relief with a minimal amount of sensory loss, and for this reason this area has often been explored electrically in cancer patients. In some cases it has produced acute anxiety attacks, which one patient vividly described as: "It's rather like the feeling of having just been missed by a car and leaped back to the curb and went B-r-r-r." Something in his guts felt very unpleasant, very unusual, and he certainly did not want to feel like that again (73). The surprising fact is that the unpleasant sensation of fear was felt in one side of the body, contralateral to the brain stimulation. Sweet (221) has reported the case of a very intelligent patient, the dean of a graduate school, who after a unilateral sympathectomy to treat his upper limb hyperhydrosis, found that his previous and customary sensation of shivering while listening to a stirring passage of music occurred in only one side and he could not be thrilled in the sympathectomized half of his body. These cases were interesting because emotions are usually experienced in a rather diffuse and bilateral fashion unless innervation has been specifically interrupted.

The role of the thalamus in the integration of fear is also suggested by the study of a female patient whose spontaneous crippling attacks of anxiety of overwhelming intensity had led to several suicide attempts and a chronic state of depression and agitation quite refractory to drugs and psychotherapy. Stimulation of the dorsolateral nucleus of the thalamus evoked precisely the same type of attack at a level of symptomatology directly proportional to the applied intensity. It was possible to find the electrical threshold for a mild anxiety or to increase it to higher levels simply by turning the dial of the stimulator. "One could sit with one's hand on the knob and control the level of her anxiety" (73).

In one of our female patients, stimulation of a similar area in the thalamus induced a typical fearful expression and she turned to either side, visually exploring the room behind her. When asked what she was doing, she replied that she felt a threat and thought that something horrible was going to happen. This fearful sensation was perceived as real, and she had a premonition of imminent disaster of unknown cause. The effect was reliable on different days and was not altered by the use of lights and a movie camera to document the finding. Her motor activity and choice of words varied according to the environmental setting, but her facial expression and acute sensation of nonspecific, unexplainable, but real fear were similar following different stimulations. The response started with a delay of less than one second, lasted for as long as the stimulation, and did not leave observable aftereffects. The patient remembered her fear but was not upset by the memory.

Some patients have displayed anxiety and restlessness when the pallidum was stimulated at frequencies above 8 cycles per second, and they also perceived a constriction or warmth in the chest (123). A few reported a "vital anxiety in the left chest," and screamed anxiously if the stimulation was repeated. Intense emotional reactions have been evoked by stimulation of the amygdaloid nucleus, but responses varied in the same patient even with the same parameters of stimulation. The effect was sometimes rage, sometimes fear. One patient explained, "I don't know what came over me. I felt like an animal" (100).

The sensation of fear without any concomitant pain has also been observed as a result of ESB of the temporal lobe (230). This effect may be classified as "illusion of fear" (174) because there was obviously no real reason to be afraid apart from the artificial electrical activation of some cerebral structures. In every case, however, fear is a cerebral interpretation of reality which depends on a variety of cultural and experiential factors with logical or illogical reasons. The fact that it can be aroused by stimulation of a few areas of the brain allows the exploration of the neuronal mechanisms of anxiety, and as a working hypothesis we may suppose that the emotional qualities of fear depend on the activation of determined structures located probably in the thalamus, amygdala, and a few other as yet unidentified nuclei. This activation usually depends on the symbolic evaluation of coded sensory inputs, but the threshold for this activation may be modified—and also reached—by direct application of ESB. Knowledge of intracerebral mechanisms of anxiety and fear will permit the establishment of a more rational pharmacological and psychiatric treatment of many suffering patients, and may also help us to understand and ameliorate the increasing level of anxiety in our civilization.

It is also known that in some tragic cases, abnormal neurological processes may be the causal factor for unreasonable and uncontrollable violence. Those afflicted may often hurt or even kill either strangers or close family members usually treated with affection. A typical example was J. P., a charming and attractive 20-year-old girl with a history of encephalitis at the age of eighteen months and many crises of temporal lobe seizures and grand mal attacks for the last ten years (60). Her main social problem was the frequent and unpredictable occurrence of rage which on more than a dozen occasions resulted in an assault on another person such as inserting a knife into a stranger's myocardium or a pair of scissors into the pleural cavity of a nurse. The patient was committed to a ward for the criminally insane, and electrodes were implanted in her amygdala and hippocampus for exploration of possible neurological abnormalities. As she was rather impulsive, confinement in the EEG recording room was impractical, and she became one of the first clinical cases instrumented with a stimoceiver, which made it possible to study intracerebral activity without restraint. . . . Depth recordings taken while the patient moved

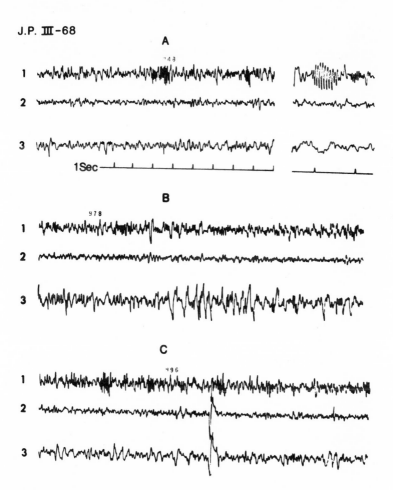

J.P. III-68

A

1

2

3

1Sec

B

978

1

2

3

C

496

1

2

3

Fig. 4. Telemetric recording of electrical activity of the brain in one of the patients [shown in an earlier illustration we have deleted—Eds.]. The location of the contacts was as follows: Channel 1: amygdaloid nucleus; Channel 2: anterior optic radiation; Channel 3: posterior optic radiation. A: spontaneous bursts appearing in Channel 1 were more prominent when the patient was psychologically excited. B: sudden spontaneous arrest of speech coincided with bursts of spikes in Channel 3. C: control recordings were unmodified by friendly behavior or by different types of motor activity such as walking and reading (60). (Illustration © 1968 The Williams & Wilkins Co., Baltimore.)

freely around the ward demonstrated marked electrical abnormalities in both amygdala and hippocampus. Spontaneous periods of aimless walking coincided with an increase in the number of high-voltage sharp waves. At other times, the patient's speech was spontaneously inhibited for several minutes during which she could not answer any questions although she retained partial comprehension and awareness. These periods coincided with bursts of spike activity localized to the optic radiation. . . . Transitory emotional excitement was related with an increase in the number and duration of 16-cycles-per-second bursts; but the patient read papers, conversed with other people, and walked around without causing any noticeable alterations in the telemetered intracerebral electrical activity.

During depth explorations, it was demonstrated that crises of assaultive behavior similar to the patient's spontaneous bursts of anger could be elicited by radio stimulation of contact 3 in the right amygdala. A 1.2 milliampere excitation of this point was applied while she was playing the guitar and singing with enthusiasm and skill. At the seventh second of stimulation, she threw away the guitar and in a fit of rage launched an attack against the wall and then paced around the floor for several minutes, after which she gradually quieted down and resumed her usual cheerful behavior. This effect was repeated on two different days. The fact that only the contact located in the amygdala induced rage suggested that the neuronal field around contact 3 was involved in the patient's behavior problem, and this finding was of great clinical significance in the orientation of subsequent treatment by local coagulation.

The demonstration that amygdaloid stimulation may induce violent behavior has also been provided by other investigators. King (128) has described the case of a woman with feelings of depression and alienation, with an extremely flat tone of voice and a facial expression which was blank and unchanging during interviews, who upon stimulation of the amygdala with 5 milliamperes had greatly altered vocal inflections and an angry expression. During this time she said, "I feel like I want to get up from this chair! Please don't let me do it! Don't do this to me. I don't want to be mean!" When the interviewer asked if she would like to hit him, the patient answered, "Yeah, I want to hit something. I want to get something and just tear it up. Take it so I won't!" She then handed her scarf to the interviewer who gave her a stack of paper, and without any other verbal exchange, she tore it into shreds saying, "I don't like to feel like this." When the level of stimulation was reduced to 4 milliamperes, her attitude changed to a broad smile, and she explained, "I know it's silly, what I'm doing. I wanted to get up from this chair and run. I wanted to hit something, tear up something—anything. Not you, just anything. I just wanted to get up and tear. I had no control of myself."

An increase in intensity up to 5 milliamperes again resulted in similar aggressive manifestations, and she raised her arm as if to strike.

It is notable that although the patients seemed to be out of control in these two instances of electrically induced aggression, they did not attack the interviewer, indicating that they were aware of their social situation. This finding is reminiscent of the behavior of stimulated monkeys who directed their aggressiveness according to previous experience and social rank and did not dare to challenge the authority of well-established bosses. Apparently ESB can induce a state of increased violent reactivity which is expressed in accordance with individual structure and environmental circumstances. We may conclude therefore that artificially evoked emotional change is only one more factor in the constellation of behavioral determinants.

PLEASURABLE EXCITATION OF THE ANIMAL BRAIN

It is surprising that in science as well as in literature more attention has been paid to suffering than to happiness. The central theme of most novels is tragedy, while happy books are hard to find; excellent monographs have been published about pain, but similar studies of pleasure are nonexistent. Typically, in the monumental *Handbook of the American Physiological Society* (75), a full chapter is devoted to pain, and pleasure is not even listed in the general subject index. Evidently the pursuit of happiness has not aroused as much scientific interest as the fear of pain.

In psychological literature the study of reward is well represented, but even there it has been considered a second-rate sensation and perhaps an artifact of a diminution of pain. It has been postulated that a truly "pleasant" sensation could not exist because organisms have a continuous tendency to minimize incoming stimuli. Pleasure was thus considered a subjective name for the diminution of drive, the withdrawal of a strong stimulation, or the reduction of pain. This "pain reduction" theory (154) has been fruitful as a basis for psychological investigations, but it is gloomy to think that we live in a world of punishment in which the only reality is suffering and that our brain can perceive different degrees of pain but no real pleasure.

Interest in the earlier ideas of hedonism has been renewed by recent experimental studies. According to this theory, pain and pleasure are relatively independent sensations and can be evoked by different types of stimuli which are recognized by separate cerebral mechanisms. Behavior is considered to be motivated by stimuli which the organism tries to minimize (pain) or by stimuli which the organism tries to maximize (pleasure). The brain is thought to have different systems for the reception of these two kinds of inputs, and the psychological state of pleasure or reward can be determined not only by the termination of pain but also by the onset of primary pleasure. The discovery of two anatomically distinct mechanisms in the brain, one for punishment, as mentioned earlier, and one for reward, provides a physiological basis for the dualistic motivation postulated in hedonism (62, 165).

The surprising fact is that animals of different species, including rats, cats, and monkeys, have voluntarily chosen to press a lever which provides electrical stimulation of specific cerebral areas. The demonstrations are highly convincing because animals which initially pressed a lever to obtain the reward of sugar pellets later pressed at similar or higher rates when electrical stimulation was substituted for food. These experiments showed conclusively that the animals enjoyed the electrical impulses which were delivered only at their own demand. Watching a rat or monkey stimulate its own brain is a fascinating spectacle. Usually each lever pressing triggers a brief 0.5-to 1.0-second brain stimulation which can be more rewarding than food. In a choice situation, hungry rats ran faster to reach the self-stimulation lever than to obtain pellets, and they persistently pressed this lever, ignoring food within easy reach. Rats have removed obstacles, run mazes, and even crossed electrified floors to reach the lever that provided cerebral stimulation.

Not all areas of the brain involved in pleasurable effects appear equally responsive. The highest lever-pressing rates (of up to a remarkable 5,000 times per hour) were recorded by animals self-stimulating in the posterior hypothalamus; excitation of rhinencephalic structures (of only about 200 times per hour) was considered moderately rewarding; and in sensory or motor areas, animals self-stimulated at merely a chance level (of 10 to 25 times per hour), and these areas were classified as neutral. As should be expected, when stimulation was shifted from rewarding areas to nuclei in the punishment system in the same animals, they pressed the lever once and never went back, showing that in the brain of the same animal there were two different groups of structures, one rewarding and the other aversive.

A systematic analysis of the neuroanatomical distribution of pleasurable areas in the rat (164) shows that 60 per cent of the brain is neutral, 35 per cent is rewarding, and only 5 per cent may elicit punishing effects. The idea that far more brain is involved in pleasure than in suffering is rather optimistic and gives hope that this predominance of the potential for pleasurable sensations can be developed into a more effective behavioral reality.

Because of the lack of verbal communication with animals, any ideas about what kind of pleasure, if any, may be experienced during ESB is a matter of speculation. There are some indications, however, that the perceived sensations could be related to anatomical differentiation of primary rewards of food and sex, because hungry animals self-stimulated at a higher rate in the middle hypothalamus, while administration of sexual hormones to castrated rats increased their lever pressing of more lateral hypothalamic points.

The controversial issue of how these findings in animals may relate to human behavior and the possible existence of areas involved in pleasure in the human brain has been resolved by the information obtained in patients with implanted electrodes.

HUMAN PLEASURE EVOKED BY ESB

On the basis of many studies during cerebral surgery, Penfield (174) has said of anger, joy, pleasure, and sexual excitement in the human brain that "so far as our experience goes, neither localized epileptic discharge nor electrical stimulation is capable of awakening any such emotion. One is tempted to believe that there are no specific cortical mechanisms associated with these emotions." This statement still holds true for the cerebral cortex, but studies in human subjects with implanted electrodes have demonstrated that electrical stimulation of the depth of the brain can induce pleasurable manifestations, as evidenced by the spontaneous verbal reports of patients, their facial expression and general behavior, and their desire to repeat the experience. In a group of twenty-three patients suffering from schizophrenia (98), electrical stimulation of the septal region, located deep in the frontal lobes, produced an enhancement of alertness sometimes accompanied by an increase in verbal output, euphoria, or pleasure. In a more systematic study in another group of patients, further evidence was presented of the rewarding effects of septal stimulation (20, 99). One man suffering from narcolepsia was provided with a small stimulator and a built-in counter which recorded the number of times that he voluntarily stimulated each of several selected points in his brain during a period of seventeen weeks. The highest score was recorded from one point in the septal region, and the patient declared that pushing this particular button made him feel "good" as if he were building up to a sexual orgasm, although he was not able to reach the end point and often felt impatient and anxious. His narcolepsia was greatly relieved by pressing this "septal button." Another patient with psychomotor epilepsy also enjoyed septal self-stimulation, which again had the highest rate of button pressing and often induced sexual thoughts. Activation of the septal region by direct injection of acetylcholine produced local electrical changes in two epileptic patients and a shift in mood from disphoria to contentment and euphoria, usually with concomitant sexual motivation and some "orgastic sensations."

Further information was provided by another group of sixty-five patients suffering from schizophrenia or Parkinson's disease, in whom a total of 643 contacts were implanted, mainly in the anterior part of the brain (201). Results of ESB were grouped as follows: 360 points were "Positive I," and with stimulation "the patients became relaxed, at ease, had a feeling of well-being, and/or were a little sleepy." Another 31 points were "Positive II," and "the patients were definitely changed . . . in a good mood, felt good. They were relaxed, at ease, and enjoyed themselves, frequently smiling. There was a slight euphoria, but the behavior was adequate." They sometimes wanted more stimulations. Excitation of another eight points evoked behavior classified as "Positive III," when "the euphoria was definitely beyond normal limits. The patients laughed out loud, enjoyed themselves, and positively liked the stimulation, and wanted more." ESB of another 38 points gave ambivalent results, and the patients expressed occasional pleasure or displeasure following excitation of the same area. From three other points, responses were termed "orgasm" because the patients initially expressed enjoyment and then suddenly were completely satisfied and did not want any more stimulation for a variable period of time. Finally, from about two hundred other points, ESB produced unpleasant reactions including anxiety, sadness, depression, fear, and emotional outbursts. One of the moving pictures taken in this study was very demonstrative, showing a patient with a sad expression and slightly depressed mood who smiled when a brief stimulation was applied to the rostral part of the brain, returning quickly to his usual depressed state, to smile again as soon as stimulation was reapplied. Then a ten-second stimulation completely changed his behavior and facial expression into a lasting pleasant and happy mood. Some mental patients have been provided with portable stimulators which they have used in self-treatment of depressive states with apparent clinical success.

These results indicate the need for careful functional exploration during brain surgery in order to avoid excessive euphoria or depression when positive or negative reinforcing areas are damaged. Emotional instability, in which the subject bursts suddenly into tears or laughter without any apparent reason, has been observed following some neurosurgical interventions. These major behavior problems might have been avoided by sparing the region involved in emotional regulation.

In our own experience, pleasurable sensations were observed in three patients with psychomotor epilepsy (50, 58, 109). The first case was V.P., a 36-year-old female with a long history of epileptic attacks which could not be controlled by medication. Electrodes were implanted in her right temporal lobe and upon stimulation of a contact located in the superior part about thirty millimeters below the surface, the patient reported a pleasant tingling sensation in the left side of her body "from my face down to the bottom of my legs." She started giggling and making funny comments, stating that she enjoyed the sensation "very much." Repetition of these stimulations made the patient more communicative and flirtatious, and she ended by openly expressing her desire to marry the therapist. Stimulation of other cerebral points failed to modify her mood and indicated the specificity of the evoked effect. During control interviews before and after ESB, her behavior was quite proper, without familiarity or excessive friendliness.

The second patient was J.M., an attractive, cooperative, and intelligent 30-year-old female who had suffered for eleven years from psychomotor and grand mal attacks which resisted medical therapy. Electrodes were implanted in her right temporal lobe, and stimulation of one of the points in the amygdala induced a pleasant sensation of relaxation and considerably increased her verbal output, which took on a more intimate character. This patient openly expressed her fondness for the therapist (who was new to her), kissed his hands, and talked about her immense gratitude for what was being done for her. A similar increase in verbal and emotional expression was repeated when the same point was stimulated on a different day, but it did not appear when other areas of the brain were explored. During control situations the patient was rather reserved and poised.

The third case was A.F., an 11-year-old boy with severe psychomotor epilepsy. Six days after electrode implantation in both temporal lobes, his fourth tape-recorded interview was carried out while electrical activity of the brain was continuously recorded and 5-second stimulations were applied in a prearranged sequence at intervals of about four minutes. The interviewer maintained an air of friendly interest throughout, usually without initiating conversation. After six other excitations, point LP located on the surface of the left temporal lobe was stimulated for the first time, and there was an open and precipitous declaration of pleasure. The patient had been silent for the previous five-minute interval, but immediately after this stimulation he exclaimed, "Hey! You can keep me here longer when you give me these; I like those." He went on to insist that the ongoing brain tests made him feel good. Similar statements with an emphatic expression of "feeling good" followed eight of a total sixteen stimulations of this point during the ninety-minute interview. Several of these manifestations were accompanied by a statement of fondness for the male interviewer, and the last one was accompanied by a voluptuous stretch. None of these manifestations appeared during the control pre-

stimulation period of twenty-six minutes or during the twenty-two minutes when other points were excited. Statistical analysis of the difference
between the frequency of pleasurable expressions before and after onset
of stimulations proved that results were highly significant ($P < 0.001$).

The open expressions of pleasure in this interview and the general
passivity of behavior could be linked, more or less intuitively, to feminine
strivings. It was therefore remarkable that in the next interview, performed in a similar manner, the patient's expressions of confusion about
his own sexual identity again appeared following stimulation to point LP.
He suddenly began to discuss his desire to get married, but when asked,
"To whom?" he did not immediately reply. Following stimulation of another point and a one-minute, twenty-second silence, the patient said, "I
was thinking—there's—I was saying *this* to you. How to spell 'yes'—y-e-s.
I mean y-o-s. No! 'You' ain't y-e-o. It's this. *Y-o-u*." The topic was then
completely dropped. The monitor who was listening from the next room
interpreted this as a thinly veiled wish to marry the interviewer, and it
was decided to stimulate the same site again after the prearranged schedule had been completed. During the following forty minutes, seven other
points were stimulated, and the patient spoke about several topics of a
completely different and unrelated content. Then LP was stimulated
again, and the patient started making references to the facial hair of the
interviewer and continued by mentioning pubic hair and his having been
the object of genital sex play in the past. He then expressed doubt about
his sexual identity, saying, "I was thinkin' if I was a boy or a girl—which
one I'd like to be." Following another excitation he remarked with evident pleasure: "You're doin' it now," and then he said, "I'd like to be a
girl."

In the interpretation of these results it is necessary to consider the
psychological context in which electrical stimulation occurs, because the
personality configuration of the subject, including both current psychodynamic and psychogenetic aspects, may be an essential determinant of
the results of stimulation. Expression of feminine strivings in our patient
probably was not the exclusive effect of ESB but the expression of already
present personality factors which were activated by the stimulation. The
balance between drive and defense may be modified by ESB, as suggested
by the fact that after one stimulation the patient said without apparent
anxiety, "I'd like to be a girl," but when this idea was presented to him
by the therapist in a later interview without stimulation, the patient
became markedly anxious and defensive. Minute-to-minute changes in
personality function, influenced by the environment and by patient-
interviewer relations, may modify the nature of specific responses, and
these variables, which are difficult to assess, must be kept in mind.

FRIENDLINESS AND INCREASED
CONVERSATION UNDER
ELECTRICAL CONTROL

Human relations evolve between the two opposite poles of love and hate which are determined by a highly complex and little understood combination of elements including basic drives, cultural imprinting, and refined emotional and intellectual characteristics. This subject has so many semantic and conceptual problems that few investigators have dared to approach it experimentally, and in spite of its essential importance, most textbooks of psychology evade its discussion. To define friendliness is difficult although its identification in typical cases is easy, and in our daily life we are continuously evaluating and classifying personal contacts as friendly or hostile. A smiling face, attentive eyes, a receptive hand, related body posture, intellectual interest, ideological agreement, kind words, sympathetic comments, and expressions of personal acceptance are among the common indicators of cordial interpersonal relations. The expression of friendship is a part of social behavior which obviously requires contact between two or more individuals. A mutually pleasurable relation creates a history and provides each individual with a variety of optic, acoustic, tactile, and other stimuli which are received and interpreted with a "friendly bias." The main characteristic of love and friendship is precisely that stimuli coming from a favored person are interpreted as more agreeable than similar stimuli originating from other sources, and this evaluation is necessarily related to neuronal activity.

Little is known about the cerebral mechanisms of friendliness, but as is the case for any behavioral manifestation, no emotional state is possible without a functioning brain, and it may be postulated that some cerebral structures are dispensable and others indispensable both for the interpretation of sensory inputs as amicable and for the expression of friendship. Strong support for this idea derives from the fact, repeatedly proved in neurosurgery, that destruction of some parts of the brain, such as the motor and sensory cortices, produces motor deficits without modifying affective behavior, while ablation of the frontal lobes may induce considerable alteration of emotional personality. Further support has been provided by electrical stimulation of the frontal lobes, which may induce friendly manifestations.

In patient A. F., mentioned earlier in connection with pleasurable manifestations, the third interview was characterized by changes in the character and degree of verbal output following stimulation of one point in the temporal cortex. Fourteen stimulations were applied, seven of them through point RP located in the inferolateral part of the right frontal

lobe cortex, and the other seven through contacts located on the cortex of the right temporal lobe and depth of the left and right temporal lobes. The interview started with about five minutes of lively conversation, and during the next ten minutes the patient gradually quieted down until he spoke only about five seconds during every subsequent two-minute period. Throughout the interview the therapist encouraged spontaneous expression by reacting compassionately, by joking with, urging, and reassuring the patient, and by responding to any information offered. The attitude never produced more than a simple reply and often not even that.

In contrast to this basic situation, there were six instances of sharp increase in verbal communication and its friendly content. Each of these instances followed within forty seconds after stimulation of point RP. The only exception was the last excitation of this point when the voltage had been changed. The increases in verbal activity were rapid but brief and without any consistency in subject material, which was typical for the patient. Qualification and quantification of the patient's conversation were made by analyzing the recorded typescript which was divided into two-minute periods and judged independently by two investigators who had no knowledge of the timing or location of stimulations. Comparison of the two-minute periods before and after these stimulations revealed a verbal increase from seventeen to eighty-eight words and a greater number of friendly remarks, from six to fifty-three. These results were highly significant and their specificity was clear because no changes in verbalization were produced by stimulation of any of the other cerebral points. It was also evident that the evoked changes were not related to the interviewer's rather constant verbal activity. It was therefore concluded that the impressive increase in verbal expression and friendly remarks was the result of electrical stimulation of a specific point on the cortex of the temporal lobe.

REFERENCES

(20) BISHOP, M. P., S. T. ELDER, & R. G. HEATH. Intracranial self-stimulation in man. *Science,* 140: 394–396, 1963.

(50) DELGADO, J. M. R. Emotional behavior in animals and humans. *Psychiat. Res. Rep.,* 12: 259–271, 1960.

(53) DELGADO, J. M. R. Free behavior and brain stimulation. Pp. 349–449 in: "International Review of Neurobiology," Vol. VI. C. C. Pfeiffer and J. R. Smythies (eds.) New York: Academic Press, 476 pp. 1964b.

(56) DELGADO, J. M. R. Aggression and defense under cerebral radio control. Pp. 171–193 in: "Aggression and Defense. Neural Mechanisms and Social Patterns." UCLA Forum in Medical Sciences, No. 7, Vol. V, C. D. Clemente and D. B. Lindsley (eds.) Berkeley: Univ. Cal. Press, 361 pp., 1967.

(58) DELGADO, J. M. R. & H. HAMLIN. Spontaneous and evoked electrical seizures in animals and in humans. Pp. 133–158 in "Electrical Studies on the Unanesthetized Brain." Estelle R. Ramey and Desmond S. O'Doherty (eds.), New York: Paul B. Hoeber, 432 pp., 1960.

(60) DELGADO, J. M. R., V. MARK, W. SWEET, F. ERVIN, G. WEISS, G. BACH-Y-RITA, & R. HAGIWARA. Intracerebral radio stimulation and recording in completely free patients. *J. Nerv. Ment. Dis.,* 147: 329–340, 1968.

(62) DELGADO, J. M. R., W. W. ROBERTS, & N. E. MILLER. Learning motivated by electrical stimulation of the brain. *Amer. J. Physiol.,* 179: 587–593, 1954.

(73) ERVIN, F. Participant in "Brain Stimulation in Behaving Subjects." Neurosciences Research Program Workshop, Dec., 1966.

(75) FIELD, J., H. W. MAGOUN, & W. E. HALL (eds.). "Handbook of Physiology. Section 1: Neurophysiology." Washington, D. C.: Amer. Physiol. Soc., Vol. I, 1959, Vols. II & III, 1960.

(87) GERARD, M. W. Afferent impulses of the trigeminal nerve. The intramedullary course of the painful, thermal and tactile impulses. *Arch. Neurol. Psychiat.* (Chicago), 9: 306–338, 1923.

(98) HEATH, R. G., "Studies in Schizophrenia. A multidisciplinary Approach to Mind-Brain Relationships." Cambridge: Harvard Univ. Press, 619 pp., 1954.

(99) HEATH, R. G. Electrical self-stimulation of the brain in man. *Amer. J. Psychiat.,* 120: 571–577, 1963.

(100) HEATH, R. G., R. R. MONROE, & W. MICKLE. Stimulation of the amygdaloid nucleus in a schizophrenic patient. *Amer. J. Psychiat.,* 111: 862–863, 1955.

(105) HESS, W. R. Stammganglien-Reizversuche. (Verh. Dtsch. physiol. Ges., Sept., 1927). *Ber. ges. Physiol.,* 42: 554–555, 1928.

(106) HESS, W. R. "Beitrage zur Physiologie d. Hirnstammes I. Die Methodik der lokalisierten Reizung. und Ausschaltung subkortikaler Hirnabschnitte." Leipzig: Georg Thieme, 122 pp., 1932.

(109) HIGGINS, J. W., G. F. MAHL, J. M. R. DELGADO, & H. HAMLIN. Behavioral changes during intracerebral electrical stimulation. *Arch. Neurol. Psychiat.,* (Chicago), 76: 399–419, 1956.

(123) JUNG, R. & R. HASSLER. The extrapyramidal motor system. Pp. 863–927 in: "Handbook of Physiology," Section 1: Neurophysiology Vol. II, J. Field, H. W. Magoun and V. E. Hall (eds.) Baltimore, Md.: Williams & Wilkins, pp. 781–1439, 1960.

(128) KING, H. E. Psychological effects of excitation in the limbic system. Pp. 477–486 in: "Electrical Stimulation of the Brain," D. E. Sheer (ed.) Austin: Univ. Texas Press, 641 pp., 1961.

(148) LORENZ, K. Ritualized fighting. Pp. 39–50 in: "The Natural History of Aggression." J. D. Carthy and F. J. Ebling (eds.) New York: Academic Press, 159 pp., 1964.

(154) MILLER, N. E. Learnable drives and rewards. Pp. 435–472 in: "Handbook of Experimental Psychology," S. S. Stevens (ed.) New York: John Wiley, 1436 pp., 1951.

(157) MONTAGU, A. "On Being Human." New York: Hawthorne, 128 pp., 2nd Ed., 1966.

(164) OLDS, J. Hypothalamic substrates of reward. *Physiol. Rev.*, 42: 554–604, 1962.

(165) OLDS, J. & P. MILNER. Positive reinforcement produced by electrical stimulation of the septal area and other regions of the rat brain. *J. comp. physiol. Psychol.*, 47: 419–428, 1954.

(174) PENFIELD, W. & H. JASPER. "Epilepsy and the Functional Anatomy of the Human Brain." Boston: Little, Brown, 896 pp., 1954.

(201) SEM-JACOBSEN, C. W. "Depth-Electrographic Stimulation of the Human Brain and Behavior: From Fourteen Years of Studies and Treatment of Parkinson's Disease and Mental Disorders with Implanted Electrodes." Springfield, Ill.: C. C. Thomas, 222 pp., 1968.

(212) SOULAIRAC, A., J. CAHN, & J. CHARPENTIER. "Pain." New York: Academic Press, 562 pp., 1968.

(214) SPIEGEL, E. A. & H. T. WYCIS. Stimulation of the brain stem and basal ganglia in man. Pp. 487–497 in: "Electrical stimulation of the Brain," D. E. Sheer (ed.) Austin: Univ. Texas Press, 641 pp., 1961.

(220) SWEET, W. H. Pain. Pp. 459–506 in: "Handbook of Physiology," Section 1: Neurophysiology. Vol. 1. J. Field, H. W. Magoun, W. E. Hall (eds.) Washington, D. C.: Amer. Physiol. Soc., 779 pp., 1959.

(221) SWEET, W. H. Participant in "Brain Stimulation in Behaving Subjects." Neurosciences Research Program Workshop. Dec., 1966.

(230) VAN BUREN, J. M. Sensory, motor and autonomic effects of mesial temporal stimulation in man. *J. Neurosurg.*, 18: 273–288, 1961.

(234) WALTER, W. G. Participant in "Brain Stimulation in Behaving Subjects." Neurosciences Research Program Workshop, Dec., 1966.

What genetic course will man steer?

Herman Muller

*INTRODUCTION   There are two major forms of ge-
netic engineering: selective breeding and genetic surgery. In the following
article a Nobel Prize-winning biologist, the late Dr. Herman J. Muller,
discusses the potential and promise of selective breeding—the program of
"germinal choice" that is already being used to produce more than 10,000
babies yearly in the United States. Citing scientific developments (for example, frozen sperm banks) that make selective breeding far more effective today than in the past, Muller goes on to argue that new programs
of germinal choice will not only offset the dilemma of "our load of mutations" but will also help avoid the difficulties and social mistakes of "old-
style" eugenics movements:*

> *The banks of germinal material that will thereby become available
> will include material derived from persons of outstanding gifts, in-
> telligence, moral fiber, and physical fitness. In this way couples desir-
> ing to have in their own families one or more children who are es-
> pecially likely to embody their own ideals of worth will be afforded
> a wide range of choice. They will be assisted by records of the lives
> and characteristics of the donors and of their relatives, and by coun-
> sel from diverse specialists, but the final choices will be their own
> and their participation will be entirely voluntary. It is to be ex-
> pected that the use of this method will increase in the course of
> coming generations and will implement, on the genetic side, a great
> advance in human brotherhood, intelligence, and bodily vigor
> [Muller, in Sonneborn, 1965].*

W e—that is, humanity—will take our biological evo-
lution into our own hands and try to steer its direction, provided that
we survive our present crises. Have we not eventually utilized, for better

Muller, H. What genetic course will man steer? *Bulletin of the Atomic Scientists*, 1968,
   24, 6–12. Reprinted by permission of Science and Public Affairs, the Bulletin of
   the Atomic Scientists. Copyright © 1970 by the Educational Foundation for Nuclear
   Science.

or worse, all materials, processes, and powers that we could gain some mastery over? And are there not means already by which we *can* influence our heredity, and other means that we are likely to gain?

We may define genetic advances by life as the gaining of abilities for making use of the environment more effectively, and for withstanding or even making use of circumstances that earlier would have been useless or hostile. By this measure, the totality of living things has certainly advanced enormously through the ages. For it has increasingly extended life's domain, increased its resources, and made it more secure. Moreover, certain lines of descent, most notably the one leading to ourselves, have ultimately advanced the most by these criteria. They, and especially we, are the ones that can overcome the greatest difficulties, and the most adverse ones. And we, the self-styled heirs of all the ages, have constituted the very luckiest, the most improbably lucky, combinations of trials of the whole lot.

The luck that allowed any line to advance genetically was of course based on the Darwinian natural selection of mutant types, and of combinations of them. Since the kind of mutation occurring cannot be influenced by the effect it will have, and since there can be ever so many more ways of harming than of improving any mechanism, vastly more mutations and combinations of them proved to be failures than successes in their influence on "genetic survival," "net multiplication," or simply "fitness." It is the *multiplication* of the successful mutants that plays the key role in evolution, for it alone allows additional successful steps sufficient chance to occur. To permit room and resources for this multiplication there must of course be correlative reduction in numbers, or extinction, of some less successful types, except when the new ones that succeed all go into virgin territory, or somehow make enough extra resources available for others too.

OUR FOREBEARS' RUN OF LUCK

Let us review briefly some clues to man's concatenation of luck having been so much greater than that of other organisms by focusing upon his ancestors of the last hundred million years, the primates. A long succession of events had already made the mammals the most advanced animals. Of the primates, remains of the most primitive known group, the prosimians, have been found in strata that also contain remains of dinosaurs. Prosimians must early have gained such physical advantages for active life in trees as opposable first digits, improved vision, equipment for a somewhat omnivorous diet, and uniparity. But they were soon pushed into the background and thus hampered in advancing futher by their more successful offshoots, the simians: monkeys and apes. Thus, they failed to gain the simians' greater maneuverability, higher curiosity, and general intelligence.

The bodily and psychological advances made by monkeys and apes gave a further basis for the advances afterward made by the apes' proto-human offshoot, which split off from the other apes some 20 million years ago. Suffice it here to call attention to the constant view forward, with its opening up of wider opportunities, permitted by the apes' arm-mobility and consequent arm-swung mode of progression, and, derived from the latter, their semi-erect posture even on the ground.

These traits put even more of a premium than before on broad awareness, versatility, and love of variety, hence too on curiosity concerning objects, both inanimate and animate, and general intelligence. The latter includes a higher ability to transfer lessons learned in a given field to another one, and to solve problems. This in turn allowed, at least in the chimpanzee, the making of very simple tools, and some hunting of game.

Meanwhile, social intelligence, affection between companions, and co-operation had also increased; the little groups of protohumans had continued to be fairly permanent and to include individuals of all ages, and could therefore profit by emphasis on these social traits. Moreover, the division into many small social groups must have promoted natural selection for the genetic bases of social intelligence, and of social traits in general. This is because genes that tend to extend maternal and brotherly feelings to other members of the closely related little group result also in mutual aid. By thus helping the group's survival, these genes actually foster their own survival even when they lead to self-sacrifice, since others of the tiny band tend to have the same genes. By the greater growth, followed by the resplitting of the more social little groups, the genetic groundwork of cooperation was increasingly strengthened in the species.

MAN IMPROVES ON LUCK

In these ways, the genetic structure must have been laid down for a line of descent which, separating off from that of other apes some 20 million years ago, could by virtue of both its bodily and mental traits evolve to get along increasingly well on the ground. By some two million years ago, its members had already become fully erect and much like ourselves in form, except for their little more than ape-size brain and large jaws. Since their lairs contain abundant broken bones of fair-sized game, as well as rough-hewn tools, they must not only have evolved much more initiative, including aggressivness, than apes, but also, and most important, they must already have accumulated a substantial amount of extragenetically transmitted experience. In other words, cultural evolution, a process so nearly unique in the human line, had begun in earnest.

Like the evolution of the genetic constitution, that of culture requires the arising, the transmitting, and the selection of innovations. But since the cultural innovations are in thought and behavior, their transmission is by some form of imitation, not heredity, even though genes must afford the abilities for these processes. Of course this form of transmission allows a much more rapid spreading than that through differential multiplication.

During these developments human foresight as well as hindsight became enhanced. Hence the initiation of cultural innovations gradually, and with the scientific technological breakthrough very rapidly, became less haphazard, unlike that of mutations. They could increasingly be preselected to advantage, more reliably and rapidly post-tested, and their transmission became faster and wider. Larger steps then became more feasible, and even necessary.

It is generally conceded that the advances of science and technology already carry the physical potential of bringing dignity, affluence, health, enlightenment, and brotherhood within the reach of all. It is also conceded that, because of the dearth of really integrative and cooperative thinking and the inertia of old ways, these very advances are misused to cause the desperate crises of fast mounting population, massive depletion of resources, mass pollution, maldistribution, mass want that knows it need not exist, inflexible privilege, mass miseducation along outgrown lines, mass deception, frenzied fanaticism, mass coercion, the threat or actuality of mass slaughter, and that of the destruction of civilization.

Thus, the changes in social conditions constitute, so far, no more than a now-foreseeable larger cultural step forward which has become mandatory for the survival of civilization. It can bring no utopia—there will never be such a status, it is to be hoped—but it will be, in a sense, only a beginning of progress on a somewhat less insecure basis.

MAN UNDERMINES HIMSELF

Just as natural mutations had to be stringently sifted by natural selection if a population were to advance or even not to deteriorate, so, in species divided into many small groups, the mutational combinations in each had to be sifted, by a longer-range natural selection, in the interests of the species as a whole. And again, genera with only one species had, other things being equal, less chance of surviving than did multi-specific ones, since any single species is so likely to prove, in the still longer run, to have been a natural error. This is shown by the fact that such a tiny per cent of species of the past have turned out to represent lines that persisted. In accord with this principle is the finding that the category with the highest per cent of survivals has been that of phyla, and that successively narrower categories have had a correspondingly decreasing survival rate.

In the case of man, it has been intrinsically dangerous for him to have so long existed as just one species. He has been saved not only by his unparalleled advantages but also by having until recently been divided into thousands of tiny bands, of at most a few score members each. In fact, as we have seen, this condition was especially favorable for the genetic enhancement of cooperative traits, including, I might add, those promoting group initiative or even—to use a harsher word—aggression. Until some two hundred generations ago the population pattern remained like this over by far the largest portion of the area inhabited by man. However, the agricultural revolution resulted in larger, denser, fewer groups, and the urban revolution greatly intensified this trend, thus practically preventing further genetic advances based on intergroup competition and even, in all probability, threatening the maintenance of those previously gained.

At the same time, intragroup natural selection, working via families and individuals, is also counteracted as much as our improving techniques can do so, by saving everyone whom they can for survival and for reproduction. They have already become highly effective in this job. This means that mutations having a net detrimental effect on body or mind may now be accumulating almost as fast as they arise. We can escape the inference that such mutations far outweigh any advantageous ones only by believing that mutations are designated by Providence for a species' direct benefit, but in that case we run contrary to the clear experimental results.

These considerations show that modern culture is used to achieve maximal saving of lives and fertility, unaccompanied by a conscious planning which would take the genetic effects of this policy into account. Our culture thus protects against elimination of mutations detrimental to bodily vigor, intelligence, or social predispositions. Hence it must allow more accumulation of detrimentals in populations than would otherwise be the case. It appears wishful thinking to suppose that there is in our type of culture a built-in selective mechanism, not designed by us intentionally, which acts over a long period so as adequately to replace the earlier positive feedback whereby the genetic constitution was advanced.

Yet degeneration by passive accumulation of mutant genes is extremely gradual in manifesting its effects. The reason for this creeping pace is that most mutant genes exert such minute effects, at least when the given gene has been received from only one parent. The problem of creeping genetic deterioration is not acute in comparison with the fast-growing menaces presented by our cultural imbalances.

The presently much more important genetic problem arising out of modern cultural conditions lies in the need for a further advance in the genetic level of those psychological endowments which have already attained a height so distinctive of man. These are cooperativeness and general intelligence, including the creativity which arises from high initiative working through high intelligence.

ADJUSTING TO NEW CONDITIONS

A stronger, more broadly acting cooperativeness is becoming imperative for adjusting to the relatively new conditions of life in large communities, and especially in the hoped-for world community of equal opportunities. Even in the scant two to four hundred generations since the ancestors of most people gave up living in tiny bands, there may have been some significant passive accumulation of retrograde genetic changes that adversely affected one's brotherly feelings toward more distant associates. So-called enlightened self-interest is no substitute. It can lead people in communities already having socially oriented practices to conform to these, though it alone would not initiate such communities. But these same conformists may, on feeling safe from exposure, engage in unfair, cut-throat competition, covert fraud, or more extreme criminality.

More modern means of bringing up the young and of otherwise influencing the mind will doubtless be much more effective than today in the development of social feelings and behavior, and the shrinkage or repression of antagonistic ones. Yet we are far from knowing to what extent practicable treatments of these kinds would be able to rival or exceed a deep and broad warmheartedness which was genetically built in. Meanwhile, the exigencies of recent culture call on us not to leave a stone unturned that could cause more of the population to be of this predisposition.

The avoidance of disaster would be far from man's only motivation in seeking a stronger, broader, brotherly love. Many of us realize the truth behind the saying "Love is what makes the world go 'round." Since such feelings and behavior have already been built into our genetic constitutions and built up in our cultures to a considerable although not now sufficient degree, we do appreciate and crave them, even for their own sakes. We have in this way been led into a situation where more brotherly love will at the same time promote our survival, help to remove the aimlessness and sense of alienation so prevalent today, and afford people deeper inner fulfillment in working for their now vast community.

As for intelligence, consider how lost most people are today if they try to grapple realistically with our bewildering ideological, social, technical, or scientific problems. In all these areas more background, penetration, and integrative ability than they have are fast becoming required. Personally, if I had an opportunity to gain greater intelligence or understanding I would have any and all means of doing so used, except where, like Faust, I had to "sell away my soul" to achieve it. Moreover, our species as a whole for a very long time made the same choice, even though unconsciously. Hence our own dominance.

In fact, in consequence of the long-continued genetic selection in that direction, intelligence and probably cooperativeness are traits which would allow artificial selection of their positive extremes without, or with minimal, upsets in other respects. This conclusion is verified by the relatively high level of vigor and of other valuable attributes which these extremes display, and by the positive correlations among nearly all these traits.

There seems no reason why there need be any limit, except that set by our intelligence, to the advances made in our science and technology, and to the creative powers they would allow us to exert. Nor do we now see any necessary limit to intelligence, although great increases in human intelligence would doubtless require, at times, breakthroughs released by anatomical or biochemical innovations in the brain or accessories of it. Such innovations—for example, the *corpus callosum*—have arisen in past mammalian genetic evolution. In culture, there have been analogous ones, such as writing.

WORKING TOWARD THE MAJOR AIMS

The most basic way of working toward the major aims is to educate everyone not later than in high school in the main principles of biology, including especially genetic and cultural evolution and their lessons for ourselves. On the heels of this should be a sketch of world history, depicting the growing unity of man.

However, with the educational background outlined, increasingly large numbers of couples who were suffering from sterility in the husband would be eager to avail themselves of means of having one or more children derived on the male side from someone they both held in deepest regard as a person physically by no means inferior while morally and mentally really outstanding. There are perhaps ten thousand children a year produced in this country by artificial insemination with semen from donors chosen by the physician; but he does not select them according to such standards and he keeps their identity secret from everyone, including the couple. Well-endowed children would be far more desired if the couples were allowed to exercise the deciding voice in the choice of the genetic father after seeing the records concerning a wide range of possible ones, considering counsel concerning them, and judging which of them have shown more of the traits preferred by the couple themselves. Are not fertile couples nowadays expected to make their own choices of their partners in marriage, and are they not in that way allowed to choose also —even though with far less directness or likelihood of getting what they prefer than by the method here proposed—the kind of children whom they themselves want?

Openness of choice regarding donors would make it desirable that the semen had usually been stored, preferably for decades, after the donors' decease. Thus the disclosure of the fact that a given person had been the donor could no longer handicap him nor open the possibility of leading to personal entanglements between him and the recipient couple. Moreover, perspective could better be gained on the possible donors' phenotypically expressed merits and their genetic reliability in passing these along—information which would be invaluable in the making of choices.

Gradually, increasing numbers of non-sterile couples also would want to take advantage of so attractive an opportunity, for at least one child in their family. The first participants would be those wanting the child spared some defect of the husband's, and other idealistic realists, who were far from subnormal. For all of them, clearly, quite open choices, made voluntarily, but after counseling and considering of the documentary evidence, would be essential. Then later, others would be proud to follow suit, letting it be known that they had done so.

There are many reasons against using secrecy in this "germinal choice." One is that adopted children usually find out that they have been adopted, as would "half-adopted" ones. The adopted child's attempt to discover his genetic derivation when (as is now usual) it is a closely guarded secret, commonly acts like a cancer in his life. On the other hand, knowledge of the facts would exert the opposite influence. Moreover, due appraisal of the data actually *requires* genetic recording of an open type. So does the making of genetic judgments about the future possibilities of an individual's germ cells, as well as the avoidance of incest, when the time comes for any given child to reproduce.

Of course the couples would be warned beforehand that genetic segregation and environmental influences allow the results of no human reproduction to be predicted, and that such selection as here depicted only *weights* the results in their favor. It would, however, be pointed out that outstandingly good performance has almost always required a combination of both favorable environment and favorable heredity, and that in heredity the child stands on the average half-way between the means of its two genetic parents.

Then as the results, so favorable on the whole, of the relatively few first trials gradually became known, ever more couples would want to follow these pioneers' example; that is how new customs usually start. Previous taboos against the practice would dwindle. In their place, a new atmosphere of hope would emerge: hope both for the rewarding results likely to accrue to the couples themselves, and hope among them and others for mankind in general. Thus a genetic leaven would tend to diffuse through the population, and also a cultural, spiritual leaven. At last *human* resources, even on the genetic side, would begin to be enhanced at an accelerating pace.

Despite the differences in choice among couples, they would wish, and should be guided, to include some of the more special gifts or predilections which tend to support or channel the two major ones of cooperative disposition and general intelligence aimed at by all. Among these are joy of life; strong feelings combined with good emotional self-control and balance; the humility to be corrected and self-corrected without rancor; empathy; thrill at beholding and at serving in a greater cause than one's self-interest; fortitude; patience; resilience; perceptivity; sensitivities and gifts of musical or other artistic types; expressivity; curiosity; love of problem-solving; and diverse special intellectual activities and drives. This list is very incomplete, the traits are complex, and many overlap and are interdependent. Physical traits also—for example, longevity, late senility, vigor, good automatic regulation, agility—should be given considerable place. No one has nearly all these mental and physical endowments, but that choice should be made which, while largely consistent with the counsel, best fits that couple's ideals.

As these more special gifts become commoner in the population they can and should be more and more combined. This process will not ultimately reduce diversity, for the resulting population of more generally well-endowed individuals will of course branch out again diversely from the higher general level so attained. Thus it will gain still greater aptitudes, of varied kinds in its different members.

In getting this project started, it is of the utmost importance that rigorous precautions be taken to insure that the persons in the group or groups undertaking it genuinely understand and favor the two major aims previously stressed. Persons who favor what *they* consider genetic improvement are of course all agreed on the major value of intelligence. However, they are far from agreed on the need for more cooperativeness, and even of those who believe they favor it a large number are gravely mistaken about its nature. That is one reason it has here been placed first, before intelligence. Many persons would today consider as desirable co-operation joint actions that would give preference to their own race, or nation, or class, or institution, or religious or provincial group, rather than to mankind as a whole. I do not mean by this to imply that mankind as a whole might never be served by one's taking sides in a dispute—far from it—but that a consistent policy of favoring one's own side just because it is one's own is contrary to the kind of cooperation needed in today's world.

Thus the group of prime-movers, to start with, must be small and carefully chosen, and guided by rules that maximally safeguard their future observance of this interpretation of social values. They should of course have as participants not only persons specialized in genetics, in the physiology of reproduction in its theoretical and medical aspects, in psychology, and in social sciences, but also representatives from the field of values and from other truly humanistic fields. In this connection, it is important to note that I have found not a few religious or ideological leaders of diverse kinds to adopt a not unfavorable attitude toward this project when it was explained. Included were representatives of the Catholic, Methodist, and Unitarian-Universalist denominations, of Judaism, official Humanism and Free-thinking. Moreover, persons brought up to Buddhism and to Shintoism have expressed approval.

As regards the attitude of the above groups toward intelligence, they should keep in mind that eminence and creative intelligence are far from the same thing, though usually confused. Truly creative intelligence is likely to break barriers that were previously observed. Therefore these creative, highly intelligent persons all too often fail to be recognized as such by their contemporaries, although they have a relatively better chance of being so recognized by the following or a still later generation. That is another reason for storing most of the semen for decades. One of the best ways for getting recognition of the fact that our own aims are not narrow or biased is to have included in the material stored that from varied races and social groups, and to raise no objection to any couple of a different race or group using such material if they want to; but they should never be pressured in either direction on this point. Of course the data seen regarding the donors will include information about their race, social class, etc., for these matters often have much bearing on the environments they had to contend with, or benefited from, and therefore on the amount of contribution from genetic sources.

The taking of extra precautions to insure a sound, forward-looking social attitude on the part of the prime movers and supporters of the project of germinal choice is made especially important by the present mores of our American society. Although it is far advanced in social outlook and practices as compared with its condition of only half a century ago—as my personal recollections can vividly attest—it has not yet advanced far enough along this road to make "performance," as measured by mundane success in our present society, a reliable clue to the possession of the two major traits here stressed.

Although the chief seeds of Western progress do lie in its science, technology, education, and struggling democracy, its most conspicuous spirit is after all that of raucous, hypocritical and often misleading salesmanship, aided by vulgar display, along with mass distractions, petty politics, and a growing militarism.

In view of this situation, still so confused and subject to strong and dangerous currents and countercurrents, unusual vigilance will be indispensable for keeping the aims of the genetic betterment group here proposed from becoming perverted.

TECHNIQUES, RESEARCH, AND PRACTICAL AIDS

As is now so well known, human spermatozoa can be kept deep-frozen at the temperature of liquid nitrogen (and lower), without deterioration during prolonged storage, even though the processes of freezing and thawing still incapacitate for fertilization a minority of them. The addition of glycerin, and, probably still better, dimethyl sulfoxide (DMSO), considerably reduces this undesired effect. At several places in this country, and in at least one abroad, banks of frozen sperm are already being kept. The infants from the deep-frozen sperm have been comparable in their normality with those from unfrozen (or unmanipulated) sperm. However, there has been no attempt so far as is known to procure for any of these banks the semen of donors who are outstanding.

Research is badly needed concerning ways of "stretching" the amount of use possible for a given sample, since suitable dilutants, long known for domestic animals, have not yet been found for man. Nor have ways yet been found of reliably fertilizing a human egg by a sperm *in vitro,* since some kind of sperm "capacitation" is needed beforehand, which normally occurs in the Fallopian tubes. Another need is to find out how immature germ cells, that could of course be kept deep-frozen like other tissues, can be caused to develop into normal spermatozoa *in vitro;* this would make possible the unlimited use of a given sample of immature germ cells.

With changing mores regarding germinal choice these services would eventually open much more possibility of choice to recipient couples, and with more choice the mores would change more rapidly, in a self-accelerating cycle. Thus the preliminary choosing of donors would become largely unnecessary. All the more necessary, however, would be the adoption of means of insuring that the counselors, and those engaged in choosing germinal material for their families, recognized and truly understood the major aims here stressed.

PROSPECTS

If to some people such discussions seem "far out," it should be remembered that they deal with measures closer to realization than those of applied gene knowledge of the traditional kind, and ever so much closer than those of "genetic surgery." In fact the latter procedures also would have the same weighty problem of aims to decide if they were not to be confined to matters which, by comparison, were trivialities. As we have seen, the germinal choice by empirical methods that is so much closer to realization still has to clear one or more technological hurdles of importance before it can be of very wide use. But these should prove readily negotiable if subjected to some concerted action.

In the empirical germinal choice project it is the matter of values that looms as by far the most important one at present. This is especially the case because so many people who would like to be associated with it fail to realize its importance, or what the major values should be, and are therefore striving to get the techniques going, willy-nilly.

We as geneticists concerned with man should see it as a part of our own responsibility not only to enlighten the public but also to promote, in the meantime, the collection, documentation, and storage of exemplary germinal material. This would be that of men who best represent the major aims of enhanced cooperativeness, based on more heartfelt, broader brotherly love and of more creative and generalized intelligence. Only in that way can we meet the obligation we all have to the multitudes to use the insights they afforded us in behalf of their and our successors.

We must avoid getting sidetracked into acceptance of the delaying procedure so prevalent in both academic and political circles, which declares: "This needs more study!" Of course it does, but it is clear that there are certain things which can and must be done at this point; also that some of us are the ones to do them, in collaboration with suitable persons in other fields, whom we must find and encourage. Chief among these immediate tasks is the starting of the practice of accumulating germinal stores and records, derived from persons who so far as we can see embody the major traits here stressed. The example thus set by us is the main present feature of this starting effort.

On the whole, physicians, especially those concerned with reproduction and the urinogenital organs, who would be willing to give up dictatorship and secrecy as principles to be adhered to in inseminations carried out under the germinal choice project, would be important to have as participants in it. But they are extremely hard to find. Meanwhile the work of getting the project going must be undertaken as soon as possible, and both medical and legal aid will eventually be forthcoming.

Thus we should not let ourselves be discouraged by the temporary difficulties. We should not only bear in mind the urgent need for success. We should also recall that, after all, man has gone from height to height, and that he is now in a position, if only he *will*, to transcend himself intentionally and thereby proceed to elevations yet unimagined. He no longer can do so unintentionally. It is up to us to do our bit in this purposive process, and to use what we know constructively, rather than remain in that ivory tower which has the writing on its wall. Our reward will be that of helping man to gain the highest freedom possible: the finding of endless worlds both outside and inside himself, and the privilege of engaging in endless creation.

Psychochemical manipulation
and social policy

David Krech

INTRODUCTION   Of all the regulatory procedures discussed in this chapter, the one that seems most able to control human behavior today, right now, is drugs. If you doubt the efficacy of drugs in regulating behavior, you have probably never taken a stiff drink, sleeping compound, tranquilizer, or stimulant, and have failed to read books like The Man with the Golden Arm *or* Naked Lunch.

What startles scientist and layman alike is the growing number of drugs that have recently been developed to assault the human brain. In 1966, Dr. Stanley Yolles, Director of the National Institute of Mental Health, predicted before a Senate subcommittee: "The next five to ten years . . . will see a hundredfold increase in the number and types of drugs capable of affecting the mind."

In the face of accelerating progress in psychopharmacology, many scientists are beginning to ponder the social implications of various behavior-controlling drugs. They are concerned not with whether a specific behavior-controlling drug will be developed, but with what will happen once it exists. One such scientist is David Krech, a psychologist at the University of California, Berkeley. In the following article he speculates about what might happen if a drug capable of raising human intelligence is perfected and introduced into society. Along the way, he shows us that behavior is a combination of psychological and chemical forces and reminds us always to be alert to the social consequences of the introduction of behavior-control procedures.

Ladies and gentlemen, prepare for a change of pace. I am not so much troubled by the mores of biomedical research and its individualistic ethics as I am by some strangely complex problems of

Krech, D. Psychochemical manipulation and social policy. *Annals of Internal Medicine,* 1967, **67,** 19–24. Reprinted by permission of the author and the Annals of Internal Medicine.

social policy that the positive, successful results of such research may soon raise, problems for which none of us are prepared.

Like all properly housebroken scientists, I can be boldly speculative in private but cautiously careful and tiresome in public. Today, however, I shall forget my scientific manners and make unseemly public leaps from animal studies to scientifically unwarranted conclusions about people. I do this because I hold that it is far less grievous a sin to be overspeculative than to be overcautious in an age where scientific knowledge is so swiftly and recklessly transduced into powerful instruments of social action for evil or good. If we are to anticipate the knowledge and forestall the evil, we must be boldly speculative. Let me proceed then without further apology.

It is my considered judgment—well, fairly well considered—that within 5 to 10 years there will be available a regimen combining psychological and chemical measures that will significantly increase the intelligence of man. This troubles me, and should trouble you, for reasons that may soon become clear. To give some substance to these predictions and forebodings, let me cite first some supporting experimental chapter and verse.

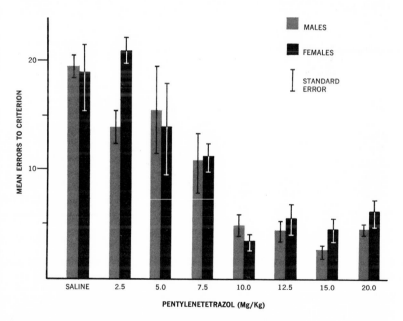

Fig. 1. Effect of pentylenetetrazol on discrimination learning in mice [Krivanek and McGaugh (1)]. (Art adapted from Krech.)

I start with Prof. James McGaugh's demonstration (1) that certain central nervous system stimulants can improve an animal's ability to learn. Figure 1 summarizes one of his recent experiments. The experimental mice were presented with the task of learning to choose a white alley leading to food over a black alley. Note that the saline control animals averaged about 20 errors before they learned always to choose the white alley, but the Metrazol® (pentylenetetrazol)-dosed animals improved with increasing strengths of the drug unit until, at the dose level of 10 mg/kg of body weight, the mice solved the problem after but 5 errors; beyond that dosage there was no appreciable improvement. There seems to be a limit to the intellectual power of even a hopped-up California supermouse. In another experiment two different strains of mice were trained to solve a simple maze (Figure 2). Note first that we had here hereditary differences in learning ability: a relatively bright strain (BALB/C) and a relatively stupid one ($C_{57}BL/6$). Secondly, note that the stupid $C_{57}BL/6$'s treated with 10 mg/kg of pentylenetetrazol did as well as their untreated but hereditarily superior colleagues. Chemotherapy

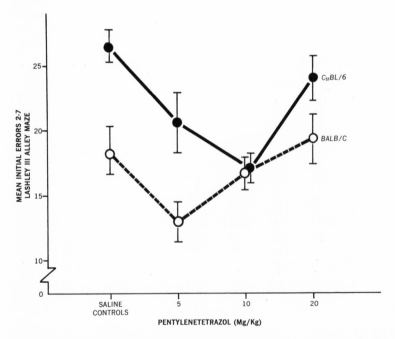

Fig. 2. Effect of pentylenetetrazol on maze learning in two strains of mice [Krivanek and McGaugh (1)]. (Art adapted from Krech.)

here compensated for the $C_{57}BL/6$'s stupid parents. In another series of experiments McGaugh found that different drugs worked differentially for different strains, individuals, and intellectual tasks. Thus, for some problems picrotoxin helped the dull animal but not the bright, while for other problems pentylenetetrazol seemed to help everyone.

Does all of this mean that we will soon be able to substitute an inexpensive get-smart pill for our expensive school enrichment programs? The answer is no, as our Berkeley experiments on the effects of experience on the brain suggest (2). Let me describe a typical experiment. At weaning age 12 rats are put into a psychologically enriched living group while their twin brothers are placed in a psychologically impoverished group. They all have the same food, of course. All 12 enriched pups live in 1 large cage equipped with inviting rat toys in a well-lighted, noisy, and busy laboratory (Figure 3). As the rats grow older, they are given various little learning tasks to master for which they are rewarded with bits of sugar. While these animals are enjoying the richest intellectual environment that Berkeley can provide for rats (but they are not on drugs!), their brothers lead quite different lives. Each impoverished animal lives out his solitary confinement in a small cage situated in a dimly lit and quiet room. It is rarely handled by its keeper and never invited to solve problems or join in fun and games with fellow rats or graduate students.

Fig. 3. Rats in the psychologically enriched environment [Bennett, Diamond, Krech, and Rosenzweig (2)]. (Photo copyright 1964 by the American Association for the Advancement of Science.)

At the age of 105 days all the rats are sacrificed, and their brains are analyzed morphologically and chemically.

This standard experiment that I have just described has been repeated dozens of times and has yielded the results that are summarized in Figure 4. As the more fortunate litter mate lives out his life in the enriched condition, the bulk of his cortex expands and grows deeper and heavier than that of his culturally deprived brother. Part of this increase in cortical mass is accounted for by an increase in the number of cortical glia cells, part by an increase in the size of the neuronal cell bodies and their nuclei, and part by an increase in the diameter of the cortical blood vessels. Biochemical changes also occur. The enriched brain shows both more acetylcholinesterase and more cholinesterase activity.

Now, what does all this mean? Let us return to McGaugh's results for a moment. Whether a drug will improve an animal's learning ability will depend, of course, upon how the drug changes the chemistry of the animal's brain. And it is now clear from our own work that the chemical status of the brain, *before the introduction of any drug,* is partly dependent upon the psychological milieu in which the animal has been living. Therefore, putting McGaugh's results and our results together, it seems clear that *how* a drug, introduced from the outside, will change the brain chemistry and, thus, affect learning will depend upon the organism's psychological environment. I am not talking about some sort of mysterious interaction between "psychological forces" and "chemical compounds." I am talking about interactions between chemical factors in the

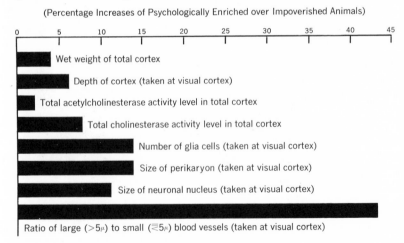

Fig. 4. Effects of stimulation and training on cerebral cortex. (Art adapted from Krech.)

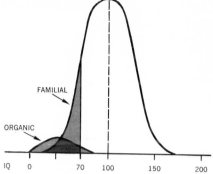

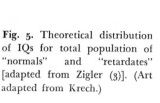

Fig. 5. Theoretical distribution of IQs for total population of "normals" and "retardates" [adapted from Zigler (3)]. (Art adapted from Krech.)

brain induced by environment and chemical factors introduced into the brain by injections or pills. This is what lay behind my opening conclusion that within a few years psychology and chemistry will be able to raise the intelligence of man significantly.

Why does this worry me? To answer this question, I shall ask you to take a very brief look at some human data (3) and then join me in an old parlor game. Figure 5 shows the theoretical IQ distribution for our population. Note that the mental retardates are separated into the so-called "organics"—comprising those retardates whose difficulties can be traced to clearly identifiable physical defects such as phenylketonuria or serious head injuries—and the "familial retardates"—made up of children with IQs between 40 and 70 in whom there has been found no clear physiological defect. The causes cited for familial retardation include defects in brain biochemistry, hereditary factors, and cultural factors; indeed, this group is often labeled "the cultural familial retardates."

Now the most likely development from the research that I have been discussing will undoubtedly produce effective treatment for many of the cultural familial retardates. But if we will be able to raise the IQs of the cultural familial retardates, how about the "cultural familial geniuses"? And what about the many millions of men, women, and children in the largest group of all—the "cultural familial mediocrities"? Let me suggest three possible answers.

The first possibility I will label "Brave New World, Mark I." Here, as shown in Figure 6, we assume that our psychological chemical procedures will raise the intelligence of all men and women so that the distribution curve would shift in the direction of higher IQ levels. Now, let us play the old parlor game of "What if?". Remember how it goes? You say, "What if, through a genetic mutation induced by radioactive fallout from our liberty-loving, anticommunist, democratic, nuclear-testing pro-

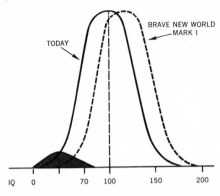

Fig. 6. Hypothetical distribution of IQs resulting from an across-the-board increase for all normals and familial retardates (*Brave New World, Mark I*) compared with current distribution. (Art adapted from Krech.)

gram, all babies were born with three arms? What changes do you foresee?" And your guests begin to speculate. Someone suggests that the whole clothing industry would have to be retooled—three sleeves instead of two; the deodorant industry would boom; speakers would have to revise their "on-the-one-hand and on-the-other-hand" clichés; handholding under the dinner table would be facilitated, leading to an increase in off-the-reservation dalliance, divorce, and eventual total moral decay. Very well. What would happen if, through psychochemistry, we raise the IQ level of most people by 20 points? What new demands would this place on our educational facilities and practices? What political changes might such a population bring about? What moral changes? How about religious practices and institutions?

Let me propose another possibility and another set of questions. You will remember that McGaugh found that some drugs can help only the duller strains and individuals of his experimental animal populations. Perhaps we shall find that with the human being we can raise only the lower IQs, the higher IQs being resistant to further improvement. Now the picture would appear as in Figure 7. In "Brave New World, Mark II" we would have relatively little spread from the brightest to the dullest. Who now will be the hewers of wood and the drawers of water and the inhabitants of the slums and the wastelands—and who, the WASPS and the gentry? What changes will all of this induce when we are all pretty much alike intellectually? How long can we remain segregated into different political, economic, and social groups?

Let me end with the "Mark III" model. You will also remember that different drugs may be effective for different kinds of problems. On the human level this means that we may be able, through psychochemistry, to raise verbal abilities in some, arithmetic reasoning in others, artistic abilities in still others. Now, who gets what raised and who decides for whom? The parent? The family pediatrician? The family physician?

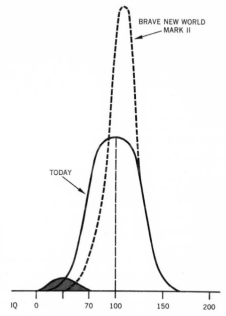

Fig. 7. Hypothetical distribution of IQs resulting from an increase restricted to the lower IQ levels (*Brave New World, Mark II*) compared with current distribution. (Art adapted from Krech.)

The school board? And on what basis do they decide? On the effectiveness of the pharmaceutical industry's advertising? On the effectiveness or the persuasiveness of detail men? On the ability to pay for the more expensive abilities? These problems—surpassingly strange in their novelty, bafflingly complex, and of serious import—are problems with which you will inevitably become intimately involved. Yet it seems clear to me that the physician alone does not have the wisdom and the knowledge to handle these matters. Here, most certainly, the physician cannot be allowed to write social policy on his prescription pad. And here, most certainly, the physician should be prepared to welcome guidance from the laity and even accede gracefully to social control.

REFERENCES

(1) KRIVANEK, J., MCGAUGH, J. C. In preparation, 1967.
(2) BENNETT, E. L., DIAMOND, M. C., KRECH, D., ROSENZWEIG, M. R. Chemical and anatomical plasticity of brain. *Science* 146: 610, 1964.
(3) ZIGLER, E. Familial mental retardation: a continuing dilemma. *Science* 155: 292, 1967.

Effect of brand preference upon consumers' perceived taste of turkey meat

James C. Makens

INTRODUCTION *It has been said there are more people on Madison Avenue devoted to controlling human behavior than all the American scientists put together. Whether such a statement is accurate remains conjecture; yet one thing is certain: the advertising industry is paid millions of dollars yearly on the premise that it* can *regulate human conduct. It is unlikely that any company would pay the thousands of dollars necessary to buy ad agency and media time if it felt that advertising could not sway people's buying behavior.*

Just how effective is advertising in controlling human behavior? After reading Joe McGinniss' The Selling of the President 1968 *or Vance Packard's* The Hidden Persuaders, *one gets the impression that it is very effective indeed. Yet, to gauge advertising's effectiveness accurately, one must turn from literary speculation to well-controlled scientific studies. Such a study is presented below. It is one of a relatively small number of research projects that have examined advertising's effectiveness. Hopefully, as growing numbers of scientists investigate the topic further, we will be in a better position to evaluate the behavior control potential of advertising.*

Several studies have been conducted to determine the ability of panelists to correctly identify selected branded products through taste experiments (Bowles & Pronko, 1948; Printers Ink, 1962; Pronko

& Bowles, 1948, 1949; Pronko & Herman, 1950; Prothro, 1953; Thumin, 1962). The products which were included in these tests were ones that are normally purchased by consumers quite frequently, such as cola beverages or beer. These were also products whose brands are normally before the consumer during time of consumption and which may be consumed individually.

Taste tests are useful tools in marketing research but not enough diverse experiments have been reported to demonstrate their range of applicability. The study to be reported offers an example of the wide application that taste tests have as useful research techniques.

The purpose of this study was to determine the effect of a well-known brand turkey on consumers' preferences based upon a measurement of their taste ratings for turkey meat.

This study is a departure from previous reported taste tests due to the characteristics of the product. A turkey is not purchased frequently nor is the brand normally displayed before the consumer when the turkey is eaten. It is also a product that is not ready for consumption at the time of purchase. Unlike cola beverages or beer, the brand of turkeys is not normally before consumers at the time of consumption and might be known only to the purchaser and/or cook. Therefore, unless those eating the turkey were told that the meat they were being served is a certain brand, it is improbable that their sense of taste would be influenced.

METHOD

The Michigan State University consumer preference panel of 150 Detroit area consumers was utilized as the test group. This panel had been in existence since 1956 and was held three times each year at Wayne State University in Detroit. The members had incomes ranging from $4,000 to $10,000; had received 12-13 years of formal education; and were between 31-45 years of age. The panel operated as an afternoon and an evening session with different individuals participating in each.

The study consisted of two different experiments. Both were included in the afternoon meeting but during the evening, only Experiment I was used. One hundred and fifty consumers participated in Experiment I and 61 participated in Experiment II.

Two different brands were used throughout the experiment. One brand had never been sold in the Detroit area and was unknown by the subjects (Ss). The other (known brand) represented a nationally advertised brand which was sold in the Detroit area at the time of the study. The Ss had previously demonstrated a majority preference for this brand over others in a ranking test held during an earlier panel. This test did not involve taste. Instead it was a four sample ranking test involving turkeys of different brands. This gave evidence that the brand designated as a known brand was indeed known and preferred by Ss. This knowledge is of particular importance in a test of this nature. The results of a questionnaire also demonstrated that the known brand had been purchased by many of the Ss within the previous year.

The unknown brand had not been used in previous experiments and was for all practical purposes completely unfamiliar to the Ss.

Experiment I

PROCEDURE. A turkey was roasted prior to the experiment and similar size samples were cut from one section of the breast. These samples were evenly divided on two ceramic plates. A cardboard carton was placed behind each plate. One carton was covered with a plastic bag bearing the known brand while the other carton was covered with a bag bearing the unknown one.

The Ss were given a sample from each of the plates and were told that these samples were taken from turkeys of the brands represented by the bags behind the plates. They were then asked to compare the taste and texture of the two samples and rank them on a card. A five-point hedonic scale, including the words Excellent, Good, Fair, Poor, and Bad, was listed for each sample. After the samples were ranked, the Ss were asked to indicate which of the two samples they preferred or if both tasted the same. The order in which the samples were tasted was reversed during the evening session.

A null hypothesis was established that there is no difference in preference for the two samples.

Experiment II

PROCEDURE. The second experiment employed similar size samples with unlike texture (tough and tender). These samples had been cut from a like section of the breasts of two turkeys. The tougher samples registered a shear value of 12 as compared to a value of 6 for the tender samples as recorded on a Warner-Bratzler Shear Press.

The Ss were not told that the textures of the samples varied. Instead, the samples were placed on two ceramic plates and were identified only by typewritten symbols (% and *) which according to Marquardt, 1963, have no preference meanings to consumers. The samples identified as * had the value of 12.

Each S was asked to indicate on a card, from which of the two brands displayed in Experiment I, he believed each sample was taken. If a S had no idea from which branded turkey a sample had been cut, he was instructed to check an appropriate blank indicating this. Thus the Ss were given three choices. They were also asked to indicate which of the samples they preferred.

A null hypothesis was established for Experiment II that there is no difference in preferences between sample % and sample *.

The second taste test immediately followed the one involving the hedonic scale. It is therefore possible that the sequence of testing may have affected the results to a certain degree.

RESULTS

Experiment I

It was necessary to assign a value to each of the adjectives before any statistical computations could be applied. The word Excellent was given a value of 5, Good was assigned a value of 4, Fair 3, Poor 2, and Bad was given a rating of 1. The statistical method employed was the Wilcoxon matched-pairs signed-rank test.

Table 1—Preferences Demonstrated for Turkey Meat Samples by Panel Members

Subject	N
Subjects who preferred sample identified as taken from known brand turkey	84
Subjects who preferred sample identified as taken from unknown brand turkey	51
Subjects who indicated no preference	15
Total	150

The results were analyzed statistically using an SD of 339.88 and an N of 111 which equaled the sum of the d's. The unknown brand had a mean score of 19.21 and a T value of 2,133 as compared to a mean score of 37.68 and a T value of 4,183 for the known brand. A value for z of 3.1 was yielded which indicated that the results were significant at the .01 level. Thus, the results of the hedonic scale indicated that Ss were influenced by the known brand even though both samples of meat were identical.

This was further strengthened by the results of the section of the test in which the Ss gave an answer reflecting their ordinal utility; i.e., they were asked to merely state a preference for one over the other. Here again the known brand was preferred as shown in Table 1. Out of a total of 150 replies which were given during the afternoon and evening panels, only 15 Ss (10%) indicated that both the samples tasted alike. Fifty-one (34%) of the Ss indicated that they preferred the unknown brand samples, and 84 (56%) indicated they preferred the known brand ones.

Experiment II

The data in Table 2 showed that the sample identified as % (tender sample) was preferred by 49 of the 61 evening panel members. This constitutes a majority preference of 80% as compared to 7% (4 Ss) who stated that they preferred the sample marked *. The remaining 8 Ss gave no reply. The results of a chi-square analysis yielded a value of 58.9 which was significant at the .01 alpha level. It is obvious that the Ss were able

Table 2—Preferences for Tough and Tender Turkey Meat by Panel Members and Their Association with Known and Unknown Brands

	Sample %	Sample *	Neither	Total
Number of persons who preferred the sample	49	4	8	61
Number of persons who said the sample was from the known brand turkey	31	3	—	34
Number of persons who said the sample was from the unknown brand turkey	17	1	—	18
Number who did not indicate which brand the sample was from	1	—	—	1

to detect a quality difference between the two samples and the null hypothesis was therefore rejected.

The results of this experiment also showed that 31 Ss (63% of the 49 Ss who preferred sample %) stated they believed it came from the known brand. A total of 17 Ss stated it came from an unknown brand and one S did not indicate its source.

Only four Ss stated a preference for the sample marked * and three of these stated they believed this sample came from the known brand. The remaining S believed it came from the unknown brand.

As a total, 34 Ss stated that the samples they preferred were taken from the known brand turkey, 18 indicated they were from the unknown brand and one S gave no indication. A chi-square analysis was performed using an expected value of 16.3 since the 49 panelists were given three equal choices. The observed values were 34, 18, and 1. The analysis yielded a value of 30.0 which was highly significant.

CONCLUSION

The use of taste tests in brand research appears to have a wider application than is indicated from the number of published studies. This study shows that taste tests may be used for as diverse a product as turkey.

Brand preference for one well-known brand turkey was strong enough to influence the perceived taste for turkey meat among the Ss. It is apparent that the Ss were influenced by the brand since a significant preference was shown for turkey samples identified as taken from a known brand versus identical ones labeled as taken from an unknown brand turkey.

Panelists were also able to detect taste differences between turkey meat samples with a shear value of 12 as compared to those with a value of 6 and preferred the latter. A significant number of Ss also stated that the samples they preferred were taken from a known brand turkey. This indicates that consumers expect a well-known brand turkey to be of superior quality to an unknown brand. It may also indicate that advertising for this particular brand has been effective. Obviously different brands of turkeys are differentiated products in the minds of consumers. This evidence should be of interest to all marketers of relatively homogenous food products as they plan an advertising and brand building program.

REFERENCES

BOWLES, J. W., JR., & PRONKO, N. H. Identification of cola beverages: II. A further study. *Journal of Applied Psychology*, 1948, **32**, 559–564.

MARQUARDT, R. A. An evaluation of the methods used in designing and analyzing consumer preference studies. Unpublished doctoral dissertation, Michigan State University, 1963.

Does the label change the taste?, *Printers Ink*, 1962, **278** (1), 55–57.

PRONKO, N. H., & BOWLES, J. W., JR. Identification of cola beverages: I. First study. *Journal of Applied Psychology*, 1948, **32**, 304–312.

PRONKO, N. H., & BOWLES, J. W., JR. Identification of cola beverages: III. A final study. *Journal of Applied Psychology*, 1949, **33**, 605–608.

PRONKO, N. H., & HERMAN, D. T. Identification of cola beverages: IV. Postscript. *Journal of Applied Psychology*, 1950, **34**, 68–69.

PROTHRO, E. T. Identification of cola beverages overseas. *Journal of Applied Psychology*, 1953, **37**, 494–495.

THUMIN, F. J. Identification of cola beverages. *Journal of Applied Psychology*, 1962, **46**, 358–360.

Classroom layout and
student participation

Robert Sommer

*INTRODUCTION   Sometimes the most successful forms
of behavior control are the most subtle: inconspicuous methods of persuasion of which the individual is often unaware. This was driven home
forcefully to one of the authors and his wife during a visit to Kennedy
Airport. Forced to wait an hour at one of the terminals, they sat down to
talk in the waiting room. Unfortunately, the chairs were so uncomfortable
they had to get up and spend their time walking and browsing around the
gift shops. At the time the author clearly remembers grumbling about the
"stupid designer who could build such useless pieces of furniture." You
can imagine his chagrin then when, a few months later, he discovered
the chairs had been purposely built to be uncomfortable! Robert Sommer,
the author of the article you will be reading, explains:*

> *In most [airline] terminals it is virtually impossible for two people
> sitting down to converse comfortably for any length of time. The
> chairs are either bolted together and arranged in rows theater style
> facing the ticket counters, or arranged back-to-back, and even if they
> face one another they are at such distances that comfortable conver-
> sation is impossible. The motive for the . . . arrangement appears
> the same as that in hotels and other commercial places—to drive
> people out of the waiting areas into cafes, bars, and shops where
> they will spend money [Sommer, 1969].*

*Sommer points out that one designer has gone so far as to develop a chair
that "exerts disagreeable pressure upon the spine if occupied for over a
few minutes. . . ." The chair is being purchased by American business-
men who don't want their customers to get too comfortable for too long
in one place.*
    *Recently, men like Sommer have been studying the impact of archi-
tectural design on human behavior. What they have found is that the*

*structures men build can very effectively regulate the way people behave.
Did you realize, for example, that the architectural design of a schoolroom could influence student participation in classroom discussion? If not,
you'll probably want to read the following article.*

My curiosity about classroom seating had been whetted
by teachers' assumptions about students' seating: the front rows contain
the most interested students, those in the rear engage in illicit activities,
students at the aisles are mainly concerned with quick departures, most
absentees come from the rear quadrant most distant from the windows,
and the straight-row arrangement inhibits discussion. Fact or fiction? Any
teacher could supply a dozen concordant or discordant examples at will.
The anecdotes seem to agree on the fact that classroom space can be divided into zones containing people who behave differently,[1] but whether
zones are selected by those people in the first place or affect them afterwards, or some combination of the two, remained unclear. If shoulder-to-
shoulder seating discouraged conversation in old folks' home, what did it
do to a student's attitude toward school and the teacher's attitude toward
the students? Does it make a student feel like raw material in an educational assembly line, something to be shaped, worked on, and processed?
Is it degrading to sit shoulder to shoulder with strangers front and back,
to be so close together to people alongside that knees touch, where privacy is impossible, and one cannot adjust his trousers without making a
public display? I tend to forget what it is like until those occasions when
I have to attend lectures held in classrooms. Without exception I have
been appalled by the closeness of the seats. Frequently the chairs are
locked together and cannot be separated without the organized cooperation of everyone in the row. The next person's notebook is practically in
front of my eyes. I am not used to focusing my attention on such a narrow field. My office desk is four times the size of a student's writing surface, and papers on the right or left side of my desk, still in good view,
would be on my neighbor's board in a classroom. Students are accustomed
to smaller working surfaces than I, but the distraction of the classroom
situation in which students are denied mobility and control of their
working spaces must be considerable.

A pioneer investigation of lighting in more than 4,000 classrooms
showed some interesting relationships between the health problems of

[1] As was mentioned [elsewhere], nurses on mental wards do this also. The spatial
categorization of people seems to be a fact of institutional life.

the students and their location within the classroom. When the typical room was divided into quadrants, half the children with chronic infections were found at the rear left quadrant of the room, i.e., the rear quadrant nearest the back window. Were a line to be projected across the room from the front mullion at an angle of 40 degrees from the plane of the windows, some two-thirds of the children with nutritional problems would be found between this line and the windows. The severity of both kinds of problems increased from this line toward the rear left quadrant of the room.[2] The author attributes some of these results to the lighting within the rooms, but it is quite apparent that selection of seats as related to social and physical factors must also be taken into account.

All this made me wonder about the connection between classroom layout and student participation. The question seemed eminently researchable, since student participation could be objectively recorded, and there were many different sorts of classrooms available. Six rooms were finally chosen for the study. Two were seminar rooms that offered horseshoe or open square arrangements of chairs and two were laboratories that offered extreme examples of straight-row arrangements. The fixed tables with their Bunsen burners, bottles, and gas valves prevented any rearrangement of chairs. Of the other two rooms, one was windowless with starkly modern decor. To contrast with this "closed room" we selected another whose long wall was composed entirely of windows and which had been described by design students on campus as light and airy.

There were two discussion leaders (TAs), each responsible for three sections of approximately 25 students each. The TAs were told that "a study of discussion groups" would take place but nothing about specific details of the study. The professor knew the entire experimental plan and gave it his enthusiastic support. There were three observers, all undergraduate students, who attended the discussion sections and recorded student participation on prepared seating charts. The observers typically sat at the rear of a room and remained inconspicuous. These sections followed standard procedures of a typical class except that, in the middle of the semester, the students changed rooms. At that time they were informed that some of the sections had complained about the rooms and it seemed fair to switch in the middle of the semester. We were surprised and even saddened by how passively the students accepted the room changes. Accustomed as they are to IBM cards of seven different colors as well as arbitrary changes in faculty adviser, class hours, and course offerings, the students were able to accept a switch in rooms after the spring vacation with equanimity.

[2] D. B. Harmon, "Lighting and Child Development," *Illuminating Engineering*, XL (April 1945), 199–228.

Our data were of two sorts, the first concerned the effects of rooms on student participation—was there more discussion in the seminar rooms than in the laboratory, more absenteeism in the windowless room, and so forth. The second concerned the *ecology of participation* or the way discussion varied as a function of location—were students in front more active than those in the rear; those in the center more active than those at the aisles? In the first instance we were comparing different rooms; in the second we were looking within each room. Comparison of rooms is of more relevance to value questions since we can determine if one room produced more discussion or fewer absences than another. Intraroom analyses involve the utilization of existing facilities by people willing to inhabit the environment but excluding those who choose to avoid it. Both questions are important to school administrators, the first in planning new facilities and the second in finding the best ways to utilize existing rooms.

All sections assigned to the seminar rooms and the open room met as scheduled, but escape behaviors were evident immediately in the laboratory and the windowless room. On the first day of classes in the laboratory, the TA handed a note to the department secretary requesting a change in room. When no action on his request was forthcoming, the TA moved his class to an empty room across the hall (also a laboratory but a more quiet one) where the class met for two periods. The second TA showed her distaste for the laboratory in comments to her students and in the fourth session moved her class outside with the avowed intention of meeting on the lawn from then on. Pressure from the professor induced her to meet in the assigned room. In the windowless room, escape behaviors were shown on two occasions. One TA brought his class outside but apparently did not find it very effective, so he met indoors after that. It is noteworthy that the students who followed the instructor out to the lawn arranged themselves in three straight rows in front of him. In the other section in the windowless room, the students officially petitioned the TA to meet outside. The request was written on the blackboard by the students, and the question was raised in class several times.

In the two seminar rooms an average of 9.0 students participated each session compared to 10.5 in the laboratory. This difference, which indicated more widespread participation in the laboratory, was statistically reliable. Although a higher proportion of people participated in the laboratory, there was a trend for greater absolute participation in the seminar rooms in terms of the larger total number of statements per class period. The implication is that a few people say more in a seminar arrangement, whereas participation is more widespread with the straight-row arrangement. There were no differences in participation between the open and the windowless rooms, nor were there significant differences between the sections in grades.

Table 1—Face-to-Face and Side Table Participation in Seminar Rooms

	Average number of voluntary statements from	
	Side tables (N = 226)	Table directly opposite instructor (N = 141)
Old seminar room 1st 6 weeks	1.63	2.42
Old seminar room 2nd 6 weeks	3.19	4.62
New seminar room 1st 6 weeks	2.89	3.69
New seminar room 2nd 6 weeks	0.88	1.97
Total: All rooms	2.08	3.15

SEMINAR ARRANGEMENT. We can now examine the way that participation was distributed in each room. With the seminar arrangement we can compare participation of students at the side tables with those sitting directly opposite the instructor. In every section in the seminar room there was more participation from people directly opposite the instructor than from those at the side tables. Students sitting away from the tables participated less than those at the tables. In the new seminar room, where the tables formed a hollow square, students avoided the chairs alongside the instructor. This was true even when the room was full—students sat on the floor or went out and secured new chairs. On the few occasions when a student occupied a chair adjacent to the instructor, he was generally silent throughout the entire period. This finding is in accord with the work on dominance relationships discussed [elsewhere].

STRAIGHT-ROW ARRANGEMENTS. The laboratory, which had been included as an extreme example of a straight-row arrangement, was a challenge to the discussion leader. One TA typically sat at the front of the instructor's desk rather than behind it, and the other encouraged her students to bring their stools up to the front bench in an unsuccessful attempt to approximate a semicircular arrangement. The high tables and uncomfortable stools resisted her efforts, and a straight-row arrangement prevailed in all discussion sections meeting in this room. The students in the front row participated more than students in subsequent rows, but students around the walls participated more than students in any row but the first. This is also consistent with the eye-contact hypothesis, since only students in the front row and the sides had a clear and relatively unobstructed view of the TA.

In the open room, which contained four rows of chairs facing the instructor, students in the front row spoke more than students in the other rows, but this was not a reliable difference. The same was true of the windowless room—the first row again participated more, but this difference was not significant either. However, the data are complicated by the fact that latecomers in both rooms tended to sit in the front row. Our observers had noted that the front row, which was considered to be "too close" to the instructor in each room, was avoided by students who came on time. Of the 51 latecomers in these two rooms, 41 ended up in the front row, five in the second row, and five in the third row. When we removed the latecomers from the tabulations, we found the previous trends were accentuated and reached statistical reliability. Students in the first row participated more than students in either the second or the third rows. The layout here was the reverse of the laboratory where, because of the noise and high tables, the choice seats were in front. Of the 41 latecomers in the laboratory, 4 ended up in the first row, 1 in the second row, 17 in the third row, 10 in the fourth row, and 9 at the sides of the room. Removing the latecomers from the participation scores in the laboratory did not alter the trends. We still found 71 per cent of the students in the first row participating compared to approximately 50 per cent of the students in the other three rows. This suggests that the relationship between location and participation must take individual choice (environmental preference) into account. When the desirable seats are in front, increased participation results because the greater stimulus value of the instructor reaches the most interested students. When the favorable seats are in the middle or rear, the increased expressive value of the instructor for students in front will tend to cancel out the fact that the most interested students are in other rows, and there will be no clear relationship between row and participation.

Table 2—Participation by Row in Conventional Classrooms

	Average number of voluntary statements from			
	Row 1 (N = 144)	Row 2 (N = 162)	Row 3 (N = 128)	Row 4 (N = 20)
Open room 1st 6 weeks	2.30	1.88	1.45	0.80
Open room 2nd 6 weeks	1.25	0.76	1.20	1.10
Windowless room 1st 6 weeks	1.00	0.78	0.97	—
Windowless room 2nd 6 weeks	2.38	1.57	1.78	—
Total: All rooms	1.77	1.23	1.32	0.95

The following year Joan Crawford repeated the study with a discussion group she was leading. By an interesting coincidence, her group also met in a small room where the front row was avoided by students.

However, this time there were ample chairs in the rear rows and, throughout the semester, the front row was entirely empty. When we checked participation in rows two to six, there was a linear relationship between amount of discussion and proximity to the instructor. Students in the second row averaged 3.7 statements per session compared to 2.6 from those in the third row, 1.5 from those in the fourth row, and 0.5 from those in the fifth row.

Jan Ebert recorded class participation in two discussion sections, one in French and the other in freshman English. Students in the French class were allowed to sit where they pleased, but students in the English class were seated alphabetically. In the French class with voluntary seating, there was a clear connection between row and participation. The vast majority of voluntary statements and questions came from the first row. There was no difference between rows in the number of times a student was called upon by the instructor. In the English section with alphabetical seating, there was not much difference between the first two rows in voluntary participation, but the students in the third row participated very little. Again there was no difference between the three rows in frequency of being called on by the instructor. Miss Ebert's results support the idea that location and prior interest interact to affect class participation. When the most interested students sit where there is maximum visual contact with the instructor, there will be a clear connection between locations and participation, but when interested students are seated elsewhere, spatial effects will be less apparent.

A recent study by Levinger and Gunner [3] using a projective test, in which students arrange geometric forms and silhouettes on a felt background, showed that students who typically sat at the rear of a classroom placed greater distance between themselves and "a professor" than did students who sat at the front of the room. In the Netherlands Dr. M. J. Langeveld states:

> The seats chosen by the pupils themselves at the beginning of the school year give important social-psychological indications. For example, at the beginning of one school-year the following pupils "happened to" sit in the hindmost row: the only son of a widow who repeated this class, the only son of a widower, a heart patient who had been spoiled very much, a boy who is strongly inclined to withdraw from the school community, an older boy who had been sent away from another school, and two pupils repeating the class ages 20 and

[3] George, Levinger and Jeannette Gunner, "The Interpersonal Grid: 1. Felt and Tape Techniques for the Measurements of Social Relationships," *Psychonomic Science,* in press.

21. And who occupies the front seats? The first three rows were occupied by five newcomers, the prefect of the class, a somewhat older boy who boards with one of the masters, three girls who have learned that they should work hard and pay attention, and three boys with the same attitude.[4]

A sensitive observer of student life in ghetto schools, Herbert Kohl advocates spatial freedom in the classroom. With freedom to move around and change seats, there is a continual shift in seating, but this, in Kohl's opinion, has not disrupted the fundamental fabric of the class. Rather the spatial freedom provides internal adjustments and compensations that avoid many possible disruptions. When feeling tense or anxious, a student might sit in the back row where he would be less likely to come into contact with others, but when he was interested in the material, he could come right up front.[5] Both Langeveld and Kohl illustrate the way that a perceptive teacher can use children's seating to gain information about the children and how they are feeling.

To test the expressive contact hypothesis that students in the center are psychologically closer to the instructor than students at the sides, we analyzed our participation data by dividing each room into a center zone and two side zones. The results from all ten sections showed that students in the center of a row participate more than students at the sides. Figure 1 shows pictorially that participation is greatest in the front row as well as within the center section of each row.

Susan Tuana mapped participation in three large lecture halls with capacities of approximately 300 students. Each hall was divided into three sections, two smaller ones at the sides, and one larger in the center. She recorded participation in six different classes (ranging from drama to anatomy) meeting in each of the rooms. Her data, then, come from 18 independent observations of as many large classes. The number of questions asked per class averaged 2.3 (with a range of zero to nine), with a trend for questioning to decrease as class size increased. Almost half of the questions came from the two front rows in the center section (very few came from the front rows in the side sections), and another third came from students sitting along the side aisles. There was very little participation from the "faceless mass" in the middle areas. This is in accord with previous results since visual contact with the instructor is better in the front rows and along the aisles.

[4] This section from Dr. Langeveld's book *Introduction to the Study of the Educational Psychology of the Secondary School* (Groningen-Batavia, 1937), p. 185, was translated and sent to [Robert Sommer] by Dr. Derk de Jonge.

[5] H. Kohl, *36 Children* (New York: The New American Library, Inc., 1967), p. 13.

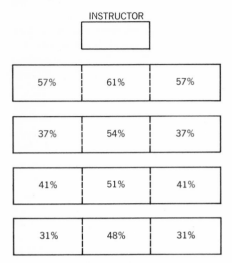

Fig. 1. Ecology of participation in straight-row classrooms. (Art adapted from Sommer.)

If we know little about what goes on inside classrooms, we know even less about what happens between classes, after class in school clubs, and to the student who does his homework as the radio on his dresser blares away. To understand the institutionalized learning process requires us to deal with a complex ecosystem that includes the community, the school building, as well as the classroom. Barker and Gump undertook one of the few studies in which the school itself was considered as an ecosystem. Comparing large and small high schools in the United States and En' land, they found that the impressive dimensions of the large school— the imposing exterior edifice, long corridors and countless rooms, the bustle of activity between classes, the masses of students, the complex table of organization of teachers and administrators—did not produce a richer learning environment than that at the smaller schools. Barker and Gump describe the small schools as small motors rather than large motors; they have all the essential parts of the larger motors, but fewer replications and differentiations of some parts. In the small schools there was more per capita participation in student government, school newspaper, drama, and musical activities.[6]

In this chapter we have omitted any discussion of learning outside the classroom. This schizophrenic posture is common to most design problems. While educational critics such as Edgar Friedenberg and Paul Goodman ask incisive questions about the relevance of contemporary education,

[6] Roger G. Barker and Paul Gump, *Big School, Small School* (Stanford: Stanford University Press, 1964).

school boards, principals, and teachers plan programs within existing structures. The basic module of school construction is the classroom containing a teacher and 20 to 30 students. At some future time the module may become the individual student in his study carrel equipped with teaching machine, TV unit, and various information retrieval devices connected to a central computer. We will then need conference rooms rather than lecture halls. At the present time, teachers are hindered by their insensitivity to and fatalistic acceptance of the classroom environment. Teachers must be "turned on" to their environment lest their pupils develop this same sort of fatalism.

The Chinese indoctrination program for prisoners of war: a study of attempted "brainwashing"*

Edgar H. Schein

INTRODUCTION To the American public there is probably no more widely known or feared method of behavior control than "brainwashing." Ever since American soldiers were brainwashed in North Korean prison camps, we have been inundated with books, movies and mass media reports on the subject—most of which treat brainwashing as a powerful new method of behavior control.

In reality, brainwashing is neither very new nor very effective. This is pointed out in the following study by Edgar Schein, a study conducted on repatriated American servicemen in 1956. His finding—that "there is nothing new or terrifying about the specific [brainwashing] techniques used by the Chinese; they invented no mysterious devices for dealing with people"—remains valid today. It is true, as Schein also points out, that the Chinese did show some originality in combining several "traditional" devices (e.g., group discussion, self-criticism, interrogation, reward and punishment, forced confessions, propaganda and information control) into an overall blueprint for mind control.

Whether brainwashing will ever be an effective form of behavior control remains to be seen. Based on the Chinese experience in North Korea, one is tempted to dismiss it as a regulatory procedure. It should be pointed out, however, that the Chinese program was carried out under the most adverse circumstances for effecting ideological conversion. First, the American servicemen had the advantage of constantly reinforcing each other against becoming more receptive to the Chinese. Second, and perhaps equally important, Americans have not been trained to think in ideological philosophical perspective, as have the Chinese. The Chinese

* The views expressed in this paper are those of the author and do not necessarily reflect the official opinion of the Department of the Army.

Schein, E. H. The Chinese indoctrination program for prisoners of war. *Psychiatry,* 1956, **19,** 149–172.

had the problem of teaching American prisoners a way of thinking as well as what to think. Considering the difficulties faced by the Chinese, one can speculate that under more favorable conditions, brainwashing might become a more effective behavior control mechanism (Karlins & Abelson, 1970) than it has heretofore been.

In this paper I shall try to present an account of the "typical" experiences of United Nations prisoners of war in Chinese Communist hands, and to interpret these experiences in a social-psychological framework. Before the return of United Nations prisoners, the "confessions" of such prominent men as Cardinal Mindszenty and William Oatis had already aroused considerable interest in so-called brainwashing. This interest was heightened by the widespread rumors of collaboration among United Nations prisoners of war in Korea. Following their repatriation in August 1953, a rash of testimonial articles appeared in the weekly magazines, some attempting to show that the Chinese Communist techniques were so terrifying that no one could withstand them, others roundly condemning the collaborative activities of the so-called "progressives" [1] as having been selfishly motivated under conditions in which resistance was possible. These various accounts fall short because they are too emotionally charged to be objective, and because they fail to have any generality, since they are usually based on the personal experiences of only one man.

The data upon which this paper is based were gathered in an attempt to form a generalized picture of what happened to the average man from the time he was captured until the time he was repatriated. The data were collected during August 1953 at Inchon, Korea, where the repatriates were being processed, and on board the U.S.N.S. General Black in transit to the United States from September 1 to September 16.

The method of collecting the data was, in the main, by intensive interviews conducted in Inchon, where the author was a member of one of the processing teams.[2] In the course of the processing, relatively objective tests and projective tests were also given the men; but intensive interviewing was felt to be preferable for gathering the data presented here, because the material to be obtained was highly novel, and because the men had been through a highly traumatic situation which might

---

[1] Commonly called *pro's* by their fellow prisoners.

[2] As part of the processing, psychiatric interviews were initiated at Inchon during the two or three days that the men were there. The procedure of processing has been described in detail by Henry A. Segal in "Initial Psychiatric Findings of Recently Repatriated Prisoners of War," *Amer. J. Psychiatry* (1954) 111:358–363.

make the eliciting of *any* information very difficult. It was also recognized that the men might find it difficult to remember, might be reluctant
to relate certain of their experiences, and might retrospectively falsify
many events.

Of approximately 20 repatriates selected at random at different
stages of the repatriation, each was asked to tell in chronological order
and in as great detail as possible what had happened to him during his
captivity. Emphasis was placed on what the Chinese or North Koreans *did*
in their handling of the prisoners and how the men reacted. The men
were particularly encouraged to relate the reactions of *others,* in order
to avoid arousing anxiety or guilt over their own behavior and thereby
blocking the flow of memories. The interviews varied in length from two
to four hours.

From these interviews a picture emerged which was recorded in the
form of a composite or typical account of the capture and imprisonment
experience. This account was then given to three psychiatrists who together had interviewed 300 men assigned to them at random. It was their
job to delete material which, on the basis of their information, was false
and to add details which had not been revealed in my 20 interviews.

On board ship I was present at a large number of psychiatric interviews and group therapy sessions, and engaged in many informal discussions with repatriates. Extended late evening "bull sessions" with repatriates were particularly informative.

Many of the traumatic prison-camp experiences could probably not
be fully communicated through verbal interviews. However, I believe
that the data are sufficiently inclusive and reliable to provide a reasonably
accurate account of prisoner-of-war experiences. The picture presented
is not to be viewed as the experience of any single person, nor as the experience of all the men. Rather, it represents a composite or typical account which, in all its details, may or may not have been true for any
one prisoner.

THE PRISONER-OF-WAR EXPERIENCE

Capture, the March, and Temporary Camps

United Nations soldiers were captured by the Chinese and North
Koreans at all stages of the Korean conflict, although particularly large
groups were captured during November and December, 1950. The conditions under which men were captured varied widely. Some men were
captured by having their positions overrun or surrounded; others ran
into road blocks and were cut off; still others fought for many days on
a shifting front before they succumbed. The situation in the front lines

was highly fluid, and there was a good deal of confusion on both sides. When a position was overrun, the men often scattered and became disorganized.

While the initial treatment of prisoners by the North Koreans was typically harsh and brutal—they often took the prisoner's clothing, gave him little if any food, and met any resistance with immediate severe punishment or death—the Chinese, in line with their over-all indoctrination policy, often tried to create an atmosphere of friendliness and leniency. Some men reported that their Chinese captors approached them with outstretched hands, saying, "Congratulations! You've been liberated." It was made clear to the man that he could now join forces with other "fighters for peace." Often the Chinese soldiers pointed out to their captives how lucky they were not to have been captured by the North Koreans. Some men reported incidents of Chinese beating off North Koreans who were "trying to hurt" American prisoners, or of punishing their own guards for being too rough or inconsiderate. The men were usually allowed to keep their clothing, and some consideration was given to the sick and wounded. However, the food and medical attention were only slightly better than that provided by the North Koreans.

For the first six to twenty-four hours after capture, a man was usually in a state of dazed shock, unable to take any kind of integrated action and, later, unable to report any kind of feeling he had had during this period. Following this, he expected death or torture at the hands of his captors, for rumors that this would happen had been widely circulated in the front lines, often based on stories of men who had fallen into North Korean hands. These fears were, however, quickly dispelled by the friendly attitude of the Chinese soldiers; and this friendly attitude and the emphasis on "peace" was the first and perhaps most significant step in making the prisoner receptive to the more formal indoctrination which was to come later.

In the next weeks or months the prisoner was exposed to great physical hardship and to a series of psychological pressures which amounted to a cyclical reactivation of fears and their relief by actual events or by extravagant promises. Implicit in most of what the Chinese said and did was the suggestion that these stresses could be brought to an end by the adoption of a "cooperative" attitude by the prisoner, although at first it was not clear just what this meant.

The men were collected behind the lines and were marched north in groups of varying sizes. The men marched only at night, averaging about 20 miles, and were kept under strict cover in the daytime. Conditions on the march were very hard. Most men reported having great difficulty eating strange and badly prepared foods; however, they were often reminded, whether true or not, that they were getting essentially the same rations as the average Chinese foot soldier. Medical care was almost nonexistent, but this too was depicted as being equally true for Chinese soldiers because of supply shortages. Almost all the men had diarrhea, many had dysentery, and most of them suffered from exposure. Every day would find a few more dead.

Although the columns were not well guarded, few escapes were attempted because the men were too weak, did not know the terrain, were on the whole poorly organized, and were afraid of the North Koreans. The few who did escape were almost always returned to the group within a short time.

During these one- to two-week marches the men became increasingly disorganized and apathetic. They developed a slow plodding gait, called by one man a "prisoner's shuffle." Lines of authority tended to break down, and the prevailing attitude was "every man for himself." Open competition for food, clothing, and shelter made the maintenance of group ties almost impossible. Everything that happened tended to be frustrating and depriving, yet there was no ready outlet for hostility, and no opportunity for constructive resistance. The only *realistic* goal was to get to prison camp where, it was hoped, conditions would be better.[3]

Uppermost in the men's minds were fantasies of food—memories of all the good meals they had had in the past, or plans for elaborate menus in the future. The only competing fantasies concerned loved ones at home, or cars, which seemed symbolically to represent the return to their homes and to freedom.

Arrival at one of the temporary camps was usually a severe disappointment. Many men reported that the only thing that had kept them going on the march was the hope of improved conditions in the camp; but they found the food as bad as ever, living conditions more crowded than before, and a continued lack of consideration for the sick and wounded. Moreover, there was now nothing to do but sit and wait. The news given the men was mostly false, playing up Communist military victories, and was, of course, particularly demoralizing. Many of the men became extremely apathetic and withdrawn, and according to some reports these apathy states sometimes became so severe as to result in death.

The Chinese continually promised improvements in conditions or

---

[3] Not all of the men participated in such severe marches. Those captured in 1951 and 1952 were sometimes taken north by truck or under less severe conditions. The sick and wounded were given somewhat more consideration, although never much in the way of medical aid. Numerous incidents were reported of Chinese guards helping men, occasionally even carrying them.

It should also be mentioned that the North Korean civilians seemed ambivalent toward the prisoners. Many of them were sadistic, but many others helped the Americans by hiding them or giving them food and clothing.

early repatriation, and failures of these promises to materialize were blamed on obstructions created by United Nations air activity or lack of "cooperation" among the prisoners. It was always made clear that only certain prisoners could hope to get a break: those who "did well," "co-operated," "learned the truth," and so on. The Chinese distributed propaganda leaflets and required the men to sing Communist songs. Apparently even guards were sensitized to finding potential collaborators among the prisoners by observing their reactions to such activities. Outright indoctrination was not attempted on the marches and in the temporary camps, but those men who finally reached one of the permanent camps were ill-prepared physically and psychologically for the indoctrination pressures they were about to face.

Life in the Permanent Prisoner-of-War Camp

Most of the permanent camps were parts of small Korean villages, often split into several compounds in different parts of the village. The camps were sometimes surrounded by a fence, by barbed wire, or by natural barriers, although sometimes not enclosed at all. While guards were posted at key places, they were not sufficiently plentiful to prevent escapes or excursions to other parts of the village. The camp usually consisted of a series of mud huts in which the men slept on the floor or on straw matting, and a schoolhouse or other permanent building which was used as administrative headquarters, for lectures, and for recreation. The various Chinese officer and enlisted billets were usually scattered through the village. Mess and latrine facilities were very inadequate, and conditions were crowded, but far better than in the temporary camps.

In camp the men were segregated by race, nationality, and rank, and were organized into companies, platoons, and squads. The squads varied in size from 10 to 15 men, who usually shared the same living area. No formal organization was permitted among the prisoners; thus, the Chinese put their own personnel in charge of the platoons and companies, and appointed certain prisoners as squad leaders without consideration of rank.

Although the daily routine in camp varied, the average prisoner arose at dawn, was required to do calisthenics for an hour or more, was assigned to various details—such as gathering wood, carrying water, cooking, repairing roads, burying other prisoners, and general maintenance of the camp—and then was given a breakfast of potato soup or some form of cereal at around eight o'clock. The rest of the morning and afternoon was usually spent on indoctrination or details. Whether there was a midday meal depended on the attitude of the prisoner, the supply of food, and the general state of the political situation. The main meal was served around five o'clock and usually consisted of vegetables, grains, rice, and occasional bits of pork fat or fish. For men on such a meager diet, details involving many miles of walking or very hard work were especially exhausting.

Recreation varied with the camp and with the political situation. During the first year or so, a heavy emphasis was placed on indoctrination, and recreation was restricted to reading Communist literature, seeing propaganda films, and playing such games as checkers and chess. As the truce talks progressed and repatriation became a possibility, conditions in the camps improved generally. Less emphasis was placed on indoctrination and more leeway was given to the prisoners to engage in recreation of their own choice. The improvement in living conditions made physical recreation more feasible, and the men were permitted to devise athletic fields and equipment. Intercamp "Olympics" conducted by the Chinese—and used by them for their own propaganda purposes—drew wide participation among the more athletically inclined, regardless of their political sentiments.

There are few data available concerning the sexual activities of the prisoners. There were Korean women available in the villages, but men seldom visited them. Reports of homosexuality were very infrequent.

THE INDOCTRINATION PROGRAM

All of these conditions in the permanent camp were, in actual practice, interlocked with the indoctrination program. This program cannot be viewed as a collection of specific techniques routinely applied, but rather as the creation of a whole set of social conditions within which certain techniques operated. Whether the Chinese manipulation of the social setting to create certain effects was intentional can only be conjectured; intentional or not, it was an important factor in such success as the indoctrination program achieved.

The Removal of Supports to Beliefs, Attitudes, and Values

On matters of opinion, people tend to rely primarily on the opinions of others for determination of whether they themselves are "right" or "wrong"—whether these opinions of others are obtained through mass media of communication or through personal interaction. All of the prisoners' accustomed sources of information concerning daily events on a local, national, or international level were cut off by the Chinese, who substituted their own, usually heavily biased, newspapers, radio broadcasts, and magazines. *The Daily Worker* from various cities was available in the camp libraries, as were numerous magazines and journals from China, Poland, Russia, and Czechoslovakia. The radio news broadcasts heard usually originated in China. And the camp headquarters had no scruples concerning accuracy in the news announcements made over the camp public-address system.

The delivery of mail from home was systematically manipulated; the evidence indicates that all mail which contained information about the war or the truce talks, or which contained favorable personal news, was withheld, while letters containing no general information, or bad personal news, were usually delivered.

Personal contact with visitors from outside the camps was very limited, mainly restricted to Communist news correspondents. For most prisoners, there was simply no way to find out accurately what was going on in the world.

The Chinese also attempted to weaken the means of consensual validation by undermining personal contacts among the men. First of all, the men were segregated by race, apparently in order to put special indoctrination pressure on members of certain minorities, especially Negroes. The men were also segregated by rank, in what appeared to be a systematic attempt to undermine the internal structure of the group by removing its leaders. Thus the noncommissioned officers, who were at first in the enlisted camps, were put into a special camp when the Chinese found out that they were quite effective in keeping the other men from various kinds of collaboration. It was reported that this segregation was often followed by a considerable increase in collaboration, particularly among the younger enlisted men.

The Chinese emphasized that rank was no longer of any significance; the entire group was now part of a wider "brotherhood"—the earlier mentioned "fighters for peace"—in which, under communism, everyone was to be equal. The Chinese sometimes put particularly young or inept prisoners in command of the squads to remind the men that former bases of organization no longer counted. While such a procedure aroused only resistance and hostility in most of the prisoners, undoubtedly a few malcontents welcomed the opportunity to gain occupancy of the favored positions that had never been available to them before.

There was also persistent emphasis on undermining all friendships, emotional bonds, and group activities. For instance, the Chinese prohibited all forms of religious expression and ruthlessly persecuted the few chaplains or others who tried to organize or conduct religious services. Bonds to loved ones at home were weakened by the withholding of mail, as the Chinese frequently pointed out to the men that the lack of mail meant that their friends and relatives no longer cared for them.

The systematic use of Chinese spies and also informers from prisoner ranks made it possible for the Chinese to obtain detailed information about almost all activities going on in camp. The men reported around their quarters and listening to that the Chinese were forever sneaking conversations or observing activities from hidden posts, and they also knew that some of their number were acting as informers. These circumstances helped to create a feeling of general distrust, and the only fully safe course was to withdraw from all intimate interaction with other prisoners.

When any semblance of effective organization appeared spontaneously among the men, the Chinese would usually immediately remove and segregate the leaders or key figures; and informal groups which might have supported resistance activities were also usually systematically broken up. The few that were not broken up either were not effective or died because of lack of internal support, thus indicating that this system of social control was highly effective. Usually groups were formed for one of three purposes—to plan for and aid in escapes, to prevent men from collaborating, or for social reasons. According to most reports, the groups organized around escape were highly ineffective. Usually such groups were quickly liquidated by being physically broken up. A few poorly planned escapes were attempted, but the marginal diet, the strangeness of the surrounding terrain, and the carefully built-up fear of the North Koreans all served to minimize escapes. When an escape did occur, the Chinese usually recovered the man easily by offering a bag of rice to anyone turning him in. The groups organized to keep men from collaborating, or to retaliate against them if they did, were usually composed of some of the more outspoken and violent resisters. One such group, labelled the "Ku Klux Klan" by the Chinese because of its militant policy, appeared to be composed mainly of men who had served some time in prison for various infractions of camp rules. They threatened potential collaborators through anonymous notes, but the number of incidents in which they followed through was relatively small. Usually the Chinese discovered their plans and, whenever they became dangerous, disrupted their activities. The third type of group consisted of prisoners who were solely interested in each other's company; one such group, made up primarily of older prisoners, was called "The Old Soldiers' Home."

A few groups remained intact even though the Chinese knew about them, perhaps because the Chinese did not consider them very dangerous, or because their leaders, as spokesmen for the prisoners, provided a valuable sounding board whenever the Chinese wanted to know how the group would react to certain changes in policy. The latter, in fact, gave such groups some power, but if this power was ever misused—that is, if the group supported an escape attempt or a theft of food, for instance— the group was quickly liquidated and its leaders were imprisoned or moved to another camp.

Various other groupings of men existed, some, such as the squad, for administrative reasons, others to support various Chinese enterprises. Soon after capture, the Chinese made a concerted effort to recruit men for a number of "peace committees" whose purpose it was to aid in the indoctrination by conducting personal interviews with resistant prisoners and to deter any resistance activity. They also were charged with such propaganda missions as the preparation of leaflets, peace petitions, and scripts for radio broadcasts—all under the guise of running such innocuous camp activities as recreation. An intercamp peace organization was also formed to draw up peace appeals and petitions to be submitted to the United Nations, carrying, of course, the endorsement of a large number of prisoners.

The members of the camp peace committees and the delegates to intercamp peace rallies were usually selected by a pseudo-democratic method. However, the men who ended up in the key positions were usually those the Chinese wanted, or, in any case, approved of—that is, men who were willing to cooperate with the Chinese, and who had sincerely or falsely convinced their captors that they were sympathetic to the Communist cause. Sometimes the election was held over and over again until the right man was chosen. At other times the men resigned themselves to the fact that all would go more smoothly if they selected at the beginning the man the Chinese wanted, for the group could be dissolved at will anyway.

Each camp also had a number of other committees operating under the peace committee. They were responsible for the daily routine affairs of the camp, such as sanitation, food, recreation, study, and entertainment. The number of noncollaborators who were allowed to be members appeared to depend on the mood of the Chinese and the degree to which they wanted to keep in touch with prisoner opinions. It is likely that with the general improvement in camp conditions in 1952 and 1953, the membership of the various committees became more representative. The peace committees were, by then, largely defunct; they had been exploited as much as possible by the Chinese and no longer served any function in their propaganda campaigns.

Various social groups formed by pro's were left intact—perhaps as a reminder to other prisoners that one way to enter into meaningful relationships with others was through common political activities for the Communists.

One of the most significant facts about the few types of groups that did exist in camp is that they were highly unstable from an internal point of view because of the possible presence of informers and spies. Mutual distrust existed especially in the peace committees and in groups sanctioned by the Chinese, because no member was ever sure whether any other member was really a pro or was just pretending to "go along." If a man was pretending, he had to hide this carefully lest a real pro turn him in to the Chinese. Yet a man who sincerely believed in the Chinese peace effort had to hide this fact from others who might be pretenders, for fear they might harm him directly or blacklist him for the future, at the same time convincing other pro's that he really was sincere.

The members of resistance groups and social groups also had to be wary of each other, because they never knew whether the group had been infiltrated by spies and informers. Furthermore, the fact that the group might be broken up at any time tended to keep any member from becoming too dependent on, or close to, another.[4]

From the point of view of this analysis, the most important effect of the social isolation which existed was the consequent emotional isolation which prevented a man from validating any of his beliefs, attitudes, and values through meaningful interaction with other men at a time when these were under heavy attack from many sources, and when no accurate information was available.

Direct Attacks on Beliefs, Attitudes, and Values

The chief method of direct indoctrination was a series of lectures that all prisoners had to attend at some time during their imprisonment. These lectures were given daily and lasted from two to three hours. Each camp had one or more political instructors who read the lectures from a prepared text. Often one instructor read while another seemed to follow a second copy of the text, as if to make sure that the right material was being presented. The lectures were direct, simple, black-and-white propaganda. They attacked the United Nations and particularly the United States on various political, social, and economic issues, at the same time glorifying the achievements of the Communist countries, and making strong appeals for "peace."

Most men reported that the anti-American material was naïve and seldom based on adequate or correct information about the United States. Even the pro-Communist arguments were sometimes weak and susceptible to attack. Occasionally a well-educated prisoner debated points on communism successfully with instructors who had little knowledge of the classical works of communism. Usually the instructors presented the neo-Communist views of writers such as Mao Tse-tung and were unable to counter the arguments of prisoners who knew Marx and Lenin. The number of prisoners with sufficient education to engage in such arguments was, however, extremely small.

The constant hammering at certain points, combined with all the other techniques used—and in a situation where the prisoners had no access to other information—made it likely that many of the Chinese argu-

---

[4] Segal (reference footnote 2) has aptly described such prisoner groups as "groups of isolates."

ments did filter through enough to make many of the men question some of their former points of view. It is also likely that any appeal for "peace," no matter how false, found a receptive audience among combat-weary troops, especially when it was pointed out that they were fighting on foreign soil and were intervening in a civil war which was "none of their business." Both lectures and didactic "interrogations" emphasized detailed predictions of what would happen to the prisoners upon repatriation, some of which turned out to be accurate.[5] The Chinese implied that certain problems which would arise would be the result of the "weakness" or "unfairness" of the democratic ideology.

Another direct technique was the distribution of propaganda leaflets and the showing of Communist films glorifying the accomplishments of the Communist regime in Russia and China, and pointing out how much more had been done by communism for the peasant and laborer than by the capitalist system. While such films might have been highly ineffectual under ordinary circumstances, they assumed considerable importance because of the sheer lack of any other audio-visual material.

Perhaps the most effective attack on existing values, beliefs, and attitudes was the use of testimonials from prisoners who were ostensibly supporting Communist enterprises. These included peace petitions, radio appeals, speeches, and confessions. The use of such testimonials had a double effect in that it further weakened group ties while presenting pro-Communist arguments. As long as the men unanimously rejected the propaganda, each of them could firmly hold to the position that his beliefs must be right, even if he could not defend them logically. However, *if even one other man became convinced, it was no longer possible to hold this position.* Each man was then required to begin examining his beliefs and was vulnerable to the highly one-sided arguments that were repeatedly presented.

Of particular importance were the germ-warfare confessions which were extracted from a number of Air Force officers and enlisted men. The Chinese made a movie of one or two of the officers giving their testimony to the "international" commission which they had set up to investigate the problem, and showed this movie in all the camps. Furthermore, one or two of the officers personally went from camp to camp and explained how United Nations forces had used these bombs; this made a powerful impression on many men who had, until then, dismissed the whole matter as a Chinese propaganda project. The great detail of the accounts, the sincerity of the officers, the fact that they were freely going from camp to

[5] The various problems that faced repatriates have been discussed by Segal, reference footnote 2, and by Robert J. Lifton in "Home by Ship: Reaction Patterns of American Prisoners of War Repatriated from North Korea," *Amer. J. Psychiatry* (1954) 110:732-739.

camp and did not look as if they were then or had previously been under any duress made it difficult for some men to believe that the accounts could be anything but true.

While it is difficult to determine how many men were convinced that the United Nations forces had used germ bombs, it is evident that serious doubts arose in the minds of many, and some admitted being still in doubt even some weeks after their repatriation. Unquestionably, personal testimonials were on the whole a far more effective propaganda weapon than any amount of direct lecturing, although they both played a part in the over-all indoctrination. In general, the older and more experienced prisoners were less susceptible to this kind of propaganda. One sergeant stated that the following kinds of reasons prevented him and others from falling for germ-warfare charges: first, germ bombs are tactically impractical and ineffective; second, the United States would probably not abandon its ethics, and germ bombs would not be consistent with those ethics; and third, even if the United States were to use weapons previously not considered ethical, it would use atom bombs in preference to germ bombs.

The Chinese also used Koreans to give testimonials concerning the barbarity of the United Nations; in one instance women and children told one of the peace committees how United Nations planes had dropped toys which exploded when children tried to pick them up. It is difficult to evaluate the effects of such propaganda, but it is not likely that many prisoners believed stories of such extremity.

Indirect Attacks on Beliefs, Attitudes, and Values

In the direct attacks which I have been discussing, the source of propaganda was external. In the indirect attacks, a set of conditions was created in which each prisoner of war was encouraged to participate in a way that would make it more possible for him to accept some of the new points of view. One attempt to accomplish this was by means of group discussions following lectures.

Most lectures ended with a series of conclusions—for example, "The South Koreans started the war by invading North Korea," or "The aim of the capitalist nations is world domination." The men were then required to break up into squads, go to their quarters, and discuss the material for periods of two hours or more. At the end of the discussion each squad had to provide written answers to questions handed out during the lecture—the answers, obviously, which had already been provided in the lecture. To "discuss" the lecture thus meant, in effect, to rationalize the predetermined conclusions.[6]

[6] During the last year or so of imprisonment, many of the features of indoctrination which earlier had been compulsory were put on a voluntary basis. Any prisoners who were interested in learning more about communism could attend special lectures

A monitor was assigned to each squad to "aid" the men in the discussion, to make sure that they stayed on the proper topic, and to collect the answers and make sure that they were the "right" ones. Initially, the monitor for most squads was an English-speaking Chinese, but whenever possible the Chinese turned the job over to one of the squad members, usually the one who was most cooperative or sympathetic to the Communist point of view. If one or more members of the squad turned in "wrong" answers—for example, saying that the North Koreans had invaded South Korea—the entire squad had to listen to the lecture again and repeat the group discussion. This procedure might go on for days. The Chinese never tired of repeating the procedure over and over again, apparently believing that group discussion had a better chance of success in converting men to their point of view than individual indoctrination.

The success of such discussions often depended on the degree of supervision. If the monitor was lax, the groups would talk about anything but the required material. But a prisoner-of-war monitor who was actively pro-Communist or a Chinese who had a good understanding of English idiom might obtain considerable discussion. Even when an issue was actively discussed, in many cases it probably reinforced the United Nations' position by providing an opportunity for the men to obtain some consensual validation. But in other cases, the deliberation on points of view other than the one they had always held caused them to question certain beliefs and values which in the past had not led to satisfactory conditions for them.

A second means of indirect attack was interrogation. Interrogations were carried on during all stages of internment, but their apparent function and the techniques utilized varied from time to time. Almost all men went through lengthy and repetitive military interrogations, but failure to answer questions seldom led to severe physical punishment. Instead, various psychological pressures were applied. For instance, all information supplied was cross-checked against earlier interrogations and against the information from other men. If an answer did not tally with other information, the respondent had to explain the discrepancy. Continuous pressure to resolve contrary answers often forced a man to tell the truth.

The Chinese tried to create the impression that they could obtain *any* information from *anyone* by the following interrogation technique: If a man continued to refuse to answer a question, despite great fatigue and continued repetition of the question, the interrogator would suddenly pull out a notebook and point out to the man the complete answer to the question, sometimes in astonishingly accurate detail. The interro-

---

and group discussions. The men who participated in such voluntary programs were known as "self-study pro's" and were given many privileges not accorded to other prisoners.

gation would then move on to a new topic and the same procedure would
be repeated, until the man could not assess whether there was indeed
anything that the Chinese did *not* know. In most cases the man was told
that others had already given information or "confessed," so why should
he hold back and suffer? [7]

A further technique was to have the man write out the question and
then the answer. If he refused to write it voluntarily, he was asked to copy
it from the notebooks, which must have seemed like a harmless enough
concession. But the information which he had copied could then be shown
to another man as evidence that he had given information of his own
volition. Furthermore, it could be used to blackmail him, because he
would have a hard time proving that he had merely copied the material.

Another type of interrogation to which almost all men were subjected involved primarily nonmilitary information. The Chinese were
very curious about all aspects of life in the Western world and asked
many questions about it, often in great detail. They also endeavored, by
means of printed forms, to obtain a complete personal history from each
prisoner, with particular emphasis on his social-cultural background, his
class status, his and his parents' occupational histories, and so on. The
purpose was apparently to determine which prisoners' histories might
predispose them toward the Communist philosophy and thus make them
apt subjects for special indoctrination.

Most men did not give accurate information. Usually the prisoner
filled out the form in terms of fictitious characters. But later he would be
required to repeat the entire procedure and would usually be unable to
remember his earlier answers. He would then be confronted with the dis-
crepancies and would be forced into the fatiguing activity of having to
invent justification after justification to resolve them.

If and when the Chinese felt that they had obtained a relatively true
account, it was used in discussion between the interrogator and the prisoner to undermine the prisoner's beliefs and values. Various points in
the life history were used to show a man the "errors" of his past life—
for example, that he or his parents had been ruthless capitalists exploit-
ing workers, yet had really received only meager benefits from such ex-
ploitation. The Chinese were particularly interested in any inconsistencies in the life histories and would focus discussion on them in order to
bring to light the motivations involved. Whenever possible, any setbacks
that a man had experienced economically or socially were searchingly
analyzed, and the blame was laid on the capitalistic system.

The fact that many men were unclear about why they were fighting

[7] Many men reported that they felt the Chinese were boasting when they told
what they knew—that they were very proud of their ability as interrogators and felt
a need to show off to their captors.

in Korea was a good lever for such discussions. The interrogator or instructor could point out the basic injustices of foreign intervention in a civil war, and simultaneously could arouse longings for home and the wish that the United Nations had never taken up the fight in the first place. It was not difficult to convince some men that being in Korea was unfair to the Koreans, to themselves, and to their families who wanted them home.

Interrogations might last for hours, days, or even weeks. In some cases the interrogator lived with his subject and tried to create an atmosphere of warmth and friendliness. The main point seemed to be to get the prisoner talking, no matter what he was talking about. The discussions sometimes became effective didactic sessions because of the friendly relationship which the interrogator built up. If there were any weaknesses or inconsistencies in a man's belief systems, once he lowered his guard and began to examine them critically, he was in danger of being overwhelmed by the arguments of the instructor. This did not, of course, occur typically. For many men such critical self-evaluation served as a reinforcement to their own beliefs and actually enabled them to expose weaknesses in the Communist arguments.

Another effective technique for getting the men to question their own beliefs and values was to make them confess publicly to wrongdoings and to "criticize" themselves. Throughout the time that the men were in camp they were required to go through these rituals over and over again, no matter how trivial the offense. These offenses usually were infractions of camp rules. Soon after the men had arrived in permanent camp they were given copies of the camp rules and were required to sign a statement that they would abide by them. Most of the men were far too hungry and cold to read several pages of script covering every aspect of camp life in such minute detail that it was practically impossible not to break one of the rules from time to time. For example, an elaborate set of rules governed where in camp a man was allowed to expectorate.

Sooner or later a minor or major infraction of the rules would occur. The man would be immediately brought up before the camp commander, where his offense would be condemned as a serious crime—one for which he, the commander would point out, could be severely punished, if it were not for the lenient Chinese policy. In line with the great show which the Chinese made of treating the prisoner as a responsible person, the fact that he had agreed in writing to abide by the rules would be emphasized. The prisoner could not now say that he had not read the rules, for this would expose him to further embarrassment. The camp commander would then ask whether the man would admit that he had broken the rule, whether he was sorry that he had done so, and whether he would promise not to behave in such a "criminal" manner in the future. If the offender agreed, which seemed at the time to be harmless enough and an easy way to get off, he would be asked to write out a confession.

Sometimes this ended the matter. But frequently the man was required to read his confession to a group of prisoners and to follow it by "self-criticism," which meant that the description of the wrong deed had to be analyzed in terms of the wrong *idea* that lay behind it, that the self had to be "deeply and sincerely" criticized in terms of a number of reasons why the idea and deed were "wrong," and that an elaborate set of promises about future conduct had to be made, along with apologies for the past. Such public self-effacement was a humiliating and degrading experience, and it set a bad precedent for other men who had been attempting to resist getting caught in this net.

Writing out confessions, reading them, and criticizing oneself for minor misconduct in camp did not seem too great a concession at first when viewed against the possibility of physical punishment, torture, or imprisonment. However, these techniques could become a psychological torture once the initial concession had been made. A man who had broken a rule and had gone through the whole ritual of criticism would shortly afterward break another rule, which would arouse increased hostility on the part of the Chinese and lead to correspondingly greater demands for confession and self-criticism. Men who had confessed at first to trivial offenses soon found themselves having to answer for relatively major ones.[8]

It should be pointed out, however, that the prisoners found numerous ways to obey the letter but not the spirit of the Chinese demands. For example, during public self-criticism sessions they would often emphasize the wrong words in the sentence, thus making the whole ritual ridiculous: "I am sorry I called Comrade Wong *a no-good son-of-a-bitch.*" Another favorite device was to promise never to "get caught" committing a certain crime in the future. Such devices were effective because even those Chinese who knew English were not sufficiently acquainted with idiom and slang to detect subtle ridicule.

There is also some evidence that the Chinese used enforced idleness or solitary confinement to encourage prisoners to consider the Communist point of view. One of the few activities available, in such circumstances, was to read Communist literature and books by Western authors who directly or indirectly attacked capitalism. The camp libraries were wholly

[8] It can be seen that such a technique of "training" a man to confess can ultimately lead to the demand that he confess not only to misdeeds and the "wrong" ideas which lay behind them, but also to "wrong" thoughts and feelings which had not even resulted in action. In conjunction with public self-appraisal, prisoners were also often encouraged to keep diaries of their activities and thoughts. Usually only those prisoners who seriously studied communism kept diaries.

made up of such literature. Those who did not have the strength or inclination to go on physically taxing details found themselves with no alternative but to spend their time reading pro-Communist material. In addition, some read because they felt so emotionally isolated from other prisoners that they could enjoy only solitary activities.

The Eliciting of Collaboration by Rewards and Punishments

For a number of propaganda purposes the Chinese seemed to want certain men to cooperate in specific ways, without caring whether they accepted communism or not. These men did not seem to enjoy as much status as other pro's and were cast off by the Chinese as soon as they had ceased to be useful. Such collaboration was elicited directly by a system of rewards and incentives on the one hand, and threats and punishments on the other.

While it is dangerous to relate complex human behavior to a simple pattern of rewards and punishments, the repatriates' accounts of life in the prisoner-of-war camps make possible a considerable number of inferences concerning the "positive" and "negative" aspects of the social environment, which were important in eliciting the kind of behavior the Chinese wanted. It was made clear to all prisoners, from the time of their capture on, that cooperation with the Chinese would produce a more comfortable state of affairs, while noncooperation or open resistance would produce a continuing marginal existence. Which rewards were of primary importance to the men varied with their current condition. On the marches and in the temporary camps physical conditions were so bad that more food, any medication, any clothing or fuel, better and less crowded living conditions, and the like constituted a powerful reward. Promises of early repatriation, or at least of marked improvement of conditions in the permanent camps, were powerful incentives which were chronically exploited.

In the permanent camps there was some improvement in the physical conditions, so that basic necessities became less effective incentives. The promise of early repatriation continued to be a great incentive, however, despite the fact that it had been promised many times before without result. Communicating with the outside world now became a major concern. To let those at home know they were alive, some prisoners began to collaborate by making slanted radio broadcasts or filling their letters with propaganda or peace appeals in order to make sure that they were sent.

As conditions continued to improve, some of the luxury items and smaller accessories to living assumed greater significance. Cigarettes, combs, soap, candy, small items of clothing, a cup of hot tea, a drink of liquor, fresh fruit, and other items of this kind were sought avidly by some men.[9] Obtaining such items from the Chinese was inextricably linked with the degree to which the prisoner was willing to "cooperate." Any tendency toward "cooperation" was quickly followed by an increase in material rewards and promises for the future.

In some cases rewards were cleverly linked with participation in the indoctrination. For example, highly valued prizes such as cigarettes or fresh fruit were offered for essays dealing with certain aspects of world politics. The winning entries were published in the camp newspaper or magazine. Usually the winning entry was selected on the basis of its agreement with a Communist point of view, and the winner was usually someone well on the road to collaboration anyway, but the whole competition succeeded in getting the men to participate—to consider the various sides of an issue and to examine their previous views critically.

The Chinese also used rewards and punishments to undermine group organization. For example, shortly after capture, a number of men were led to believe that if they made radio broadcasts to the United Nations lines they would be repatriated early. The content of the broadcasts was not specified, but the men agreed to make them in the hope of letting their relatives know that they were alive. These men were then conspicuously assembled in front of other prisoners and were taken to a special location some distance away, where the broadcasts were to be made. In the meantime, other prisoners were encouraged to believe that these men were obtaining special privileges because they were "cooperating" in bringing "peace" to Korea.

The actual content of the radio messages turned out to be a peace appeal which tacitly condemned the United Nations, and a statement that the prisoners were being well treated by the Chinese. When the men saw the messages that they were to read, some of them refused to make the broadcast, despite threats of severe punishment. Other men agreed to make the broadcast but tried to code a message into the prescribed text, and still others hoped that the recipients of the broadcasts would somehow know that they were under duress. At least their families would know that they were alive if they broadcasted something.

When these men rejoined the other prisoners, they found that they had aroused the suspicion and hostility of many, especially since the Chinese showed their "appreciation" by ostentatiously bestowing favors on them. In order to retain these special privileges—and having in any case incurred the hostility or even ostracism of their own group—some of these

[9] A number of men reported that black-market activities flourished among the prisoners. Those items of value which men did not wish to use themselves were bartered or sold to other men. Even valuable medicines could sometimes be obtained only by bartering with pro's who had obtained them from the Chinese.

men continued to collaborate, rationalizing that they were not really harming the United Nations cause. They became self-appointed secret agents and attempted to infiltrate the Chinese hierarchy to gather "intelligence information," in which capacity they felt that they could actually aid the United Nations cause.

Among the most effective rewards used by the Chinese were special privileges and certain symbolic rewards, such as rank and status in the prison hierarchy. Perhaps the most important of the privileges was freedom of movement; the pro's had free access to the Chinese headquarters and could go into town or wherever they wished at any time of the day or night. They were given certain preferred jobs, such as writing for the camp newspaper, and were excused from the more unpleasant chores around the camp. They were often consulted by the Chinese in various policy matters. They received as a status symbol a little peace dove to be worn in the lapel or a Mao Tse-tung button which served as an identification badge. And many rewards were promised them for the future; they were told that they were playing a vital role in the world-wide movement for "peace," and that they could enjoy positions of high rank in this movement if they stayed and continued to work for it.

If one asks why men "fell" for this kind of line—why they were able to believe this kind of promise—one must look to the circumstances described earlier. These men had no sources of contrary information to rely on, and once they had collaborated even a little they were ostracized by their buddies, thus losing the support of the group which might have kept them from collaborating further.

Just as the probability of collaborative behavior could be increased through the use of rewards, the probability of resistance could be decreased through negative or painful stimulation. Usually threats of punishment were used when prisoners refused to "cooperate," and actual punishment was meted out for more aggressive resistance. Threats of death, nonrepatriation, torture, reprisals against families, reduction in food and medication, and imprisonment were all used. While the only one of these threats which was carried out with any degree of consistency was imprisonment, which sometimes involved long periods of solitary confinement, the other threats were nevertheless very effective and the possibility that they might be carried out seemed very real. Especially frightening was the prospect of nonrepatriation, which seemed a likely possibility before the prisoner lists were exchanged at Panmunjom. The threat of death was also effective, for the men knew that they could be killed and listed officially as having died of heart failure or the like.[10] With regard

[10] There is evidence that the Chinese sometimes staged "executions" in order to elicit cooperation. A prisoner might be marched out into a field, an empty gun placed to his head, and the trigger actually pulled. This procedure first created a state of high

to food and medication, the men could not determine whether they were actually being punished by having these withheld, or whether the meager supply was merely being reserved for "deserving" prisoners.

An effective threat with officers was that of punishing the whole group for which the officer was responsible if he personally did not "cooperate." The incidence of such group punishment was not revealed in the accounts, but it is clear that if an officer did "cooperate" with the Chinese, he was able both to relieve his own fears and to rationalize his cooperation as being the only means of saving the men for whom he was responsible.

Reinforcing all these threats was the vague but powerful fear of the unknown; the men did not know what they were up against in dealing with the Chinese and could not predict the reactions of their captors with any degree of reliability. The only course that led to a consistent reduction in such tension was participation in Chinese enterprises.

Overt punishment varied with the offense, with the political situation, and with the person administering it. Shortly after capture there were numerous incidents of brutality, most of them committed by North Koreans. During early interrogations the Chinese frequently resorted to minor physical punishment such as face-slapping or kicking when answers were not forthcoming, but a prisoner who continued to be silent was usually dismissed without further physical punishment.

Physical punishments in permanent camps had the effect of weakening rather than injuring the men. They varied from severe work details to such ordeals as standing at attention for long periods; being exposed to bright lights or excessive cold; standing on tiptoe with a noose around the neck; being confined in the "cage," a room too small to allow standing, sitting, or lying down; being thrown in the "hole," a particularly uncomfortable form of solitary confinement; or being kept in filthy surroundings and denied certain essentials for keeping clean. Those who were *chronically* uncooperative were permanently segregated from the rest of the group and put into special camps where more severe forms of discipline backed by harsher punishments were in effect. Basically, the "lenient policy" applied only to those men whom the Chinese hoped they could use.

More common forms of punishment for minor infractions were social in character, intended to degrade or embarrass the prisoner in front of his fellows. Public confessions and self-criticisms were the outstanding forms of such punishment, with blackmail being frequently used if a prisoner had once collaborated to any extent. There is *no* evidence that

---

anxiety and then a state of grateful relief when it was discovered by the prisoner that he would not be executed after all.

the Chinese used any drugs or hypnotic methods, or offered sexual objects to elicit information, confessions, or collaborative behavior. Some cases of severe physical torture were reported, but their incidence is difficult to estimate.

General Principles in All Techniques

Several general principles underlay the various phases of the Chinese indoctrination, which may be worth summing up at this point. The first of these was *repetition*. One of the chief characteristics of the Chinese was their immense patience in whatever they were doing; whether they were conducting an interrogation, giving a lecture, chiding a prisoner, or trying to obtain a confession, they were always willing to make their demand or assertion over and over again. Many men pointed out that most of the techniques used gained their effectiveness by being used in this repetitive way until the prisoner could no longer sustain his resistance. A second characteristic was the *pacing of demands*. In the various kinds of responses that were demanded of the prisoners, the Chinese always started with trivial, innocuous ones and, as the habit of responding became established, gradually worked up to more important ones. Thus after a prisoner had once been "trained" to speak or write out trivia, statements on more important issues were demanded of him. This was particularly effective in eliciting confessions, self-criticism, and information during interrogation.

Closely connected with the principle of pacing was the principle of constant *participation* from the prisoner. It was never enough for the prisoner to listen and absorb; some kind of verbal or written response was always demanded. Thus if a man would not give original material in question-and-answer sessions, he was asked to copy something. Likewise, group discussions, autobiographical statements, self-criticisms, and public confessions all demanded an active participation by the prisoner.[11]

In their propaganda campaign the Chinese made a considerable effort *to insert their new ideas into old and meaningful contexts.* In general this was not very successful, but it did work for certain prisoners who were in

[11] The Chinese apparently believed that if they could once get a man to participate he was likely to continue, and that eventually he would accept the attitudes which the participation expressed. However, it may have also been true that the interrogators, for instance, were in danger of losing face with their own group if they could not produce concrete evidence that they had obtained some information; at times they seemed to want any kind of answers, so long as they had something to show in headquarters as proof that they had done their job. Similarly, the material obtained at the end of the group discussions was perhaps used as evidence that the instructors were doing their jobs properly. Thus it is possible that part of the aim was a check by the Chinese on each other.

some way not content with their lot in the United States. The obtaining of autobiographies enabled each interrogator to determine what would be a significant context for the particular person he was dealing with, and any misfortune or setback that the person had suffered served as an ideal starting place for undermining democratic attitudes and instilling communistic ones.

No matter which technique the Chinese were using, they always structured the situation in such a way that the correct response was followed by some form of *reward*, while an incorrect response was immediately followed by *threats* or *punishment*. The fact that the Chinese had complete control over material resources and had a monopoly of power made it possible for them to manipulate hunger and some other motives at will, thereby giving rewards and punishments their meaning.

Among the various propaganda techniques employed by the Chinese, their use of *prestige suggestion* was outstanding. The average prisoner had no way of disputing the germ-warfare confessions and testimonials of Air Force officers, or the conclusions of an investigation of the germ-warfare charges by ostensibly impartial scientists from many nations.

Among the positive propaganda appeals made, the most effective was probably the *plea for peace*. The Chinese presented an antiwar and laissez-faire ideology which strongly appealed to the war-weary combat soldier.

In addition, the Chinese used a number of *manipulative tricks,* which were usually successful only if the prisoner was not alert because of fatigue or hunger. One such trick was to require signatures, photographs, or personal information for a purpose which sounded legitimate, then using them for another purpose. Some prisoners reported that they were asked to sign "camp rosters" when they first arrived in camp and later found that they had actually signed a peace petition.

In essence, the prisoner-of-war experience in camp can be viewed as a series of problems which each man had to solve in order to remain alive and well integrated. Foremost was the problem of physical privation, which powerfully motivated each man to improve his living conditions. A second problem was to overcome the fears of nonrepatriation, death, torture, or reprisals. A third problem was to maintain some kind of cognitive integration, a consistent outlook on life, under a set of conditions where basic values and beliefs were strongly undermined and where systematic confusion about each man's role in life was created. A fourth problem was to maintain a valid position in a group, to maintain friendship ties and concern for others under conditions of mutual distrust, lack of leadership, and systematically created social disorganization. The Chinese had created a set of conditions in which collaboration and the acceptance of communism led to a resolution of conflicts in all these areas.

REACTIONS TO THE INDOCTRINATION

It is very difficult to determine after the fact what happened in this highly complex and novel situation—what it was really like for the men who had to spend several years in the Chinese prisoner-of-war camps. Each set of experiences had a highly personal and unique flavor to it, making generalized conclusions difficult.

I may illustrate the problem by discussing *ideological change* and *collaboration*. Both of these were responses to the indoctrination, broadly conceived, *but neither necessarily implies the other*. It was possible for a man to collaborate with the enemy without altering his beliefs, and it was equally possible for a man to be converted to communism to some degree without collaborating.

Obviously, it is necessary to define these responses, even though any precise definition will to some degree distort the actual events. *Collaboration* may be defined as any kind of behavior which helped the enemy: signing peace petitions, soliciting signatures for peace petitions, making radio appeals, writing radio scripts, writing false information home concerning conditions in the camps (or recording statements to this effect), writing essays on communism or working for the Communist-controlled newspaper, allowing oneself to be photographed in "rigged" situations, participating in peace rallies or on peace committees, being friendly with the enemy, asking others to cooperate with the enemy, running errands for the enemy, accepting special privileges or favors, making false confessions or pro-enemy speeches, informing on fellow prisoners, divulging military information, and so on.

Nothing about ideological conversion is implied in this definition. A man who engaged in any of these collaborative behaviors because he wanted an extra cigarette was just as much a collaborator as one who did so because he wanted to further the Communist cause. Moreover, the definition does not take into account the temporal pattern of such behavior. Many men collaborated at one time during their imprisonment when one set of conditions existed, but did not collaborate at other times under other conditions. The man who moved from collaboration to resistance was obviously different from the man who moved from resistance to collaboration. Perhaps most important of all, this definition says nothing about the particular pattern of motivations or circumstances that drove a man to the first collaborative act and subsequently into a situation in which it was difficult to stop collaborating.

Yet such a concept of collaboration has an advantage in its reference to *overt* behavior. It was such behavior which the other men in camp reacted to and which often formed the basis for later judgments of a man by his government, family, and friends, although different motives were often imputed by different sources for such behavior. The motives that lay behind the behavior are of obvious importance and must be understood, but it should also be recognized that conjectures of motives are more precarious than analyses of behavior.

Ideological change may be defined as a reorganization of political beliefs, which could vary from acquiring mild doubts concerning some aspects of the democratic ideology to the complete abandonment of this ideology and a total embracing of communism. The latter I shall label *conversion.* The problem of measuring the *degree* of ideological change is complicated by the lack of good behavioral criteria for measuring such a process of reorganization of beliefs. One might be tempted to say that anyone could be termed a convert who actively attempted to convince others of the worth of communism, who took all the advanced courses in camp, and who was able to demonstrate in his overt behavior a disregard for democratic values. But such behavior might also characterize a relatively intelligent man who had begun to read Communist literature out of boredom, only to find that both his friends and the Chinese took this as evidence of his genuine interest in communism. He might then be ostracized by his friends and pressed into collaboration by the Chinese, who, it was rumored, severely punished anyone who deceived them.

Of all the prisoners, 21 refused repatriation; one might assume that these represent the total number of converts, but such a criterion is inadequate on at least two grounds. On the one hand, some converts would undoubtedly have been sent back to the United States to spread communism and form a potential fifth column. On the other hand, some collaborators who had not changed ideologically might have been afraid to return, knowing that court-martial proceedings and personal degradation probably awaited them.

One might think that the identification of such men could be made successfully by others who were collaborators and possibly converts. However, anyone who had been and remained a convert would *not* identify other converts. On the other hand, a collaborator who had repudiated communism and his own collaborative activities would be likely to implicate as many others as possible in order to make his own behavior look better. Allegations from known collaborators are therefore very unreliable.

Thus it is more difficult to determine how the prisoners responded to indoctrination techniques ideologically than it is to determine what overt collaboration occurred. What the prisoners *did* is, relatively speaking, a matter of fact; why they did it is a matter of conjecture. In presenting a classification of types of reactions and the motivation patterns or situations that elicited them, one must rely primarily on the *consensus* of the accounts of the repatriates and must recognize the possible biases that can arise in such an analysis after the fact. I am not implying that each prisoner could be placed into one of the categories to be presented below; it is more likely that each man fell into several categories at any given time, and, moreover, that his motivation-situation complex shifted as different sets of circumstances presented themselves.

The "Get-Alongers"

The predominant reaction of prisoners was to establish a complex compromise between the demands of the Chinese and the demands of their own ideology. This kind of behavior was labeled "playing it cool" by the men, and consisted primarily in a physical and emotional withdrawal from all situations which might arouse basic conflict. Men who reacted in this way were unwilling to do anything that did not have to be done, and learned after some months to "suspend" their feelings about most events, no matter how provoking they might be. This was not an easy adjustment to maintain, since the prisoner had to make some concessions to the Chinese to avoid the more severe physical or psychological pressures, at the same time avoiding cooperating to such an extent as to arouse the suspicion and hostility of his fellow prisoners. The safest course was to withdraw emotionally both from the Chinese and from the rest of the prisoner group; this withdrawal was made easier by the apathy and physical weakness induced by life under marginal conditions.[12]

Most of the men who achieved this kind of compromise successfully without too great a toll on their personality were well integrated and retained secure and stable group identifications from before their prisoner-of-war experience. Their judgment concerning the extent to which they could collaborate safely had to be relatively unimpaired, and they had to be able to evaluate objectively and dispassionately threats made by the Chinese.

At the beginning, while the noncommissioned officers were still in the enlisted camps, many of them were able—partly because of their strong identification with the Army, and partly because of their wider experience—to help the other men carry out such a compromise solution. In many situations they were able to give advice that appears to have been

[12] For Puerto Ricans and other foreign nationals whose knowledge of English was very shaky, the problem was easily solved. These men conveniently forgot what little English they knew, and, because the Chinese did not have instructors who could speak their languages, they were permitted to withdraw to a relatively comfortable existence of doing details or routine chores. A few others successfully convinced the Chinese that they were illiterate or in some other way incapacitated for study. Some men resolved the conflict by volunteering for all the heavy or unpleasant details, but obviously such a solution was available only to the physically strong and healthy.

sound from all points of view; thus they would help the other men com-
pose answers to questions that would be sufficiently pro-Communist to satisfy the Chinese but not extreme enough to arouse the suspicion of other
prisoners or to be called treasonable. They would also advise the other
men on the wisdom of cooperating in the lectures, of trying to escape,
and so on.

The Resisters

A number of men developed chronic resistance as their main mode
of behavior in camp, refusing to go along with even the most trivial of
Chinese requests. This lack of cooperation varied from passive resistance
to active, organized obstructionism. Such men were a great trial to the
Chinese, who labeled them "reactionaries" and either imprisoned them,
if they felt they had some justification, or segregated them in special
camps. According to the dynamics involved, these men seem to have fallen
into four somewhat separate classes.

THE OBSTRUCTIONIST. These men were characterized by a life-long pattern of indiscriminate resistance to all forms of authority,[13] and had histories of inability to get along in the United Nations Army just as they
were unable to get along with the Chinese. They openly defied any attempt to get them to conform, and performed deeds which other prisoners
considered heroic, such as withstanding severe torture. Usually these men
spent a major part of their internment in the camp prison, in solitary
confinement, or in the "hole."

THE IDEALIST OR MARTYR. These men had unusually powerful identifications with groups whose ideology demanded that they actively resist all
forms of pressure from the Chinese. The best example would be the man
who was deeply religious and whose faith demanded absolute noncooperation with a "Godless enterprise" of the type the Chinese represented.

THE ANXIOUS GUILT-RIDDEN PERSON. This was the man who was afraid
of his own inclination to be tempted by the positive rewards that the Chinese offered for collaboration, and who could handle these impulses only
by denying them and overreacting in the other direction. He was chronically guilt-ridden over his unpatriotic and antisocial impulses and ab-
solved himself by indulging in exaggerated forms of resistance.

THE WELL-INTEGRATED RESISTANCE LEADER. Probably the majority of
resisters fell into this class, although there is no way to estimate their
number. Because of extensive experience in difficult situations and a thorough understanding of the military, they were able systematically to organize other men and to set important precedents for resistance. Most of

---

[13] This pattern has been well described by Lifton, reference footnote 5.

the commissioned and noncommissioned officers fell into this group.[14] The chief characteristic of these men seemed to be their ability to make valid judgments concerning possible courses of action in a situation in which there was little information on which to base such judgments. They had to be able to guess what Chinese reactions would be, what United Nations reactions would be, and most important, how to handle the other prisoners.

The Cooperators

This group is the most difficult to delineate, since I am attempting to include not only those whom the Chinese considered progressives but all those who collaborated to any significant extent. The accounts of prisoners concerning men who collaborated make possible the discrimination of six somewhat separate patterns of motivation for such behaviors.

THE WEAKLING. This was the man who was chronically unable to resist any form of authority, and who was unable to withstand any degree of physical or psychological discomfort. Such men probably became collaborators very soon after their internment, with a minimum of ideological involvement, because it was the easiest way. They often found that the more they collaborated, the more collaboration was demanded of them. They were highly susceptible to threats of blackmail by the Chinese, who could exhibit the evidence of their collaboration to the other prisoners or the United Nations authorities. From the point of view of these men, collaboration was an acceptable adjustment under the physical strains of internment, and they developed elaborate rationalizations to justify their behavior and to convince themselves that they would not suffer for it in the future.

THE OPPORTUNIST. These men exploited the role of pro for all its material benefits, again without any ideological involvement, and with little consideration for the future welfare of themselves or others. They were characterized chiefly by their lack of stable group identifications either inside or outside the Army. They met all situations as they arose and tried to make the most out of them for themselves.

THE MISGUIDED LEADER. A minority of commissioned and noncommissioned officers engaged in various types of collaborative activities under the firm impression that they were furthering the United Nations cause and resisting the enemy. Their primary error was one of judgment.

[14] I have already mentioned the role of noncommissioned officers in helping the "get-alongers" to maintain a compromise role; my mention of them here is an illustration of the fact that this is not a classification of the men, as such, but a classification of behavior. Thus, just as the noncommissioned officers displayed leadership in many instances in compromise, so they also functioned as resistance leaders whenever possible.

They reasoned that the best way to resist indoctrination was to go along with it, to find out what the Chinese were up to, to get into the inner circle so as to better plan resistance. In most cases, they managed merely to set a bad precedent for other prisoners, who felt that if their superiors were getting special privileges they should be getting them as well. These officers, like others, found that once they had begun to collaborate it was difficult to stop. Some of these men were probably weakling types who personally preferred the path of least resistance, but who, because of their responsible positions, had to develop adequate rationalizations. They could not see that their course of action was highly inappropriate; they saw only a justification which met their own needs.

THE BORED OR CURIOUS INTELLECTUAL. Of the very small number of men who had superior education, some turned to Communist literature out of boredom or curiosity, and then found that they had aroused both the hostility of their own group and the expectations of the Chinese that they would collaborate. Only a few managed to interest themselves in the Communist literature without falling into this dilemma. More often, material rewards for the intellectual's interest resulted in his ostracism from his own group, and drove him in the direction of collaboration. Some of these men were fooled by the promise of early repatriation in return for collaboration, and they felt that their collaboration would be sufficiently minor not to damage their own futures. These men, like those previously described, seldom became ideologically confused or converted. Essentially they used bad judgment in an ambiguous situation.

THE "LOW-STATUS" PERSON. The man who was most vulnerable *ideologically* was one who had never enjoyed any kind of secure or rewarding status position either in his home community or in the Army. This type included the younger and less intelligent, the malcontent, and the man whose social reference groups made the attainment of status difficult— that is, the member of various racial, religious, national, or economic minority groups. These men had little realization of the benefits of democracy because they had never experienced them in a meaningful way. They felt that the society was more to blame for their failures than they were. Such men were ready to give serious consideration to an ideology that offered remedies for their misfortunes. As pro's within the Communist hierarchy they could, for the first time, enjoy some measure of status and privilege, and the Chinese wisely promised them important roles in the future of the "peace movement." Some of these men were probably among those who declined repatriation—perhaps out of fear, when they realized how seriously they had jeopardized their position in the Army and at home, perhaps in order to stay with the cause which had for the first time allowed them to be important. It is difficult to determine whether such men underwent a complete ideological conversion, but there is no doubt that they gave serious consideration to the Communist cause, at least to the limit of their intellectual capacity.[15]

The accounts of the repatriates were unclear regarding the reactions of members of the various minority groups, especially the Negroes. The Communist technique of segregating the Negroes and giving them special indoctrination was probably a tactical error. Many Negroes felt that if they were going to be segregated they might as well be segregated in the United States—that there was nothing new or better about communism in this respect. Moreover, the propaganda given them was too extreme; even the very low-status Negro knew that his circumstances in the United States were not as bad as the Communists painted them.

However, because of the low-status category of most of the Negroes, the positive appeals made to them must have struck responsive chords in some. They had an opportunity to be leaders and to enjoy fully equal status if they became pro's, and they could rationalize that they would be able to improve the position of their race by participating in Communist peace movements which advocated equality. It is not possible to determine to what extent these positive appeals outweighed the deterrents, and thus to estimate the degree to which ideological change occurred among the Negroes. In any case, the Chinese probably could have persuaded more Negroes to collaborate and to embrace communism had they not made the fundamental errors of segregation and poor propaganda.

THE COMMUNIST SYMPATHIZER. This was the man who, even before he had joined the Army, was sympathetic to the Communist cause and who, therefore, felt no conflict about his course of action in the prisoner-of-war camp. However, if there were loyal Communists in the camps, it is unlikely that the Chinese divulged their identity by calling them pro's, since they would be of far more use as undercover agents.

Attitudes toward Progressives

The reaction of most men toward the pro's was one of perplexity, fear, and hostility. They could not understand how anyone could "swallow the junk" the Chinese were presenting, yet they were afraid that they too might be swayed, for among the pro's were many men like themselves. If the pro was a "weak-minded guy" or a man who did not have the stamina to resist the physical pressures, other men felt some sympathy for him, but at the same time they resented the extra privileges that his weak-

---

[15] The men who were most vulnerable to ideological appeals were not necessarily the ones the Chinese encouraged to become pro's. There is considerable evidence that the Chinese were quite selective in giving important jobs to prisoners and that they favored more mature and stable ones. Thus the younger, less intelligent, and less stable person was exploited by the Chinese in the same manner as he had probably been exploited before. The Chinese made what use they could of such men and then rejected them when they ceased to be useful.

ness gained for him. If the pro was perceived to be an opportunist, he was hated and threatened with retaliation during internment or following repatriation. If the pro was a person who had status or rank, the men felt perplexed and afraid; they could not decide what they themselves should do, especially if such a pro tried to convince them that it was acceptable to collaborate.

The pro's were very conspicuous in camp by their identification symbols, by their special privileges—which they did not hesitate to flaunt—and by the fact that they usually congregated around camp headquarters. This made them ideal scapegoats and targets for hostility.

They were ostracized by the other prisoners who often refused even to carry on conversations with each other when a pro was present, forcing the pro's into interaction with each other. Thus they tended to form tightly knit groups, which continued even after the end of their internment. The men accused the pro's of informing, imputed to them many motives about which they themselves felt guilty, and attributed any punishment they suffered to some report by a pro. They threatened the pro's with physical violence, but were usually prevented by the Chinese from carrying out such threats. Later, on board ship, the men frequently said that they would now "get even," but the low rate of incidents suggests that no realistic plans underlay the threats. Perhaps most men felt too guilty about their own actual or fantasied collaboration to be comfortable about retaliating against those who had succumbed to the temptations.

The attitudes of the pro's varied with their motivations. Those who had been tricked or "seduced" into collaborating before they could fully realize the consequences remained aloof from other prisoners because they felt guilty and afraid. The opportunists or low-status prisoners felt their collaboration to be entirely justified by the prison-camp situation and viewed noncollaborators as "fools who don't know a good thing when they see it." They tried to persuade others to collaborate—in some cases because they sincerely believed part of the Chinese propaganda, and in other cases because they knew that the Chinese would reward them still further if they succeeded. Many pro's tried hard to remain liked both by the Chinese and by the other prisoners, but few succeeded. Since the Chinese presented themselves as benevolent captors, the pro's were the only group in camp who could consistently be used as an outlet for all the hostility engendered by the prison-camp situation.

THE EFFECTIVENESS OF THE INDOCTRINATION TECHNIQUES

By disrupting social organization and by the systematic use of reward and punishment, the Chinese were able to elicit a considerable amount of collaboration. This is not surprising when one considers the tremendous effort the Chinese made to discover the weak points in individual prisoners, and the unscrupulousness with which they manipulated the environment. Only a few men were able to avoid collaboration altogether —those who adopted a completely negativistic position from the moment of capture without considering the consequences for themselves or their fellow prisoners. At the same time the number of men who collaborated to a sufficient extent to be detrimental to the United Nations cause was also very small. The majority collaborated at one time or another by doing things which seemed to them trivial, but which the Chinese were able to turn to their own advantage. Such behavior did not necessarily reflect any defection from democratic values or ideology, nor did it necessarily imply that these men were opportunists or neurotics. Often it merely represented poor judgment in evaluating a situation about which they had little information, and poor foresight regarding the reactions of the Chinese, other prisoners, and people back home.

The extent to which the Chinese succeeded in converting prisoners of war to the Communist ideology is difficult to evaluate because of the previously mentioned hazards in measuring ideological change, and because of the impossibility of determining the *latent* effects of the indoctrination. In terms of *overt* criteria of conversion or ideological change, one can only conclude that, considering the effort devoted to it, the Chinese program was a failure. Only a small number of men decided to refuse repatriation—possibly for reasons other than ideological change[16]—and it was the almost unanimous opinion of the prisoners that most of the pro's were opportunists or weaklings. One can only conjecture, of course, the extent to which prisoners who began to believe in communism managed to conceal their sympathies from their fellows and the degree to which repatriates are now, as a result of their experience, predisposed to find fault with a democratic society if they cannot make a go of it.

It is difficult to determine whether to attribute this relative failure of the Chinese program to the inadequacy of their principles of indoctrination, to their technical inefficiency in running the program, or to both these factors. In actual practice the direct techniques used were usually ineffective because many of the Chinese instructors were deficient in their knowledge of Western culture and the English language. Many of their facts about America were false, making it impossible for them to obtain a sympathetic audience, and many of their attempts to teach by means of group discussion failed because they were not sensitive to the subtle ways

[16] A discussion of some background factors in the lives of these men is presented by Virginia Pasley in *21 Stayed;* New York, Farrar, Strauss & Cudahy, 1955. Unfortunately her study is inconclusive because she did not investigate the background factors in a control group of men who decided to be repatriated.

in which prisoners managed to ridicule them by sarcasm or other language devices. The various intensive pressures brought to bear on single prisoners and the fostering of close personal relationships between prisoner and instructor were far more effective in producing ideological change, but the Chinese did not have nearly enough trained personnel to indoctrinate more than a handful of men in this intensive manner.

The technique of breaking up both formal and spontaneous organization was effective in creating feelings of social and emotional isolation, but it was never sufficiently extended to make the prisoners completely dependent on the Chinese. As long as the men lived and "studied" together, there remained opportunities for consensual validation and thus for resisting indoctrination. However, as a means of social control this technique was highly effective, in that it was virtually impossible for the prisoners to develop any program of organized resistance or to engineer successful communication with the outside by means of escapes or clandestine sending out of information.

The most powerful argument against the intellectual appeal of communism was the low standard of living which the men observed in the Korean villages in which they lived. The repatriates reported that they were unable to believe in a system of values which sounded attractive on paper but which was not practiced, and they were not impressed by the excuse that such conditions were only temporary.

Most men returned from prison camp expressing a strong anti-Communist feeling and a conviction that their eyes had, for the first time, been opened to the real dangers of communism. Many men who had taken little interest in politics before returned with the feeling that they now knew what the United States was fighting for in Korea, and expressed a willingness to continue the fight wherever necessary. Hostility toward the Communists was expressed in such violent proposals as blowing up the *Daily Worker* building or deporting all registered Communists to Korea so that they could see the system in operation firsthand. The repatriates' attitude implied that anything labeled "Communist" had to be destroyed, and anything or anyone against communism had to be supported to the greatest possible extent; types of communism or types of approaches in dealing with communism were not evaluated separately.

It was, of course, difficult to determine the strength and stability of sentiments expressed a few days or weeks after repatriation. In some men these feelings undoubtedly represented an attempt to overcome the guilt that they felt for having collaborated or wavered in their beliefs. In other men they represented simply the accumulated hostility of two to three years of unrelieved frustration and deprivation. But, curiously, this hostility was seldom verbalized against the Chinese as such; it was always the Communists or the pro's who were the targets. The men were confused about the Chinese because they were so inconsistent; they never felt that they could understand or predict the Chinese reaction to anything.

In summary, it can be said that the Chinese were successful in eliciting and controlling certain kinds of behavior in the prisoner population. They were less successful in changing the beliefs of the prisoners. Yet this lack of success might have been due to the inefficiency of a program of indoctrination which could have been highly effective had it been better supported by adequate information and adequately trained personnel.

Collaboration with the enemy occurs to a greater or lesser extent in any captive population. It occurred in the Japanese and German prisoner-of-war camps during World War II. But never before have captured American soldiers faced a *systematic effort* to make them collaborate and to convert them to an alien political ideology. The only precedent in recent history was the handling of political prisoners by the Nazis, described by Bettelheim.[17] By means of extreme and degrading physical and psychological torture the Nazis attempted to reduce the prison population to an "infantile" state in which the jailer would be viewed with the same awe as the child views his father. Under these conditions, the prisoners tended, in time, to identify with the punitive authority figures and to incorporate many of the values they held, especially with respect to proper behavior in camp. They would curry the favor of the guards, would imitate their style of dress and speech, and would attempt to make other prisoners follow camp rules strictly.

It is possible that such a mechanism also operated in the Chinese prison camps. However, the Nazis attempted, by brutal measures, to reduce their prisoners to docile slave laborers, while the Chinese attempted, by using a "lenient policy" and by treating the prisoners as men in need of "education," to obtain converts who would actively support the Communist point of view. Only those prisoners who showed themselves to be "backward" or "reactionary" by their inability to see the fundamental "truths" of communism were treated punitively.

The essence of this novel approach is to gain complete control over those parts of the physical and social environment which sustain attitudes, beliefs, and values, breaking down interactions and emotional bonds which support the old beliefs and values, and building up new interactions which will increase the probability of the adoption of new beliefs and values. If the only contacts a person is permitted are with persons who *unanimously* have beliefs different from his own, it is very likely that

---

[17] Bruno Bettelheim, "Individual and Mass Behavior in Extreme Situations," *J. Abnormal and Social Psychol.* (1943) 38:417–452.

he will find at least some among them with whom, because of growing emotional bonds, he will identify and whose beliefs he will subsequently adopt.

Is the eliciting of collaborative behavior in itself sufficient to initiate the process of ideological change? One might assume that a person who had committed acts consonant with a new ideology might be forced to adopt this ideology in order to rationalize his behavior. This might happen especially if the number of possible rationalizations were limited. The situation in the prison camps, however, allowed the men to develop rationalizations which did not necessarily involve Communist premises. Furthermore, it is likely that whatever rationalizations are adopted, they will not acquire the permanence of beliefs unless supported by social reinforcements. When the prisoners reentered the democratic setting, most of them gave up whatever Communist premises they might have been using to rationalize their collaboration and found new rationalizations that attempted to explain, from the standpoint of democratic premises, why they had collaborated. Apart from the technical difficulties the Chinese experienced in running their indoctrination program, they were never able to control social interactions to a sufficient extent to reinforce in meaningful social relationships the Communist rationalizations for collaboration.

Taken singly, there is nothing new or terrifying about the specific techniques used by the Chinese; they invented no mysterious devices for dealing with people. Their method of controlling information by controlling the mass media of communication has been a well-known technique of totalitarian governments throughout history. Their system of propagandizing by means of lectures, movies, reading materials, and testimonials has its counterparts in education and in advertising. Group discussions and other methods requiring participation have their counterparts in education and in psychiatry. The possibility that group discussion may be fundamentally superior to lectures in obtaining stable decisions by participants has been the subject of extensive research in American social psychology. The Chinese methods of interrogation have been widely used in other armies, by the police, by newspaper reporters, and by others interested in aggressively eliciting information. Forced confessions and self-criticism have been widely used techniques in religious movements as a basis for conversion or as a device to perpetuate a given faith. The control of behavior by the manipulation of reward and punishment is obviously the least novel of all the techniques, for men have controlled each other in this way since the beginning of history.

Thus the only novelty in the Chinese methods was the attempt *to use a combination of all these techniques and to apply them simultaneously* in order to gain complete control over significant portions of the physical and social environment of a group of people. Such an ambitious effort applied on such a large scale is probably unique in the Communist movement, and perhaps in the *Chinese* Communist movement. In order to understand and evaluate this attempt to create ideological uniformity, it is necessary to view the techniques cited in terms of a social-psychological model which does justice to the complexity of this combination. Attempts such as Meerloo's [18] or Winokur's [19] to conceptualize the process of brainwashing in terms of a simple conditioning or learning model seem not only to be premature, but to ignore the most important factor —the simultaneous application of many techniques of social and behavioral control.

Before brainwashing can be properly understood, far more information must be gathered on its operation within China and within the Communist party as a whole; factors which the Chinese have succeeded in manipulating must be built into social-psychological researches on social conformity and attitude change; theoretical models must be constructed which will give a properly weighted emphasis to the variety of factors which probably operate in brainwashing; and personality concepts must be developed which can be used convincingly to categorize the behavior of people subjected to an attack on their most fundamental beliefs and values.

And most important, those who are attempting to understand brainwashing must look at the facts objectively, and not be carried away by hysteria when another country with a different ideology and with different ultimate ends succeeds in eliciting from a small group of Americans behavior that is not consonant with the democratic ideology.

[18] Joost A. M. Meerloo, "Pavlovian Strategy as a Weapon of Menticide," *Amer. J. Psychiatry* (1954) 110:809–813.

[19] George Winokur, " 'Brainwashing'—A Social Phenomenon of Our Time," *Human Organization* (1955) 13:16–18.

Strategies of
hypnotic interrogation

Peter B. Field and Samuel F. Dworkin

.INTRODUCTION *It might surprise the reader to know that some of the most widely publicized methods of behavior control are in reality the most ineffective in regulating human actions. So it is with hypnosis, a field in which no sizable amount of scientific evidence has ever been accumulated to indicate that a person in a hypnotic trance can be made to do something he would not voluntarily do in a waking state.*

Dr. Brown, in his book Techniques of Persuasion, *seems to capture the consensus of scientific opinion about hypnosis when he claims that ". . . the committing of socially reprehensible acts under hypnosis cannot be excluded as a possibility, but it is of far too rare and unreliable a nature to be counted on by those with evil intentions" (Brown, 1963).*

We have included a recent scientific investigation of hypnosis that underscores, once again, the general inadequacy of such a procedure for controlling behavior. Reading the study should make one appreciate the important role scientists play in assessing the relative effectiveness of various behavior control methods.

A. INTRODUCTION

One of the most fascinating questions in research on hypnosis is whether a hypnotized subject can be induced to reveal information that he wishes to conceal. A more precise formulation would be to ask what conditions increase the probability of detection of concealed information during hypnosis. Are some techniques of interrogation—and some strategies of concealment—more effective than others? How effectively can a hypnotized subject withhold information from an interrogator? Are the most hypnotizable individuals especially likely to reveal information?

We know that under some circumstances hypnotic interrogation can

Field, P. B., & Dworkin, S. F. "Strategies of hypnotic interrogation." *Journal of Psychology,* 1967, **67**, 47–58. By permission of authors and The Journal Press.

elicit information. For example, ideomotor questioning methods in hypnotherapy (5) have sometimes located information of clinical value. In these methods, the hypnotized patient may be told that a movement of his right hand or a finger will mean "yes," and a movement of his left hand or another finger will mean "no"; he is then asked questions to which he may not consciously know the answer. Watkins (11) has used hypnotic interrogation as a means of overcoming conscious resistance to revealing information. He reported demonstrations in which he successfully obtained information from military personnel who had been directly ordered by a superior officer not to reveal it. Although these results indicate that under some conditions hypnotic interrogation is successful, Watkins did not attempt to specify which conditions favored successful interrogation and which conditions prevented it. Since he worked only with excellent hypnotic subjects, he implied that hypnotizability was correlated with responsiveness to hypnotic interrogation. However, it remains an open question what results would have been obtained with less highly selected subjects.

Orne (7) has reviewed some of the problems confronting anyone who attempted to use hypnosis to interrogate enemy prisoners of war. His discussion is based on an extrapolation from the current state of knowledge in clinical and experimental hypnosis, inasmuch as there is "an utter dearth of literature concerning the actual use of hypnosis in interrogation." He concluded that the hypnotized subject may lie, withhold information, or confuse fantasy with reality; that studies indicating that hypnosis may induce antisocial behavior are open to the criticism that the laboratory is a pseudoreality situation in which subjects feel protected no matter what they are asked to do; and that the hypnotic induction of antisocial acts (including revealing of confidential information) appears to depend upon a pre-existing positive relationship between subject and hypnotist.

Interrogation under hypnosis has certain points in common with interrogation under drugs. In both cases there may occur alterations in consciousness, apparent weakening of self-control, and occasional revelation of information in spite of a continued wish to keep it secret. Redlich, Ravitz, and Dession (9) instructed nine subjects to conceal items of information during interviews conducted under sodium amytal. The subjects invented a "cover story" to help conceal the shame- or guilt-producing incidents. The authors found that three subjects maintained the cover story, two revealed the true story, two made partial admissions, one admitted a probable fantasy as the truth, and one maintained the cover story except for a slip of the tongue. Clark and Beecher (1) used large amounts of hypnotic, narcotic, analeptic, and hallucinogenic drugs to break down a cover story and detect concealed information. In spite of the fact that their subjects seemed at different times semicomatose, euphoric, mildly delirious, loquacious, panicky, etc., only two of 20 students betrayed the cover story by slips of the tongue. The results of these studies indicate that, although interrogation under drugs can sometimes be effective, there are many exceptions. These studies do not tell us what techniques were most successful, nor do they indicate what strategies of concealment were used by the subjects.

Interest in hypnotic interrogation has been stimulated by its potential usefulness in police work or in legal proceedings. In one recent case (10), a defendant in a murder trial was hypnotized in a courtroom setting and questioned by a psychiatrist, by his own attorney, and by the prosecutor. Such cases raise many questions concerning the accuracy of information elicited under hypnotic interrogation. Such cases also suggest that the difficulty of hypnotizing a person against his will may not be a conclusive objection to the practical use of hypnotic interrogation. The subject may freely consent to hypnosis in the hope of proving his innocence or mitigating his guilt.

The purpose of the present study was to create a laboratory analogue of hypnotic interrogation, and to use it to study the interplay of forces in this situation. In our research, one experimenter instructed the subject to allow himself to be hypnotized by a second experimenter, but to conceal an item of information (a number) from him. The second experimenter then capitalized upon the hypnotic state to try to induce the subject to reveal the number. These instructions were designed to create a conflict between the hypnotic impulse to reveal the information and the conscious motive to conceal the information. The authors wished to find how easy or difficult it was for unselected subjects to conceal information under these conditions, to find the detection strategies that were most effective, and to find what strategies of concealment were spontaneously adopted by the subject.

B. METHOD AND PROCEDURE

1. Subjects, Instructions, and Tests

Subjects were 35 paid volunteer college students and recent graduates recruited through notices on college bulletin boards. They ranged in age between 18 and 28. No subject had previously participated in hypnosis research. Each subject was tested individually in a hospital psychology-research laboratory. Of these 35 subjects, 26 were assigned to an experimental group and nine to a control group. The control subjects were treated identically to experimental subjects except that they merely read the interrogation techniques and the preinterrogation hypnotic induction, and were instructed to guess how they would have responded if they had actually undergone the interrogation. A control group of this kind was suggested by Orne's (8) discussion of methods to control the demand characteristics of the psychological experiment. In order to determine whether subjects are responding to a real variable or just to their hypotheses about the experiment, it is necessary to obtain some estimate of what subjects think they are to do or what they think will happen. One way to obtain this estimate is to instruct some subjects to read a description of the experiment, and then try to judge what the experiment is all about or how they would have responded.

Three interrogation techniques were developed through pretests, during which the authors discarded techniques that depended on specialized hypnotic ability—such as the ability to have hallucinations—in order to obtain techniques that are applicable to many subjects. One technique was based on one of Watkins' interrogation methods. In this technique the subject is instructed to imagine the number at the back of his mouth, imagine its moving forward, and finally speak the number. The second technique centered around the implantation of guilt and the reduction of it through revealing the number. The third technique was based on lie-detection methodology: the subject is instructed to make an involuntary movement when he hears the number read aloud.

Each subject was given the Stanford Hypnotic Susceptibility Scale, Form A (12), and an inventory measure of subjective hypnotic depth (3). After these tests the following instructions were given:

> I am going to let you pick a card with a number on it. This number will be somewhere between zero and nine. You are to remember this number very carefully. Now take one of these cards. Now write down the number you have selected. After we are through here Dr. ——— will try to find out which number you have selected. You will try as hard as you can to avoid telling him the number. Dr. ——— will hypnotize you to find out what the number is, and you will enter hypnosis. What I want you to do is to try to conceal the information from Dr. ———. When he asks you what number you saw, you will not tell him. When he asks you to go into hypnosis once again, you will of course enter hypnosis. Even though you are deeply hypnotized, you will not tell him the number. You have a good chance to do this successfully. If you think that you may have given the number away at some point, keep trying to conceal it, because Dr. ——— may not be aware of whether the number has been revealed. Now write down the number once again. Now do you have any questions?
>
> If the subject asks "Can I tell a lie?" he is told, "That's up to you. Just conceal the number you picked."

The subject was then transferred to the second experimenter in another room. (Random selection determined which of the two experimenters would take the role of the first experimenter or the interrogator with any given subject.) He was then rehypnotized by the Eye Closure induction of the Stanford Hypnotic Susceptibility Scale, Form B (12), and two of the items on this scale were administered (finger lock and arm rigidity). Next the hypnotized subject was asked "What number did you pick?" This question served to establish whether the subject would reveal the information in reply to a simple question, without elaborate interrogation methods. After this, the three interrogation techniques given below were presented to each subject, with the order of administration of the three techniques randomized for each subject. After the interrogation, hypnosis was terminated; and the subject was given a postinterrogation questionnaire, another hypnosis inventory, and an interview. These instruments obtained information on reactions during the experiment and ratings on the difficulty of resisting each interrogation technique.

2. *Interrogation Techniques*
A. NUMBER MOVING FORWARD.

Now you remember the number you picked very clearly, but everything else about the number is getting hard to remember, very hard to remember. You cannot remember what Dr. —— told you about the number, you cannot remember what you are supposed to do with the number. And now, is it getting more difficult to remember the instructions Dr. —— gave you about the number? [*Record reply.*] You seem to be just watching what is happening as if from a distance, watching yourself sitting deeply hypnotized in your chair, remembering only the number and nothing else, and you know that soon your voice and your mouth will start to work automatically and involuntarily and say the number. Now imagine the number at the back of your mouth. Imagine the number written very clearly at the back of your mouth. And you still have trouble remembering anything that Dr. —— said about this number. Now a little later, you will find that the number begins to travel forward in your mouth. It will begin to move forward in your mouth, and when it gets to your lips you will speak it loudly and clearly. You will feel a powerful wish to reveal the number you picked, and no matter how hard you try to conceal it, you will not be able to conceal it. And now the number is coming forward in your mouth, and soon your mouth will say it out loud. The number is now moving forward, it's now on the tip of your tongue, now at your teeth, your lips—what's the number? [*Record reply.*] All right, that's fine. And now you can remember very clearly what Dr. —— said, and everything else. There is no number in your mouth, you are no longer watching yourself from a distance, and your mouth is no longer working automatically. Just relax.

B. GUILT.

Now think how much you dislike the instructions Dr. —— gave you. He told you to conceal a number from me, and you greatly dislike to do this. You even feel angry at Dr. —— for putting you in this uncomfortable position. And now you can think back to some time in the past when you felt guilty about doing something your conscience told you not to do, such as taking something that did not belong to you, or doing something you should have been punished for. And you remember this feeling of guilt, or shame, because you are feeling it very clearly once again. But now you feel guilty and ashamed about keeping the number secret from me, and that feeling of shame and guilt is getting stronger because I asked you for the number and you tried to keep it a secret from me. And now is your conscience beginning to bother you for not telling me the number? [*Record reply.*] This feeling is getting much stronger, much stronger. You will feel a powerful wish to reveal the number you picked, and no matter how hard you try to conceal it, you will not be able to conceal it. And when you tell me the number, you will feel much better right away. You will feel relieved, greatly relieved, when you tell me the number. What Dr. —— told you was wrong, completely wrong, and you will feel so much better now when you tell me the number, right now. What's the number? [*Record reply.*] That's fine. You no longer feel guilty or ashamed. All the guilty feeling is going away. You know that you did nothing wrong. You no longer dislike the instructions Dr. —— gave you, and you do not feel angry at him. Just relax.

C. LIE-DETECTION.

Now soon I will tap my pen on the table, like this (*tap*). When I do, you will make some kind of reaction to it. For example, your face may change expression, or your whole body may move around in your chair, or something else, but in any case you will make some kind of response when I tap my pen on the table. Even if you try to prevent the response, you will make it anyway. When I tap my pen on the table, you will make some kind of response. [*Tap pen loudly, record response.*] All right, now I'm going to say all the numbers between zero and nine, and when I get to the number you picked, you will make an even stronger response to it. When I say the number you picked, you will make some automatic, involuntary response, even stronger than the response you just made, much stronger. Your whole face may change expression, or your body may move around when you hear the number. You will feel a powerful wish to reveal the number you picked, and no matter how hard you try to conceal it, you will not be able to conceal it. And now soon I will start to count, and you will find yourself responding automatically, without thinking. There is no way you can prevent the response. You think only of the number you picked, and you know you will make some noticeable, obvious response when you hear me say it. You will respond only to the number you picked—you will not respond to any other number. And now I will count, and you will respond without thinking.

0, 1, 2, 3, 4, 5, 6, 7, 8, 9, 3, 5, 8, 0, 4, 7, 2, 1, 9, 6. [*Record movements, gestures.*] All right, that's fine. Now you will no longer make any special response when you hear the number. You can forget all about making some special response to the number.

C. RESULTS

Six of the 26 subjects (23 per cent) revealed the information during one or more of the interrogations, while 20 subjects successfully concealed it (Table 1). No subject revealed the information in response to the simple question asked by the interrogator just before the three experimental interrogations. A sign test on the six subjects who revealed the information indicates that the experimental interrogations were more effective than a simple question in eliciting information (.05 level).

Table 1 shows that five of the eight instances in which subjects were

Table 1—Effectiveness of Different Interrogation Techniques

| Subject | Interrogation techniques | | |
	Number-moving	Guilt	Lie detection
B	Conceal	Reveal	Conceal
L	Conceal	Conceal	Reveal
A	Reveal	Conceal	Reveal
M	Conceal	Conceal	Reveal
W	Conceal	Reveal	Reveal
F	Conceal	Conceal	Reveal
20 additional subjects all showed this pattern:	Conceal	Conceal	Conceal
Total reveal	1	2	5

unable to conceal information occurred during the lie-detection interrogation, whereas only one instance of inability to conceal occurred during the number-moving-forward technique, and only two during the guilt technique. These very small numbers do not by themselves establish one technique as statistically superior to another. However, the initial impression of the possible superior effectiveness of the lie-detection technique is confirmed by attitude rating scales. After termination of hypnosis, each interrogation technique was rated on a six-point scale (from "Very easy to resist" = 1 to "Very hard to resist" = 6). An analysis of variance indicates that the mean ratings for each technique vary significantly (.001 level). Tukey's test for a significant gap indicates that the lie-detection technique was rated significantly more difficult to resist than the number-moving-forward technique (.05 level), and the latter significantly more difficult to resist than the guilt technique (.05 level; means of 4.00, 3.31, and 2.46 respectively).

Table 2 compares the experimental subjects who actually revealed the information with the control subjects who were instructed to guess

Table 2—Number of Subjects Revealing and Concealing Information in Interrogation and Control Groups

Variable	Experimental hypnotic interrogation	Control guessing own responses
Reveal	6	8
Conceal	20	1

Note: Difference between experimental and control groups significant at .01 level.

how they would have responded if they had actually undergone the interrogation. The two groups did not differ significantly in hypnotizability. A two-tailed Fisher exact probability test indicates that the guessing control group revealed information significantly more often than the experimental interrogation group (.01 level). In other words, subjects expect hypnotic interrogation to be more effective than it actually is.

The six subjects who revealed the information had significantly higher Stanford hypnotizability scores than the 20 subjects who successfully concealed the information (means of 9.33 and 6.30 respectively, $t = 2.39$, 24 df, .05 level). However, this relationship between hypnotizability and an increased probability of revealing information was not observed in the guilt technique of interrogation. Both subjects who revealed the information during the guilt interrogation had Stanford hypnotizability scores of 6, while the mean Stanford score for the remaining 24 subjects was 7.08.

The subjective hypnotic depth during the interrogation was assessed through comparing a 38-item inventory of hypnotic experiences obtained after the Stanford Form A with a repetition obtained after the interrogation. The interrogation hypnosis was rated slightly, but significantly, less deep than the Stanford Form A hypnosis (mean difference = 2.23, t for correlated means = 3.42, 25 df, .01 level). Change scores were also examined on individual items. In other words, items checked as "True" during one hypnosis and "False" during the other hypnosis were compared, and use was made of McNemar's (6) chi-square test for the significance of changes, corrected for continuity. This analysis suggests that the interrogation hypnosis was characterized by increased ability to resist. The following two items discriminated the two hypnoses most effectively, both at the .02 level. These items were denied about the interrogation hypnosis and affirmed about the Stanford Form A hypnosis: "I could not have stopped doing the things the experimenter suggested even if I tried," and "I felt uninhibited." In other words, during interrogation the subject feels that he is more able to oppose the experimenter's suggestions, and he also feels more inhibited or less responsive. Another item indicating that subjects felt they could have awakened more easily during the Stanford Form A hypnosis than during the interrogation hypnosis (.05 level) was the only item that significantly reversed this trend toward greater subjective self-control during the interrogation hypnosis.

Five of the 26 subjects attempted not only to withhold the information but also to deceive the interrogator into making a wrong guess about which number was concealed. These five subjects, who did not differ significantly from the remaining subjects in hypnotizability, were all successful in concealing the information. Three subjects attempted to do this by choosing a single incorrect response and giving it during the interrogation. This tactic was generally successful in misleading the interrogator into thinking he had successfully extracted the concealed number, especially when the subject appeared to be hesitant or compelled to reveal the number. Two subjects gave deceptive bodily movements to several different incorrect numbers during the lie-detection interrogation. Although this tactic was successful in concealing the true number, it revealed the fact that the subject was lying and did not mislead the interrogator into making a wrong guess about which number was concealed.

D. DISCUSSION

The results indicate that two extreme hypotheses are unwarranted: the group tested showed neither uniform ability to resist the hypnotic interrogation nor uniform ability to conceal information. This finding is consistent with Hilgard's (4) report that, in subjects motivated to resist hypnotic suggestions, both the resistance and the suggestions are partially effective. If the present results can be generalized, they suggest that hypnotic interrogation has some effectiveness only with a minority of subjects who are quite easily hypnotized, and is undependable with average or poor hypnotic subjects. This conclusion must be qualified by the fact that we used a relatively brief (15-minute) hypnotic induction, which of course was not effective with all subjects, and which did not produce a uniform level of hypnosis in everyone. Other possible factors that might qualify this finding include the lack of hypnotic pretraining of subjects and the absence of polygraphic instrumentation. Moreover, in police interrogation, subjects may be more highly motivated to resist (although more uncertain about exactly what must be concealed); subtle probing under hypnosis rather than blatant interrogation may be employed; and subjects may fake hypnosis or may fake hypnotic susceptibility. In any practical situation, outcome variables such as the utility or reward value of withholding information, of misleading the interrogator, and of being judged guilty or else cleared, will play important roles in determining behavior under interrogation.

Since there are no procedures that guarantee either completely successful interrogation or perfectly successful concealment under hypnotic interrogation, it may be convenient to conceive of behavior under interrogation in terms of imperfect strategies of concealment by the subject competing with imperfect strategies of detection by the interrogator. For example, the interrogator's chances of successful detection of information rise with the hypnotizability of his subject. It also seems plausible, although not directly tested in this study, that subjects who are unable to resist hypnotic interrogation in experimental settings may be the ones who will be unable to resist "real-life" hypnotic interrogation. Consequently, the interrogator's decision on using hypnotic interrogation would probably be influenced by any accurate estimate he could obtain of the subject's hypnotizability (and perhaps of the subject's ability to resist a preliminary, innocuous interrogation). Ideally, the interrogator should obtain this information while still preventing the subject from countermanipulating by faking hypnosis, hypnotizability, or inability to resist a preliminary interrogation. Of course, most subjects need not adopt such exotic countermanipulations. The most natural tactics of motivated withholding and deception were usually successful in this experiment.

The control subjects, who tried to guess their responses from reading the interrogation suggestions, overestimated the power of hypnosis and underestimated the ability of the experimental subjects to resist. This seems to indicate that subjects fail to realize that a hypnotized person has powerful resources of resistance that he can use to oppose unwelcome suggestions. One implication of this finding is that a credible threat of hypnotic interrogation may be more powerful than its actual use, as suggested by Estabrooks (2) and Orne (7). If the subject can be convinced that hypnosis will really be used, he may reason that he might as well confess, since he cannot beat hypnosis—just as some subjects confess at the prospect of a polygraph. A second implication of this finding is that, from the standpoint of controls for demand characteristics (8), the most solid finding of the present study is the ability of subjects to resist, not the fact that a few were unable to do so. In other words, since the control subjects expected hypnosis to be more powerful than it was, the fact that most subjects were able to conceal information cannot be attributed to mere compliance with a perceived experimental hypothesis, or to the subjects' expectations about hypnosis. The finding that the few subjects who attempted to do so were able to lie successfully under hypnosis confirms this general picture of substantial amounts of successful resistance to hypnotic interrogation.

The most difficult technique for subjects to resist was the lie-detection technique, the next most difficult was the number-moving-forward technique, and the easiest technique to resist was the guilt technique. Data on actual revelations of information were not clearcut statistically, but were consistent with the conclusion that the lie-detection technique was one of the more difficult techniques to resist. One possible explanation of these results is that the lie-detection technique capitalizes upon involuntary, automatic responses, while the other techniques involve more voluntary, conscious cognitive processes. For example, the lie-detection technique requires only a primitive bodily movement, while the other techniques require verbal responses. The guilt and lie-detection techniques may lie at opposite ends of a continuum from persuasion to suggestion, voluntary to automatic, or aware to unaware. The practical implication is that an interrogator is more likely to be successful with hypnosis if he uses it to manipulate automatic, involuntary responses rather than voluntary, cognitive, or verbal processes. This conclusion is not surprising in view of the fact that involuntary, automatic processes are very important components of hypnotic phenomena.

This conclusion is supported by the failure to find a relationship between hypnotizability and susceptibility to the guilt technique. If the guilt technique is a relatively cognitive, verbal, or conscious manipulation, it may work as well without hypnosis or without the use of hypnotizable subjects. This conclusion must be qualified because of the very small number of subjects (only two) who revealed the information under guilt interrogation. Although we used a guessing-control group, we did not use a control group that underwent interrogation without hypnotic induction.

Consequently, we cannot be completely sure that an induction of hypnosis is essential in producing any of the results reported in this paper.

Subjects tended to feel less deeply hypnotized during hypnotic interrogation than during the Stanford Form A, apparently because they felt more able to resist during the interrogation. In addition, however, some subjects may have lessened the conflict over revealing *vs.* concealing by allowing their hypnotic depth to lighten. It is also possible that the interrogation hypnosis may not have seemed as extensive or varied as the Stanford Form A, and therefore may not have seemed as deep.

E. SUMMARY

Three techniques of hypnotic interrogation were compared. The technique rated most difficult to resist was an involuntary movement in response to mention of the concealed item of information. The strategy rated easiest to resist was implantation of guilt. Although a majority of subjects concealed the item of information, 23 per cent revealed it. Hypnotizability was correlated with susceptibility to hypnotic interrogation. A control group guessing what responses they would have made under interrogation overestimated the power of hypnosis and underestimated the ability of subjects to resist.

REFERENCES

(1) CLARK, L. D., & BEECHER, H. K. Psychopharmacological studies on suppression. *J. Nerv. & Ment. Dis.,* 1957, **125**, 316–321.

(2) ESTABROOKS, G. H. *Hypnotism* (2nd ed.). New York: Dutton, 1957.

(3) FIELD, P. B. An inventory scale of hypnotic depth. *Internat. J. Clin. & Exper. Hypn.,* 1965, **13**, 238–249.

(4) HILGARD, E. R. Ability to resist suggestions within the hypnotic state: Responsiveness to conflicting communications. *Psychol. Rep.,* 1963, **12**, 3–13.

(5) LE BARON, G. I., JR. Ideomotor signalling in brief psychotherapy. *Amer. J. Clin. Hypn.,* 1962, **5**, 81–91.

(6) MCNEMAR, Q. *Psychological statistics* (2nd ed.). New York: Wiley, 1955.

(7) ORNE, M. T. The potential uses of hypnosis in interrogation. In Biderman, A. D., & Zimmer, H. (Eds.), *The manipulation of human behavior.* New York: Wiley, 1961. Pp. 169–215.

(8) ORNE, M. T. On the social psychology of the psychological experiment: With particular reference to demand characteristics and their implications. *Amer. Psychol.,* 1962, **17**, 776–783.

(9) REDLICH, F. C., RAVITZ, L. J., JR., & DESSION, G. H. Narcoanalysis and truth. *Amer. J. Psychiat.,* 1951, **107**, 586–593.

(10) TEITELBAUM, M. Admissibility of hypnotically adduced evidence and the Arthur Nebb case. *St. Louis Univ. Law J.*, 1963, 8, 205–214.

(11) WATKINS, J. G. Antisocial compulsions induced under hypnotic trance. *J. Abn. & Soc. Psychol.*, 1947, 42, 256–259.

(12) WEITZENHOFFER, A. M., & HILGARD, E. R. Stanford Hypnotic Susceptibility Scale: Forms A and B. Palo Alto, Calif.: Consulting Psychologists Press, 1959.

Excerpt from
"Truth" drugs

Lawrence Z. Freedman

*INTRODUCTION   What has been scientifically de-
termined concerning hypnosis—that it is not an effective behavior control
procedure—also is true of another mass media favorite: truth serum. This
was pointed out in 1960 by psychiatrist Lawrence Freedman in an article
in* Scientific American. *His conclusion is sufficient to make the point we
want to emphasize about "truth drugs": that the person who depends on
them to control another's behavior is relying on a very unreliable and
resistible form of coercion.*

In sum, experimental and clinical findings indicate that
only individuals who have conscious and unconscious reasons for doing
so are inclined to confess and yield to interrogation under the influence
of drugs. On the other hand, some are able to withhold information and
some, especially character neurotics, are able to lie. Others are so sug-
gestible or so impelled by unconscious guilt that they will describe, perhaps in response to suggestive questioning, behavior that never in fact
occurred. The material produced is not "truth" in any sense of conforming with empirical fact.

Serious wrong can be done both to the embryonic science of criminology and to the administration of justice if this procedure is employed
as a fact-finding instrument.

part 3:

Behavior control via interpersonal and group influence

The influence of others—the power of an individual or group to control the behavior of another—is one of the most pervasive and exhaustively documented findings in contemporary social science.* It is also one of the oldest, dating back at least to 1898, when Norman Triplett conducted the first social psychological experiment and discovered that whether children worked alone or in groups made a difference in their performance on a spool-winding task.

Some of the best and most important work on interpersonal and group influence was done by researchers in the 1950s. For example, the power of groups in regulating members' behavior was documented in many different settings, including military academies (Dornbusch, 1955); industrial shops (Homans, 1951; Roy, 1952); doctors' offices (Coleman, Katz, & Menzel, 1957); churches (Kelley, 1955); and neighborhoods (Festinger et al., 1950; Whyte, 1953). Findings from studies in the past decade continue to illuminate the pervasive control by groups, even over things as basic as a person's own perceptions (Koslin et al., 1968; Lambert et al., 1960).

The following four selections will show the reader some instances in which man functions as a behavior control agent; where interpersonal or group influence is used to regulate human actions. Some of these ac-

* Evidence to support this claim can be found in Chapter 3 (pp. 41–67) of M. Karlins and H. Abelson's *Persuasion* (New York: Springer, 1970).

tions are relatively innocuous, like crossing an intersection; others, not so innocuous, like administering painful shocks to a protesting human subject. What makes control by others particularly insidious is that the manipulated individual is often unaware that his behavior is being regulated. As you read through the articles, you may ask yourself: "Would I have behaved differently under the same circumstances?"

Status factors in pedestrian violation of traffic signals

Monroe Lefkowitz, Robert R. Blake and Jane Srygley Mouton

INTRODUCTION   One does not have to know some-one to be influenced by him. So pervasive is the influence of others that a person's behavior can sometimes be regulated by the actions of a total stranger (see, e.g., Asch, 1956; Bryan & Test, 1967; Freed, Chandler, Mouton, & Blake, 1955; Kimbrell & Blake, 1958; Sherif, 1952). Such was the case in the following study, where people's willingness to obey traffic signals was influenced by the actions and "status" (style of dress) of indi-viduals they had never met before.

A social factor of importance in determining the re-action a given prohibition will evoke—whether conformance or violation —is the respondent's knowledge of the behavior the restriction has pro-duced in others (1). More people will conform when they see others con-forming to a restriction, while knowledge that violations occur will in-crease the probability of infraction. The validity of these statements for a typical situation involving a prohibition has been demonstrated by an experiment dealing with reactions to signs forbidding entry to a building (2). When test subjects saw that another person violated the sign, they also violated it significantly more frequently than when they saw that another person had reacted in compliance with the prohibition.

PROBLEM

The power of others to increase or decrease the strength of a prohi-bition is probably a function of "who the others are." Blake and Mouton

Lefkowitz, M., Blake, R. R., & Mouton, J. S. Status factors in pedestrian violation of traffic signals. *Journal of Abnormal and Social Psychology*, 1955, **51**, 704–706. Copy-right 1955 by the American Psychological Association, and reproduced by permission.

(1) proposed that the perceived status of the person whose behavior serves as a model will be an important factor in determining the rate of violation. "High status figures known to violate a given law will have greater influence in weakening it than if only low status people are known to be violators. The same holds for conformance. When high status individuals are known to accept the prohibition it should have the effect of making the law more acceptable than if only low status people are known to conform."

The present paper is concerned with testing the validity of the statements relating status of the violator who serves as a model to the reaction a prohibition provokes in others. Perceived status quality of the person whose behavior toward a prohibition served as model for others was systematically varied. The basic hypothesis was that a naive subject facing a prohibition will more likely violate or conform when a high status person serves as a model for conformance or violation than when a low status person does so.

Experimental Situation

PROHIBITION SITUATION. The prohibition was a pedestrian traffic signal that flashed from "wait" to "walk" alternatively with the red, amber, and green signals regulating the flow of motor traffic. During every fifty-five second interval, the "wait" signal flashed for forty seconds and the "walk" for fifteen. Observations were made during the "wait" signal when the sign forbade movement across the street.

A counterbalanced design was employed with respect to daily time periods for observations and locations of the "wait-walk" signals. Data were collected on three successive afternoons during the hours from 12 to 1, 2 to 3, and 4 to 5 respectively. The "wait-walk" signals were located at three street corners at right angles to the main thoroughfare in the central commercial section of Austin, Texas. An observer located approximately 100 feet away from the corner recorded the data. Police officers were not on duty at the locations during the time intervals when data were collected, but arrangements for conducting the experiments had been made with the Traffic Department of the Austin Police Department.

SUBJECTS. With the exception of children and physically handicapped people, the 2,103 pedestrians passing the three locations during the three test intervals served as subjects.

COVARIATIONS IN PERCEIVED STATUS OF AND VIOLATION BY THE MODEL. Two aspects of social background were covaried in the experimental design suggested by Helson's adaptation-level theory (3). One was the behavior of an experimenter's model who either complied with or violated the "wait" signal. The second was the perceived status of the experimenter's model. The experimenter's model was a 31-year-old male. By changing his clothing the model's perceived status was either high or low. For half the conformance reactions and half the violation responses, the experimenter's model was dressed in clothing intended to typify a high status person, with a freshly pressed suit, shined shoes, white shirt, tie and straw hat. Well-worn scuffed shoes, soiled patched trousers and an unpressed blue denim shirt served to define the model as a low status person for the remaining half of the conforming and violating conditions. The rate of pedestrian violation observed during the same time intervals and at the same test locations with the experimenter's model absent served as the neutral or control condition.

The experimental design permitted both social background factors to be varied simultaneously. For example, at 12:00 noon on one day the experimenter's model, dressed in one status attire, conformed to the "wait" stimulus by crossing the street when the signal changed to "walk." The procedure was repeated for each of five trials, with the number of subjects conforming or violating recorded. Following these trials, pedestrians were observed for five additional trials under the neutral condition in which the experimenter's model was absent. The experimenter's model returned to the scene dressed in the other status attire and violated the "wait" signal by crossing the street once at approximately the midpoint of each "wait" interval for the same number of trials. The inverse order for conforming and violating trials was followed the next day, and so on.

CRITERIA FOR SCORING VIOLATION. Two criteria were used in assessing whether pedestrians were violating the "wait" signal. Only subjects standing with the experimenter's model before he crossed the street were included in the data. Pedestrians reaching or passing the white line in the center of the street while the signal still flashed "wait" were recorded as violators. By using the center line as the criterion for scoring violation and conformity, errors of judgment as to pedestrian intent were reduced to a minimum. All others meeting the first criterion but not the second were recorded as conforming with the prohibition.

RESULTS

Results from the several experimental and control conditions are presented in Tables 1 and 2. Examination of column totals demonstrates that the presence of a model of either high or low perceived status complying with the signal prohibition did not increase the rate of pedestrian conformance beyond that observed for the control condition. Since the rate of conformance under neutral conditions was so high (99 per cent), the present study did not permit a valid test of the proposition that seeing another person conform increased rate of conformity ($x^2 = 1.30$, 1 *df*). However, the presence of a model of either high or low perceived status violating the prohibition increased the pedestrian violation rate above that for the control condition. The χ^2 (48.04, 1 df) between control and experimental conditions is significant beyond the 1 per cent level of confidence. This finding is consistent with results from the comparable part of the experiment dealing with the violation of a sign forbidding the entry of a building (2).

Table 1—Reactions of Test Subjects to Experimental Treatments and Control Conditions

	Reactions of Experimenter's Model							
Status Attire of Experimenter's Model	Conforming		Control‡		Violating		Total	
	Pedestrian conforms	Pedestrian violates	Pedestrian conforms	Pedestrian violates	Pedestrian conforms	Pedestrian violates	Pedestrian conforms	Pedestrian violates
High N*	351	3	347	3	250	40	948	46
%†	99	01	99	01	86	14	95	05
Low N	420	1	395	5	276	12	1091	18
%	100	00	99	01	96	04	98	02
Total N	771	4	742	8	526	52	2039	64
%	99	01	99	01	91	09	97	03

‡The entries in the high and low status rows represent control observations made under conditions identical with the observations for the high and low status conditions except that the experimenter's model was absent.

* The unequal N's are due to slight variations in the flow of pedestrians under counterbalanced test conditions.

† Figures rounded to the nearest per cent.

Table 2—χ^2 Values for Differences Between Conditions

Conditions	χ^2	df	Level of Significance
Conforming model vs. control	1.30	1	—
Violating model vs. control	48.04	1	.01
High status violating model vs. control	44.59	1	.01
Low status violating model vs. control	3.88	1	.05
High status condition: violating model vs. conforming model	44.56	1	.01
Low status condition: violating model vs. conforming model	16.22	1	.01
Violating condition: high status model vs. low status model	16.61	1	.01

The relationship between status and violation is shown in cell frequencies across rows of Table 1. When a perceived high status model was seen to violate the prohibition, 14 per cent of pedestrians violated the signal restricting movement. The χ^2 of 44.59 (1 df) for the difference in pedestrian violation between the high status violation and the control condition, and the χ^2 of 44.56 (1 df) for the difference between perceived high status violation and perceived high status conformance are both significant beyond the 1 per cent level. The results demonstrate that when a high status person violated a prohibition, there was a significant increase in the rate of violation by pedestrians. An examination of differences in pedestrian violations that were provoked by a violating person of low status contrasted with both a low status person who conforms ($\chi^2 = 16.22$, 1 df) and also with the control condition where the low status person was absent ($\chi^2 = 3.88$, 1 df) leads to the conclusion that the low status violator increased the pedestrian violation rate beyond that typical for either of the other two conditions. Such findings demonstrate that with a person whose perceived status quality was either high or low acting as a model by violating a prohibition, the pedestrian violation rate was increased significantly beyond that occurring when the model either conformed or was absent.

From the standpoint of the hypothesis stated in the introduction, the significant comparison is that between violation rates when the status of the violator was shifted from low to high. Changing the status of the violator from low to high through creating differences in attire increased pedestrian violations from 4 per cent to 14 per cent. The χ^2 of 16.61 (1 df) for this difference in violation rate is significant at the 1 per cent level. Such findings point to the conclusion that if a situation contains a violator, a significantly greater number of pedestrians will violate the signal when the status model is high rather than low. This finding confirms the prediction given in the introduction. The behavior of others is not of equal weight in determining the readiness to violate a prohibition. Rather the higher the status of the perceived violator the greater the reduction in conformance to a prohibition by pedestrians in the same situation.

SUMMARY

Pedestrians violated the prohibition of an automatic traffic signal more often in the presence of an experimenter's model who violated the prohibition than when the latter conformed or was absent. Significantly more violations occurred among pedestrians when the nonconforming model was dressed to represent high social status than when his attire suggested lower status.

REFERENCES

(1) BLAKE, R. R., & MOUTON, JANE S. Present and future implications of social psychology for law and lawyers. *Symposium Issue, Emory Univ. J. Public Law*, 1955, 3, 352–369.

(2) FREED, A. M., CHANDLER, P. J., MOUTON, JANE S., & BLAKE, R. R. Stimulus and background factors in sign violation. *J. Pers.*, 1955, **23**, 499.

(3) HELSON, H. Adaptation-level as a basis for a quantitative theory of frames of reference. *Psychol. Rev.*, 1948, **55**, 297–313.

Shooting an elephant

George Orwell

INTRODUCTION The previous article examined the power of one person, acting alone, to manipulate the behavior of a specified individual. The following selection deals with the power of many individuals, acting in harmony, to regulate an individual's actions. As you may imagine, behavior control effectiveness is greatly enhanced through such concerted action (a college student might well remain at odds with a fraternity brother, but how often can he oppose his entire fraternity?). Just how effective such multiple influence can be is graphically described by George Orwell, as he tells us the real reason for shooting an elephant.

In Moulmein, in Lower Burma, I was hated by large numbers of people—the only time in my life that I have been important enough for this to happen to me. I was sub-divisional police officer of the town, and in an aimless, petty kind of way anti-European feeling was very bitter. No one had the guts to raise a riot, but if a European woman went through the bazaars alone somebody would probably spit betel juice over her dress. As a police officer I was an obvious target and was baited whenever it seemed safe to do so. When a nimble Burman tripped me up on the football field and the referee (another Burman) looked the other way, the crowd yelled with hideous laughter. This happened more than once. In the end the sneering yellow faces of young men that met me everywhere, the insults hooted after me when I was at a safe distance, got badly on my nerves. The young Buddhist priests were the worst of all. There were several thousands of them in the town and none of them seemed to have anything to do except stand on street corners and jeer at Europeans.

All this was perplexing and upsetting. For at that time I had already made up my mind that imperialism was an evil thing and the sooner I

chucked up my job and got out of it the better. Theoretically—and secretly, of course—I was all for the Burmese and all against their oppressors,
the British. As for the job I was doing, I hated it more bitterly than I can
perhaps make clear. In a job like that you see the dirty work of Empire
at close quarters. The wretched prisoners huddling in the stinking cages
of the lock-ups, the grey, cowed faces of the long-term convicts, the scarred
buttocks of the men who had been flogged with bamboos—all these op-
pressed me with an intolerable sense of guilt. But I could get nothing into
perspective. I was young and ill-educated and I had had to think out my
problems in the utter silence that is imposed on every Englishman in the
East. I did not even know that the British Empire is dying, still less did I
know that it is a great deal better than the younger empires that are going
to supplant it. All I knew was that I was stuck between my hatred of the
empire I served and my rage against the evil-spirited little beasts who
tried to make my job impossible. With one part of my mind I thought
of the British Raj as an unbreakable tyranny, as something clamped
down, *in saecula saeculorum,* upon the will of prostrate peoples; with
another part I thought that the greatest joy in the world would be to
drive a bayonet into a Buddhist priest's guts. Feelings like these are the
normal by-products of imperialism; ask any Anglo-Indian official, if you
can catch him off duty.

One day something happened which in a roundabout way was en-
lightening. It was a tiny incident in itself, but it gave me a better glimpse
than I had had before of the real nature of imperialism—the real motives
for which despotic governments act. Early one morning the sub-inspector
at a police station the other end of the town rang me up on the phone
and said that an elephant was ravaging the bazaar. Would I please come
and do something about it? I did not know what I could do, but I wanted
to see what was happening and I got on to a pony and started out. I took
my rifle, an old .44 Winchester and much too small to kill an elephant,
but I thought the noise might be useful *in terrorem.* Various Burmans
stopped me on the way and told me about the elephant's doings. It was
not, of course, a wild elephant, but a tame one which has gone "must."
It had been chained up as tame elephants always are when their attack of
"must" is due, but on the previous night it had broken its chain and
escaped. Its mahout, the only person who could manage it when it was in
that state, had set out in pursuit, but he had taken the wrong direction
and was now twelve hours' journey away, and in the morning the elephant
had suddenly reappeared in the town. The Burmese population had no
weapons and were quite helpless against it. It had already destroyed somebody's bamboo hut, killed a cow and raided some fruit-stalls and devoured
the stock; also it had met the municipal rubbish van, and, when the

driver jumped out and took to his heels, had turned the van over and inflicted violence upon it.

The Burmese sub-inspector and some Indian constables were waiting for me in the quarter where the elephant had been seen. It was a very poor quarter, a labyrinth of squalid bamboo huts, thatched with palm-leaf, winding all over a steep hillside. I remember that it was a cloudy stuffy morning at the beginning of the rains. We began questioning the people as to where the elephant had gone, and, as usual, failed to get any definite information. That is invariably the case in the East; a story always sounds clear enough at a distance, but the nearer you get to the scene of events the vaguer it becomes. Some of the people said that the elephant had gone in one direction, some said that he had gone in another, some professed not even to have heard of any elephant. I had almost made up my mind that the whole story was a pack of lies, when we heard yells a little distance away. There was a loud, scandalised cry of "Go away, child! Go away this instant!" and an old woman with a switch in her hand came round the corner of a hut, violently shooing away a crowd of naked children. Some more women followed, clicking their tongues and exclaiming; evidently there was something there that the children ought not to have seen. I rounded the hut and saw a man's dead body sprawling in the mud. He was an Indian, a black Dravidian coolie, almost naked, and he could not have been dead many minutes. The people said that the elephant had come suddenly upon him round the corner of the hut, caught him with its trunk, put its foot on his back and ground him into the earth. This was the rainy season and the ground was soft, and his face had scored a trench a foot deep and a couple of yards long. He was lying on his belly with arms crucified and head sharply twisted to one side. His face was coated with mud, the eyes wide open, the teeth bared and grinning with an expression of unendurable agony. (Never tell me, by the way, that the dead look peaceful. Most of the corpses I have seen looked devilish.) The friction of the great beast's foot had stripped the skin from his back as neatly as one skins a rabbit. As soon as I saw the dead man I sent an orderly to a friend's house nearby to borrow an elephant rifle. I had already sent back the pony, not wanting it to go mad with fright and throw me if it smelled the elephant.

The orderly came back in a few minutes with a rifle and five cartridges, and meanwhile some Burmans had arrived and told us that the elephant was in the paddy fields below, only a few hundred yards away. As I started forward practically the whole population of the quarter flocked out of their houses and followed me. They had seen the rifle and were all shouting excitedly that I was going to shoot the elephant. They had not shown much interest in the elephant when he was merely ravaging their homes, but it was different now that he was going to be shot. It was a bit of fun to them, as it would be to an English crowd; besides, they wanted the meat. It made me vaguely uneasy. I had no intention of shooting the elephant—I had merely sent for the rifle to defend myself if necessary—and it is always unnerving to have a crowd following you. I marched down the hill, looking and feeling a fool, with the rifle over my shoulder and an ever-growing army of people jostling at my heels. At the bottom, when you got away from the huts, there was a metalled road and beyond that a miry waste of paddy fields a thousand yards across, not yet ploughed but soggy from the first rains and dotted with coarse grass. The elephant was standing eighty yards from the road, his left side towards us. He took not the slightest notice of the crowd's approach. He was tearing up bunches of grass, beating them against his knees to clean them and stuffing them into his mouth.

I had halted on the road. As soon as I saw the elephant I knew with perfect certainty that I ought not to shoot him. It is a serious matter to shoot a working elephant—it is comparable to destroying a huge and costly piece of machinery—and obviously one ought not to do it if it can possibly be avoided. And at that distance, peacefully eating, the elephant looked no more dangerous than a cow. I thought then and I think now that his attack of "must" was already passing off; in which case he would merely wander harmlessly about until the mahout came back and caught him. Moreover, I did not in the least want to shoot him. I decided that I would watch him for a little while to make sure that he did not turn savage again, and then go home.

But at that moment I glanced round at the crowd that had followed me. It was an immense crowd, two thousand at the least and growing every minute. It blocked the road for a long distance on either side. I looked at the sea of yellow faces above the garish clothes—faces all happy and excited over this bit of fun, all certain that the elephant was going to be shot. They were watching me as they would watch a conjuror about to perform a trick. They did not like me, but with the magical rifle in my hands I was momentarily worth watching. And suddenly I realised that I should have to shoot the elephant after all. The people expected it of me and I had got to do it; I could feel their two thousand wills pressing me forward, irresistibly. And it was at this moment, as I stood there with the rifle in my hands, that I first grasped the hollowness, the futility of the white man's dominion in the East. Here was I, the white man with his gun, standing in front of the unarmed native crowd—seemingly the leading actor of the piece; but in reality I was only an absurd puppet pushed to and fro by the will of those yellow faces behind. I perceived in this moment that when the white man turns tyrant it is his own freedom that he destroys. He becomes a sort of hollow, posing dummy, the conventionalised figure of a sahib. For it is the condition of his rule that he shall spend his life in trying to impress the "natives" and so in every crisis he has got to do what the "natives" expect of him. He wears a mask, and his face grows to fit it. I had got to shoot the elephant. I had committed myself to doing it when I sent for the rifle. A sahib has got to act like a sahib; he has got to appear resolute, to know his own mind and do definite things. To come all that way, rifle in hand, with two thousand people marching at my heels, and then to trail feebly away, having done nothing—no, that was impossible. The crowd would laugh at me. And my whole life, every white man's life in the East, was one long struggle not to be laughed at.

But I did not want to shoot the elephant. I watched him beating his bunch of grass against his knees, with that preoccupied grandmotherly air that elephants have. It seemed to me that it would be murder to shoot him. At that age I was not squeamish about killing animals, but I had never shot an elephant and never wanted to. (Somehow it always seems worse to kill a *large* animal.) Besides, there was the beast's owner to be considered. Alive, the elephant was worth at least a hundred pounds; dead, he would only be worth the value of his tusks—five pounds, possibly. But I had got to act quickly. I turned to some experienced-looking Burmans who had been there when we arrived, and asked them how the elephant had been behaving. They all said the same thing: he took no notice of you if you left him alone, but he might charge if you went too close to him.

It was perfectly clear to me what I ought to do. I ought to walk up to within, say, twenty-five yards of the elephant and test his behaviour. If he charged I could shoot, if he took no notice of me it would be safe to leave him until the mahout came back. But also I knew that I was going to do no such thing. I was a poor shot with a rifle and the ground was soft mud into which one would sink at every step. If the elephant charged and I missed him, I should have about as much chance as a toad under a steam-roller. But even then I was not thinking particularly of my own skin, only the watchful yellow faces behind. For at that moment, with the crowd watching me, I was not afraid in the ordinary sense, as I would have been if I had been alone. A white man mustn't be frightened in front of "natives"; and so, in general, he isn't frightened. The sole thought in my mind was that if anything went wrong those two thousand Burmans would see me pursued, caught, trampled on and reduced to a grinning corpse like that Indian up the hill. And if that happened it was quite probable that some of them would laugh. That would never do. There was only one alternative. I shoved the cartridges into the magazine and lay down on the road to get a better aim.

The crowd grew very still, and a deep, low, happy sigh, as of people who see the theatre curtain go up at last, breathed from innumerable throats. They were going to have their bit of fun after all. The rifle was a beautiful German thing with cross-hair sights. I did not then know that in shooting an elephant one should shoot to cut an imaginary bar running from ear-hole to ear-hole. I ought therefore, as the elephant was sideways on, to have aimed straight at his ear-hole; actually I aimed several inches in front of this, thinking the brain would be further forward.

When I pulled the trigger I did not hear the bang or feel the kick— one never does when a shot goes home—but I heard the devilish roar of glee that went up from the crowd. In that instant, in too short a time, one would have thought, even for the bullet to get there, a mysterious, terrible change had come over the elephant. He neither stirred nor fell, but every line of his body had altered. He looked suddenly stricken, shrunken, immensely old, as though the frightful impact of the bullet had paralysed him without knocking him down. At last, after what seemed a long time—it might have been five seconds, I dare say—he sagged flabbily to his knees. His mouth slobbered. An enormous senility seemed to have settled upon him. One could have imagined him thousands of years old. I fired again into the same spot. At the second shot he did not collapse but climbed with desperate slowness to his feet and stood weakly upright, with legs sagging and head drooping. I fired a third time. That was the shot that did for him. You could see the agony of it jolt his whole body and knock the last remnant of strength from his legs. But in falling he seemed for a moment to rise, for as his hind legs collapsed beneath him he seemed to tower upwards like a huge rock toppling, his trunk reaching skyward like a tree. He trumpeted, for the first and only time. And then down he came, his belly towards me, with a crash that seemed to shake the ground even where I lay.

I got up. The Burmans were already racing past me across the mud. It was obvious that the elephant would never rise again, but he was not dead. He was breathing very rhythmically with long rattling gasps, his great mound of a side painfully rising and falling. His mouth was wide open—I could see far down into caverns of pale pink throat. I waited a long time for him to die, but his breathing did not weaken. Finally I fired my two remaining shots into the spot where I thought his heart must be. The thick blood welled out of him like red velvet, but still he did not die. His body did not even jerk when the shots hit him, the tortured breathing continued without a pause. He was dying, very slowly and in great agony, but in some world remote from me where not even a bullet could damage him further. I felt that I had got to put an end to that dreadful noise. It seemed dreadful to see the great beast lying there, powerless to move and yet powerless to die, and not even to be able to finish him. I sent back for my small rifle and poured shot after shot into his heart and down his throat. They seemed to make no impression. The tortured gasps continued as steadily as the ticking of a clock.

In the end I could not stand it any longer and went away. I heard later that it took him half an hour to die. Burmans were arriving with dahs and baskets even before I left, and I was told they had stripped his body almost to the bones by the afternoon.

Afterwards, of course, there were endless discussions about the shooting of the elephant. The owner was furious, but he was only an Indian and could do nothing. Besides, legally I had done the right thing, for a mad elephant has to be killed, like a mad dog, if its owner fails to control it. Among the Europeans opinion was divided. The older men said I was right, the younger men said it was a damn shame to shoot an elephant for killing a coolie, because an elephant was worth more than any damn Coringhee coolie. And afterwards I was very glad that the coolie had been killed; it put me legally in the right and it gave me a sufficient pretext for shooting the elephant. I often wondered whether any of the others grasped that I had done it solely to avoid looking a fool.

Social reinforcement

Allen D. Calvin

INTRODUCTION Often an individual or group attempts to regulate the behavior of a particular person by rewarding his "correct" behavior and punishing his "incorrect" behavior. Such sanctions can take many forms: a slap across the face, the "silent treatment," a key to the executive washroom. Sometimes verbal reinforcement is used to control a person's actions and bring him into line with the wishes of others. It is surprising how effective such reinforcement can be. A case in point is Allen Calvin's study below. With 24 members of an introductory psychology class, Calvin ran an experiment to answer this question: Could simple verbal reinforcement serve to regulate the choice of wearing apparel among college coeds?

A. INTRODUCTION

1. Subjects

As one of the outside reading assignments in my introductory class, all of the students read Skinner's *Walden Two* (2). In last year's spring semester class, as in previous classes, the book provoked a spirited discussion of social reinforcement. Several of the students suggested that we attempt to actually demonstrate the effect of social reinforcement in our college environment. The following is a report of the results of this undertaking.

B. METHOD

1. Subjects

The Ss were the approximately 550 members of the student body at Hollins College, except for the 24 members of my introductory class who served as the Es. Hollins is a liberal arts girls' school whose student body is composed primarily of upper-middle and lower-upper class Protestant whites.

Calvin, A. D. "Social reinforcement." *The Journal of Social Psychology*, 1962, **56,** 15–19.
By permission of author and The Journal Press.

2. *Procedure*

Almost all of the girls eat lunch in the dining hall which is open from 11:30 A.M. until 1:15 P.M. The lunch period was divided into two shifts, and two girls from my introductory class served as *E*s on each shift. This gave us a total of four *E*s each day. The girls who served as *E*s on a particular day were selected at random from volunteers from the class as a whole. Since extra credit was given for acting as an *E*, there were always plenty of volunteers, and an attempt was made to let everyone serve as an *E* approximately the same number of times. The *E*'s task was to count the number of students wearing the color clothes that we were interested in on a particular day. Each *E* made her judgments independently.

If any *S* asked what the *E*s were recording, they were told that it was a survey to see how many people ate lunch at various times of the lunch hour. No one questioned this explanation.

On Thursday, April 10, 1958, the *E*s tabulated the number of students at lunch who wore blue clothes. Only large outer garments such as dresses, sweaters, skirts, coats, and the like counted. After lunch on this date, all the members of the class had been instructed to reward any students seen wearing blue clothes at any time with such expressions as, "My, that is a nice looking sweater," "That coat certainly is attractive," etc.

The *E*s checked the lunch periods for blue clothes every Tuesday and Thursday for the remainder of the month of April and again on May 13. After April 22, they stopped the reinforcing of blue clothes. Beginning April 22 in addition to counting the number of *S*s wearing blue clothes the *E*s also determined the number of *S*s wearing red, and they continued to count the number of *S*s wearing red every Tuesday and Thursday through May 13. After lunch on April 24 the class began to reinforce red and continued to do so through May 13.

C. *RESULTS*

There was quite often a slight difference between the *E*s in their judgment of the number of *S*s wearing the designated color, and when this occurred, their observations were averaged, and the average score was used for that period.

Let us look at the results for blue first. On the initial check the day before social reinforcements was begun 25 per cent of the *S*s wore blue. Five days later after reinforcement the percentage had risen to 37 per cent. The average percentage wearing blue on succeeding check days during the reinforcement period was 38 per cent. The next check day covered a period in which blue was not reinforced, and the reinforcement of red had not begun—the percentage of blue dropped to 27 per cent. Five days later another check was made. During this five-day period blue was not reinforced but red was, and the percentage wearing blue rose, reaching 35 per cent. The final check was made two weeks later after a period of non-reinforcement of blue but with reinforcement of red. At this time the percentage wearing blue had returned to 38 per cent.

A Chi-square between the first day prior to reinforcement (25 per cent wearing blue) and the first day after reinforcement (37 per cent wearing blue) was computed and a Chi-square of 17.03 was obtained. The Chi-square between the first day prior to reinforcement (25 per cent wearing blue) and the weighted mean of all the reinforcement check days (38 per cent wearing blue) was 17.64. The Chi-square between the first day prior to reinforcement (25 per cent wearing blue) and the weighted mean of all the post-reinforcement check days (34 per cent wearing blue) was 9.11. The Chi-square between the first day prior to reinforcement (25 per cent wearing blue) and the weighted mean of all the other check days combined (36 per cent wearing blue) was 12.46. A Chi-square of 6.64 is significant at the .01 level.[1]

A comparison of the last reinforcement check day (38 per cent wearing blue) with the first post-reinforcement check day (27 per cent wearing blue) yielded a Chi-square of 12.95. A comparison of the last reinforcement check day (38 per cent wearing blue) with the weighted mean of the other two post-reinforcement check days (37 per cent) gave a Chi-square of .21.

Now let us look at the results for red. For this color there were two check days prior to reinforcement. The percentage wearing red on the first check day was 13 per cent, and on the next check day 11 per cent. After five days of reinforcement, the percentage wearing red rose to 22 per cent. During the next four check days, all with red reinforced, the average percentage wearing red was 18 per cent.

[1] One of the assumptions for Chi-square is independence which we do not have in the present experiment, and the Chi-square test for correlated proportions cannot be applied here. However, Edwards points out (1, p. 91) that when a correlation is positive, failure to take into account the correlation in a Chi-square analysis increases the likelihood that we will fail to reject the null hypothesis, i.e., the Chi-square becomes overly conservative. Thus, making the reasonable assumption that our correlation is positive, we are most likely underestimating the actual level of significance in the Chi-square analyses in the present experiment. Since all but one of our differences were of such a large magnitude that the Chi-square we obtained were all greater than that required for significance at the 1 per cent level, this probable "over conservatism" would not likely alter the analyses presented here. The one exception is in the case of the Chi-square between reinforcement and post-reinforcement for blue where red too was being reinforced, and in this case with a Chi-square of .21 it seems highly unlikely that we have committed a Type II error, although such a possibility cannot be eliminated with certainty.

The Chi-square between the weighted mean of the two check days prior to reinforcement (12 per cent wearing red) and the first day after reinforcement (22 per cent wearing red) was 14.34. The Chi-square between the weighted mean of the two check days prior to reinforcement (12 per cent wearing red) and the weighted mean of all the reinforcement check days (19 per cent wearing red) was 8.86. As mentioned previously, a Chi-square of 6.64 is significant at the .01 level.

D. DISCUSSION

The fact that marked increases occurred with two different colors after social reinforcement increased the general prestige of reinforcement theory tremendously in the eyes of the students. However, it was necessary to point out that we could not unequivocally attribute the increase of the wearing of the reinforced color to the social reinforcement since we had only a one-group design. What was needed for a definitive experiment was another college population with the same characteristics as Hollins which would have been treated in the same manner except for the social reinforcement. In spite of this limitation, the present findings are certainly encouraging for the hypothesis that social reinforcement can markedly influence behavior of the kind studied in the present investigation. It would be desirable for some psychologists in a setting more conducive to a multi-group design, for example, in a military or prison situation, to follow up and extend the present findings.

The behavior of the Ss during the post-reinforcement period is interesting. The initial drop in the percentage of Ss wearing blue followed by a return to the percentage of blue worn during the reinforcement period might be due to the fact that we were reinforcing red during the post-reinforcement rise for blue; thus, a person previously reinforced for blue—when reinforced for red—may have been "reminded" of previous blue reinforcements. Particularly if the reinforcements came from the same individuals for both red and blue, considerable response generalization could reasonably be expected. This hypothesis, of course, must be verified experimentally before much confidence can be placed in it.

Some of the Es suggested that we try some social punishment, i.e., tell the Ss that they looked bad whenever we saw them wearing blue. However, the possible consequences of such an approach were too disquieting to allow us to carry out the proposal. Again it is hoped that some psychologist in a setting better suited for such an attempt will try it, as such data would certainly be highly valuable for behavior theory. In this regard, it is interesting to note that a large number of the Es reported that as they continued to go about reinforcing Ss, they became very "popular." Shades of Dale Carnegie! Perhaps "How to Win Friends and Influence People" boils down to making oneself a secondary reinforcer. One can't help but wonder what would have happened to our *E*s "popularity" if we had tried social punishment. . . .

E. SUMMARY

An attempt was made to use social reinforcement to alter the color of the clothes worn by female college students. Twenty-four Hollins College students served as *E*s while the rest of the approximately 550 students served as *S*s. Marked changes occurred in the expected direction after social reinforcement. Because of the limitation of a one-group design, the results cannot be considered as definitive, but they certainly are encouraging for the hypothesis that behavior of the nature studied in the present investigation can be changed by social reinforcement.

REFERENCES

(1) EDWARDS, A. L. *Experimental design in psychological research.* New York: Rinehart, 1950.
(2) SKINNER, B. F. *Walden two.* New York: Macmillan, 1948.

Group pressure and action against a person

Stanley Milgram

INTRODUCTION How often has this happened in our juvenile courts: an adolescent with no previous criminal record is brought before the judge. When asked why he broke the law he replies: "I wouldn't have done this by myself. I did it to go along with the gang." The youngster might well be telling the truth; people often do things in groups they would not do alone—and sometimes the things they do are not very nice.

Consider, for example, the following study. In it Stanley Milgram shows how group pressure can encourage a person to perform an anti-social act. Milgram's findings underscore, once again, the power of groups in controlling a person's behavior. Remember, however, that group influence can be utilized to regulate behavior for good or evil ends. Properly directed, "group power" can give the individual the strength he needs to live a happier, more meaningful life.

A great many variations of a paradigm provided by Asch (1951) show that there is an intelligible relationship between several features of the social environment and the degree to which a person will rely on others for his public judgments. Because it possesses merits of simplicity, clarity, and reconstructs in the laboratory powerful and socially relevant psychological processes, this paradigm has gained widespread acceptance as a basic technique of research on influence processes.

One feature that has been kept constant through the variations on Asch's work is that verbal judgment has been retained as the end product and basic index of conformity. More generally, a *signal* offered by the subject as representing his judgment has been the focus of study. Most often the signal has taken the form of a verbal pronouncement (Asch, 1956;

Milgram, S. Group pressure and action against a person. *Journal of Abnormal and Social Psychology*, 1964, **69**, 137–143. Copyright 1964 by the American Psychological Association, and reproduced by permission.

Milgram, 1961), though mechanical devices which the subject uses to signal his judgment have also been employed (Crutchfield, 1955; Tuddenham & MacBride, 1959).

A distinction can be made between *signal conformity* and *action conformity* in that the immediate consequence of the former is purely informational; the subject states his opinion or reports on his perception of some feature of the environment. Action conformity, on the other hand, produces an immediate effect or alteration in the milieu that goes beyond a contribution of information. It refers to the elicitation of a *deed* by group forces, the induction of an act that is more than communicative in its effect. The act may be directed toward the well being of another person (e.g., a man is induced by group pressure to share bread with a beggar) or it may be oriented toward nonsocial parts of the environment (a delinquent is induced by gang pressure to throw a rock at a shop window).

There is little reason to assume a priori that observations made with regard to verbal conformity are automatically applicable to action. A person may pay lip service to the norms of a group and then be quite unwilling to carry out the kinds of behavior the group norms imply. Furthermore, an individual may accept and even promulgate a group standard at the verbal level, and yet find himself *unable* to translate the belief into deeds. Here we refer not to the distinction between overt compliance and private acceptance, but of the relationship between a genuinely accepted belief and its transformation into behavior.

The main point of the present experiment is to see if a person will perform acts under group pressure that he would not have performed in the absence of social inducement. There are many particular forms of action that can be inserted into a general group-pressure experimental design. One could study sorting IBM cards, or making paper cutouts, or eating crackers. Convenience makes them attractive, and in several valuable experiments investigators have used these tasks to good advantage (Frank, 1944; French, Morrison, & Levinger, 1960; Raven & French, 1958). But eventually social psychology must come to grips with significant behavior contents, contents that are of interest in their own right and are not simply trivial substitutes for psychologically meaningful forms of behavior. Guided by this consideration, a relatively potent form of action was selected for shaping by group pressure. We asked: Can a group induce a person to deliver punishment of increasing severity to a protesting individual? Whereas Asch and others have shown in what manner group pressure can cause a person to pronounce judgments that contradict his thinking, the present study examines whether group pressure causes a person to engage in acts at variance with his uninfluenced behavior.

METHOD

The details of subject recruitment, subject composition, experimenter's introductory patter, apparatus, and learning task have been described elsewhere (Milgram, 1963) and need only be sketched here.

Subjects consisted of 80 male adults, ranging in age from 20 to 50 years, and distributed in equal numbers, ages, and occupational statuses in the experimental and control conditions.

Procedure for Experimental Condition

GENERAL. The basic experimental situation is one in which a team of three persons (including two confederates) tests a fourth person on a paired-associate learning task. Whenever the fourth party makes a mistake the team punishes him with an electric shock. The two confederates suggest increasingly higher shock levels; the experimenter observes in what degree the third member of the team (a naive subject) goes along with or resists the confederates' pressure to increase the voltage levels.

DETAILS. Four adults arrive at a campus laboratory to participate in a study of memory and learning. On arrival each subject is paid $4.50. The experimenter explains that a variety of roles must be performed in the experiment, and that to make role assignments fairly, subjects are to draw printed slips from a hat, each slip designating a particular experimental role. Actually, three of the adults are confederates, and only one naive subject is tested each hour. The drawing is rigged so that the naive subject is always assigned the position, Teacher 3, and Confederate B is always the Learner. The role assignments, which the subjects read from the drawn slips, are as follows:

Role title	Participant	Task
Teacher 1	Confederate C	First, you will read word pairs to the learner. Then you will read a stimulus word along with four possible answers.
Teacher 2	Confederate A	When the learner gives his answer, your task is to indicate whether he is correct or incorrect. When he has erred you will provide him with the correct answer.
Teacher 3	Naive subject	Whenever the learner gives an incorrect answer, you will administer punishment by activating a shock generator.
Learner	Confederate B	Your task will be to learn a list of word pairs read to you by Teacher 1.

The experimenter explains that the purpose of the experiment is to study the effects of punishment on memory in a context of "collective teaching." Confederate B is taken to an adjoining room and in full view of the others is strapped into an electric-chair apparatus. The experimenter explains the nature of the learning task to the Learner and, passing over a remark made by the Learner concerning a mild heart condition, takes the three teachers to the main experimental room.

They are seated before an imposing shock generator whose essential feature is a horizontal line of 30 lever switches, labeled 15–450 volts, in 15-volt increments. Verbal designations are spread along the line of switches reading: Slight Shock, Moderate Shock, Strong Shock, Very Strong Shock, Intense Shock, Extreme Intensity Shock, and Danger: Severe Shock.

The experimenter restates that the Learner is to be tested on a paired-associate learning task (see Milgram, 1963, for details). Teachers are told that the Learner must be shocked each time he errs in the learning task. The experimenter explains how the level of shock is to be determined:

> Now the amount of punishment given on any trial is decided by the teachers themselves. Each of you will suggest a shock level. And the shock actually administered will be the lowest level suggested by any of the three teachers. In order to keep the experiment running smoothly, give suggested levels in this order: Teacher 1, submit your bid first; Teacher 2, submit your bid second; and Teacher 3, submit your bid third. Remember you can stick to one level or raise or lower your level as you desire, but on any trial, the punishment administered will be the lowest level suggested by any teacher on that trial.

Thus the naive subject finds himself in a position in which, on any trial, he can effectively control the maximum shock administered to the Learner, e.g., the ground rules of the experiment would permit him to hold the shock level down to 15 volts throughout the laboratory session. On the other hand he may go along with or move in the direction of the group choice. It is the naive subject who actually administers the shock by depressing the appropriate lever on the generator (i.e., he always emerges from the rigged drawing as Teacher 3).

The three teachers each have their roles spelled out for them again, and there remains only the task of giving each a sample shock from the generator before the experiment gets under way.

BEHAVIOR OF TEACHERS 1 AND 2 (CONFEDERATES). According to a prearranged schedule the two confederates at the shock generator call for a one-step increase in the shock level each time the Learner errs. On the first error they both call for Shock Level 1 (15 volts); on the twentieth error they both call for Shock Level 20 (300 volts), and so forth. Their constant unanimity is rendered credible by having Teacher 1 play a somewhat domineering, and Teacher 2 a somewhat submissive type. The confederates, played by adult actors, appear indifferent to the complaints of the Learner.

BEHAVIOR OF THE LEARNER. According to a prearranged schedule the Learner responds to the learning task by providing answers in the proportion of three wrong answers to each correct one. There are a total of 40 trials, 30 of them being critical (occasions when the Learner answers incorrectly).

The Learner's responses are not limited to providing answers. As the shocks administered to him become stronger, he grunts, protests, and demands to be let out of the experiment. Each complaint of the Learner is, in fact, prerecorded on magnetic tape, and is coordinated to a specific shock level. The protests and expressions of discomfort follow spontaneously the administration of an electric shock.

The Learner indicates no discomfort until the 75-volt shock is administered, at which time there is a slight grunt in response to the punishment. Similar reactions follow the 90- and 105-volt shocks, and at 120 volts the Learner shouts to the experimenter that the shocks are becoming painful. Painful groans are heard on the administration of the 135-volt shock, and at 150 volts the Learner cries out that he wants to be released from the experiment, complaining of a heart disturbance. Cries of this type continue with generally rising intensity, so that at 180 volts, the Learner cries out "I can't stand the pain," and by 285 volts his response to the shock is clearly an agonized scream. At 300 volts the victim shouts in desperation that he will no longer provide answers to the memory test, and so forth through 450 volts. In other words, increases in shock level are met by increasingly severe reactions from the person being punished.

It is to be remembered that this is merely a *potential* series of responses. If a shock no higher than the 75-volt level is administered, only a grunt is heard. As a point of procedure, protests were not repeated at the same shock level, e.g., after the first grunt was used in response to Shock Level 75, no further complaints were introduced until and if a higher shock level were used.

EXPERIMENTAL MEASURES. The principal experimental measure, therefore, is the level of shock administered by the subject on each of the 30 critical trials. The shock levels were automatically recorded by an Esterline-Angus event recorder wired directly into the shock generator, providing us with a permanent record of each subject's performance.

POSTEXPERIMENTAL SESSION. An interview and debriefing session were held immediately after each subject's performance. A variety of background measures was obtained, as well as qualitative reactions to the experimental situation.

Control Condition

The purpose of the control condition is to determine the level of shock the naive subject administers to the Learner in the absence of group influence. One naive subject and one confederate (the Learner) perform in each session. The procedure is identical to that in the experimental condition, except that the tasks of Confederates A and C are collapsed into one role handled by the naive subject. References to collective teaching are omitted.

The naive subject is instructed to administer a shock each time the Learner errs, and the naive subject is told that as teacher he is free to select any shock level on any of the trials. In all other respects the control and experimental procedures are identical.

RESULTS

Figure 1 shows the mean shock levels for each critical trial in the experimental and control conditions. It also shows a diagonal representing the stooge-group's suggested shock level on each critical trial. The degree to which the experimental function moves away from the control level and toward the stooge-group diagonal represents the effects of group influence. Inspection indicates that the confederates substantially influ-

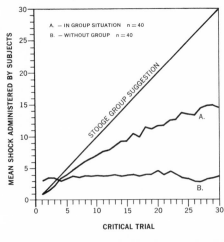

Fig. 1. Mean shock levels in experimental and control conditions over 30 critical trials. (Art adapted from Milgram.)

enced the level of shock administered to the Learner. The results will now be considered in detail.

In the experimental condition the standard deviation of shock levels rose regularly from trial to trial, and roughly in proportion to the rising mean shock level. However, in the control condition the standard deviation did not vary systematically with the mean through the 30 trials. Representative mean shock levels and standard deviations for the two conditions are shown in Table 1. Hartley's test for homogeneity of variance

Table 1—Representative Mean Shock Levels and Standard Deviations in the Experimental and Control Conditions

Trial	Experimental condition		Control condition	
	Mean shock level	SD	Mean shock level	SD
5	4.03	1.19	3.35	2.39
10	6.78	2.63	3.48	3.03
15	9.20	4.28	3.68	3.58
20	11.45	6.32	4.13	4.90
25	13.55	8.40	3.55	3.85
30	14.13	9.59	3.38	1.89

confirmed that the variances in the two conditions were significantly different. Therefore a reciprocal-of-the-square root transformation was performed before an analysis of variance was carried out.

As summarized in Table 2, the analysis of variance showed that the overall mean shock level in the experimental condition was significantly higher than that in the control condition ($p < .001$). This is less interesting, however, than the differing slopes in the two conditions, which show the group effects through the course of the experimental session.[1] The analysis of variance test for trend confirmed that the slopes for the two conditions differed significantly ($p < .001$).

Examination of the standard deviations in the experimental condition shows that there are large individual differences in response to group pressure, some subjects following the group closely, others resisting effectively. Subjects were ranked according to their total deviation from the confederates' shock choices. On the thirtieth critical trial the most conforming quartile had a mean shock level of 27.6, while the mean shock level of

[1] On the first four trials the control group has a higher mean shock than the experimental group; this is an artifact due to the provision that in the experimental condition the shock actually administered and recorded was the lowest suggested by any member of the group; when the subject called for a shock level higher than that suggested by the confederates, it was not reflected in the data. (This situation arose only during the first few critical trials.) By the fifth critical trial the group pressure begins to show its effect in elevating the mean shock level of the naive subjects.

**Table 2—Analysis of Variance of Shock Levels Administered
in the Experimental and Control Conditions**

Source	df	SS	MS	F
Total between individuals	79	966,947.1	12,239.8	
Between experimental conditions	1	237,339.4	237,339.4	25.37*
Between individuals	78	729,607.7	9,353.9	
Within individuals	2,320	391,813.5	168.9	
Between trials	29	157,361.7	5,426.3	96.04*
Trials × Experimental conditions (Trend)	29	106,575.4	3,675.0	65.04*
Remainder	2,262	127,876.4	56.5	

* $p < .001$.

the least conforming quartile was 4.8. Background characteristics of the experimental subjects were noted: age, marital status, occupation, military experience, political preference, religious affiliation, birth-order information, and educational history. Less educated subjects (high school degree or less) tended to yield more than those who possess a college degree ($x^2_{df = 1} = 2.85$, $p < .10$). Roman Catholic subjects tended to yield more than Protestant subjects ($x^2_{df = 1} = 2.96$, $p < .10$). No other background variable measured in the study was associated with amount of yielding, though the number of subjects employed was too small for definite conclusions.

The shock data may also be examined in terms of the *maximum* shock administered by subjects in the experimental and control conditions, i.e., the highest single shock administered by a subject throughout the 30 critical trials. The information is presented in Table 3. Only 2 control subjects administered shocks beyond the tenth voltage level (at this point the Learner makes his first truly vehement protest), while 27 experimental subjects went beyond this point. A median test showed that the maximum shocks administered by experimental subjects were higher than those administered by control subjects ($x^2_{df = 1} = 39.2$, $p < .001$).

The main effect, then, is that in the experimental condition subjects were substantially influenced by group pressure. When viewed in terms of the mean shock level over the 30 critical trials, as in Figure 1, the experimental function appears as a vector more or less bisecting the angle formed by the confederates' diagonal and control slopes. Thus one might be tempted to say that the subject's action in the experimental situation had two major sources: it was partly determined by the level the subject would have chosen in the control condition, and partly by the confederates' choice. Neither one nor the other entirely dominates the average behavior of subjects in the experimental condition. There are very great individual differences in regard to the more dominant force.

Table 3—Maximum Shock Levels Administered in Experimental and Control Conditions

Verbal designation and voltage indication	Number of subjects for whom this was maximum shock	
	Experimental	Control
Slight Shock		
15	1	3
30	2	6
45	0	7
60	0	7
Moderate Shock		
75	1	5
90	0	4
105	1	1
120	1	1
Strong Shock		
135	2	3
150	5	1
165	2	0
180	0	0
Very Strong Shock		
195	1	0
210	2	0
225	2	0
240	1	0
Intense Shock		
255	2	0
270	0	0
285	1	0
300	1	0
Extreme Intensity Shock		
315	2	0
330	0	0
345	1	0
360	2	0
Danger: Severe Shock		
375	0	1
390	0	0
405	1	0
420	2	0
XXX		
435	0	0
450	7	1

DISCUSSION

The substantive contribution of the present study lies in the demonstration that group influence can shape behavior in a domain that might have been thought highly resistant to such effects. Subjects are induced by the group to inflict pain on another person at a level that goes well beyond levels chosen in the absence of social pressure. Hurting a man is an action that for most people carries considerable psychological significance; it is closely tied to questions of conscience and ethical judgment. It might have been thought that the protests of the victim and inner prohibitions against hurting others would have operated effectively to curtail the subject's compliance. While the experiment yields wide variation in performance, a substantial number of subjects submitted readily to pressure applied to them by the confederates.

The significance of yielding in Asch's situation is sometimes questioned because the discriminative task is not an issue of self-evident importance for many subjects (Bronowski).[2] The criticism is not easily extended to the present study. Here the subject does not merely feign agreement with a group on a perceptual task of undefined importance; and he is unable to dismiss his action by relegating it to the status of a trivial gesture, for a person's suffering and discomfort are at stake.

The behavior observed here occurred within the framework of a laboratory study presided over by an experimenter. In some degree his authority stands behind the group. In his initial instructions the experimenter clearly legitimized the use of any shock level on the console. Insofar as he does not object to the shocks administered in the course of the experiment, his assent is implied. Thus, even though the effects of group pressure have been clearly established by a comparison of the experimental and control conditions, the effects occurred within the context of authoritative sanction. This point becomes critical in any attempt to assess the relative effectiveness of *conformity* versus *obedience* as means of inducing contravalent behavior (Milgram, 1963). If the experimenter had not approved the use of all shock levels on the generator, and if he had departed from the laboratory at an early stage, thus eliminating any sign of authoritative assent during the course of the experiment, would the group have had as powerful an effect on the naive subject?

There are many points of difference between Asch's investigation and the procedure of the present study that can only be touched upon here.

1. While in Asch's study the *adequate* response is anchored to an external stimulus event, in the present study we are dealing with an internal, unbound standard.

[2] J. Bronowski, personal communication, January 10, 1962.

2. A misspoken judgment can, in principle, be withdrawn, but here we are dealing with action that has an immediate and unalterable consequence. Its irreversibility stems not from constraints extrinsic to the action, but from the content of the action itself: once the Learner is shocked, he cannot be unshocked.

3. In the present experiment, despite the several sources of opinion, there can be but a single shock level on each trial. There is, therefore, a competition for outcome that was not present in the Asch situation.

4. While in the Asch study the focus of pressure is directed toward the subject's judgment, with distortion of public response but an intermediary stage of influence, here the focus of pressure is directed toward performance of action itself. Asch's yielding subject may secretly harbor the true judgment; but when the performance of an action becomes the object of social pressure, there is no comparable recourse to a covert form. The subject who performed the act demanded by the group has yielded exhaustively.

5. In the Asch situation a yielding subject engages in a covert violation of his obligations to the experimenter. He has agreed to report to the experimenter what he sees, and insofar as he goes along with the group, he breaks this agreement. In contrast, in the present experiment the yielding subject acts within the terms of the "subject-experimenter contract." In going along with the two confederates the subject may violate his own inner standards, and the rights of the Learner, but his relationship with the experimenter remains intact at both the manifest and private levels. Subjects in the two experiments are faced with different patterns of social pressure and violate different relationships through social submission.

REFERENCES

ASCH, S. E. Effects of group pressure upon the modification and distortion of judgment. In H. Guetzkow (Ed.), *Groups, leadership, and men.* Pittsburgh: Carnegie Press, 1951.

ASCH, S. E. Studies of independence and conformity: I. A minority of one against a unanimous majority. *Psychol. Monogr.,* 1956, **70** (9, Whole No. 416).

CRUTCHFIELD, R. S. Conformity and character. *Amer. Psychologist,* 1955, **10,** 191–198.

FRANK, J. D. Experimental studies of personal pressure and resistance. *J. gen. Psychol.,* 1944, **30,** 23–64.

FRENCH, J. R. P., JR., MORRISON, H. W., & LEVINGER, G. Coercive power and forces affecting conformity. *J. abnorm. soc. Psychol.,* 1960, **61,** 93–101.

MILGRAM, S. Nationality and conformity. *Scient. American,* 1961, **205,** 45–51.

MILGRAM, S. Behavioral study of obedience. *J. abnorm. soc. Psychol.,* 1963, **67,** 371–378.

RAVEN, B. H., & FRENCH, J. R. P. Legitimate power, coercive power, and observ-ability in social influence. *Sociometry*, 1958, 21, 83–97.

TUDDENHAM, R. D., & MACBRIDE, P. The yielding experiment from the subject's point of view. *J. Pers.*, 1959, 27, 259–271.

part 4:

Dispositional and cultural factors in behavior control

Part 4 presents evidence indicating that man's behavior is controlled in part by his biological characteristics and cultural experiences. Because a person's body and his culture are so much a part of him, he sometimes fails to realize the regulating powers of such factors in his everyday life. Yet, recent evidence indicates that these factors are important and do control a wide variety of human actions. Did you know, for example, that:

- A person's heredity might predispose him to commit anti-social acts (Montagu, 1968)?
- Genetic factors play a role in the etiology of schizophrenia (Heston, 1970; Meehl, 1962)?
- The way a person governs the space around him varies from culture to culture (Hall, 1966)?
- The language a person speaks determines, in part, the way he conceptualizes his world (Whorf, 1939, 1941)?
- Peoples' perceptions vary from culture to culture (Segall, Campbell & Herskovits, 1963)?

Just *how* and *why* biological and cultural factors play a role in behavior determination will be examined in the following selections.

Chromosomes and crime

Ashley Montagu

*INTRODUCTION   When we ask what causes people
to commit crimes, there are always two important factors: the dispositional
and situational determinants of anti-social behavior. Each human being
is a biological organism living in a social context, and thus his behavior
is always the joint outcome of hereditary and environmental influences.
One should keep this in mind when reading Ashley Montagu's provocative work,* Chromosomes and Crime. *When we speak of hereditary factors
playing a role in anti-social behavior, it is always understood that such
factors* alone do not *cause deviant actions, but, rather, that they increase
the likelihood of such actions taking place under certain environmental
conditions.**

A re some men "born criminals"? Is there a genetic basis
for criminal behavior? The idea that criminals are degenerates because
of "bad genes" has had wide appeal.

Johann Kaspar Spurzheim and Franz Joseph Gall, the inventors of
phrenology early in the 19th Century, associated crime with various bumps
on the head, reflecting the alleged structure of the particular region of the
brain within. Later in the last century, Cesare Lombroso, an Italian crim-
inologist, listed physical stigmata by which criminals might be recognized.
Lombroso's marks of degeneration included lobeless and small ears, re-
ceding chins, low foreheads and crooked noses. These traits supposedly
foretold of a biological predisposition to commit crimes.

In more recent years, Earnest A. Hooton of Harvard and William
H. Sheldon of New York claimed to have found an association between
body type and delinquent behavior. These claims, however, were shown
to be quite unsound.

* In the past two years studies have been conducted which cast some doubt on
the proposed relationship between chromosomes and crime. At this time further investigations are being undertaken with an eye to determining once and for all if a
person's genetic makeup might be involved in his anti-social behavior.

Reprinted from *Psychology Today* Magazine, October, 1968. Copyright © Communica-
tions/Research/Machines/Inc.

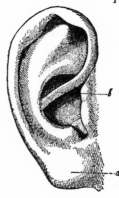

Fig. 1. Criminal ear—one of Lombroso's marks of degeneration, from *Criminal Man* by Gina Lombroso Ferrero, Putnam's, 1911. (Art adopted from Montagu.)

Of all the tales of "bad blood" and "bad genes," perhaps the two most famous are those of the "Jukes" and the "Kallikaks." The tale of the Jukes was first published in 1875 by Richard L. Dugdale, a New York prison inspector. In his report, "The Jukes: A Study in Crime, Pauperism, Disease, and Heredity," Dugdale covers seven generations, 540 blood relatives and 169 related by marriage or cohabitation. Although Dugdale did not invent the Jukes, he often fell back upon his imagination to bolster his theory of the hereditary causes of crime when the facts failed. When information about individuals was hard to come by, Dugdale resorted to characterizations as "supposed to have attempted rape," "reputed sheep-stealer, but never caught," "hardened character" and the like.

The Kallikaks were studied by Henry H. Goddard, director of a school for the mentally retarded in New Jersey. In his report published in 1912, he followed the fortunes and misfortunes of two clans of Kallikaks. Both were descended from the same Revolutionary War soldier. The bad Kallikaks sprang from this soldier's union with a feeble-minded girl, who spawned a male so bad that he became known as "Old Horror."

"Old Horror" fathered 10 other horrors and they in turn became responsible for the hundreds of other horrible Kallikaks traced by Dr. Goddard. All of the good Kallikaks were descendants, of course, from the Revolutionary War soldier's marriage with a Quaker woman of good blood. Since none of the good Kallikaks seems to have inherited any "bad genes," something rather strange must have occurred in the lineage, for we know that a certain number of the good offspring should have shown some "degenerate" traits.

The Jukes and the Kallikaks are sometimes quoted as examples of what "good" and "bad" genes can do to human beings. While it is possible that a genetic defect may have been involved in some of these pedigrees, the disregard by the investigators of environmental effects renders

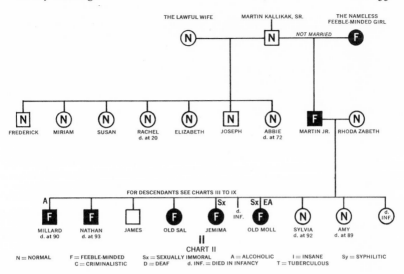

Fig. 2. The good and the bad Kallikaks, from *The Kallikak Family* by Henry H. Goddard, © Macmillan, 1912 (copyright renewed 1940 by Henry H. Goddard). (Art adapted from Montagu.)

their work valueless except for their quaint, anecdotal style of reporting.

The question of whether a man's genetic make-up may be responsible for his committing acts of violence has again come forward in the courts.

In France this year, Daniel Hugon was charged with the murder of a prostitute. Following his attempted suicide, he was found to be of XYY chromosomal constitution. Filled with remorse, Hugon had voluntarily surrendered to the police. His lawyers contended that he was unfit to stand trial because of his abnormality.

Richard Speck, the convicted murderer of eight nurses in Chicago in 1966, also is reported to be an XYY. Tall, mentally dull, with an acne-marked face and a record of 40 arrests, Speck presents a characteristic example, both genotypically and phenotypically, of the XYY type. Whether he was "born to raise hell" as a consequence of his chromosomal constitution, or whether his impoverished social environment would have been a sufficient condition, or whether both were necessary for his fateful development, no one at the moment is in a position to say.

The possible link between an XYY chromosomal constitution and criminals first came to light three years ago in a study of prison hospital inmates. In December 1965, Patricia A. Jacobs and her colleagues at Western General Hospital in Edinburgh published their findings on 197 mentally abnormal inmates undergoing treatment in a special security institution in Scotland. All had dangerous, violent or criminal propensities.

Seven of these males were found to be of XYY chromosomal constitution, one was an XXYY, and another an XY/XXY mosaic. Since on theoretical grounds the occurrence of XYY males in the general population should be less frequent than the XXY type (the latter type occurs in some 1.3 out of 1,000 live births), the 3.5 per cent incidence of XYY males in a prison population was a highly significant finding.

There is still too little information available concerning the frequency of XYY males among the newly born or adults, but there is little doubt that the frequency found by Jacobs and her colleagues is substantially higher than that in the general population. Few laboratories yet are able to do chromosome studies on a large scale, so information available is based on limited population samples from small areas. Current estimate of the frequency of XYY males at birth range from 0.5 to 3.5 per 1,000.

Jacobs also found that the XYY inmates were unusually tall, with a mean height of 6 feet 1.1 inches. Males in the institution with normal XY chromosomal constitution had a mean height of 5 feet 7 inches.

Since publication of the paper by Jacobs and her co-workers, about a dozen other reports have been published on XYY individuals, and all the reports confirm and enlarge upon the original findings. [*See illustration, page 199.*] However, in many of these cases only inmates 6 feet or more in height were selected for study, so care must be taken in interpreting the findings.

In a sample of 3,395 prison and hospital inmates, 56 individuals were XYY, nine others had supernumerary Ys in one combination or another. Only eight of the inmates were XXY. Supernumerary Y chromosomes in any other combination are only one-fifth as frequent as the XYY—a significant fact that suggests it is the YY complement in the presence of a *single* X chromosome that constitutes the most frequent anomaly.

However, the presence of an extra Y chromosome, in any combination, appears to increase the chances of trouble. It also seems that the presence of an extra X chromosome, no matter what the number of extra Y chromosomes may be, in no way reduces the chance of trouble.

The Y chromosome, so to speak, seems to possess an elevated aggressiveness potential, whereas the X chromosome seems to possess a high gentleness component.

It appears probable that the ordinary quantum of aggressiveness of a normal XY male is derived from his Y chromosome, and that the addition of another Y chromosome presents a double dose of those potencies that may under certain conditions facilitate the development of aggressive behavior.

Of course, as with any chromosome, this does not mean that the genes are directly responsible for the end-effect. Rather, the genes on the sex chromosomes exercise their effects through a long chain of metabolic pathways. The final physiological or functional expression results from the interaction of the genes with their environments.

Genes do not determine anything. They simply influence the morphological and physiological expression of traits. Heredity, then, is the expression, not of what is given in one's genes at conception, but of the reciprocal interaction between the inherited genes and the environments to which they've been exposed.

Genes, chromosomes, or heredity are not to be interpreted, as so many people mistakenly do, as equivalent to fate or predestination. On the contrary, the genetic constitution, the genotype, is a labile system, capable of being influenced and changed to varying degrees.

Unchangeability and immutability are not characteristics of the genetic system. The genetic code for any trait contains a set of specific instructions. The manner in which those instructions will be carried out depends not only on those instructions but also upon the nature of their interaction with other sets of instructions as well as with their environments.

The phenotype, that is the visible product of the joint action of genes and the environment, is variable. The idea of genetic or hereditary preformation is as incorrect and unsound as is the doctrine of hereditary predestination. In discussing the behavioral traits so frequently associated with the XYY type, these facts must be especially borne in mind.

How does the XYY chromosomal aberration originate? Most probably the double Y complement is produced during formation of the sperm. During the process of meiosis, in which chromosomes divide and duplicate themselves, normal separation of the sex chromosomes leads to two kinds of sperm—those with an X chromosome, and those with a Y chromosome. If an X sperm fertilizes a normal X ovum, an XX individual (normal female) will result. If the Y sperm fertilizes the ovum, a normal XY male will result.

Failure of the sex chromosomes to separate normally is called nondisjunction. There are two divisions during meiosis. If nondisjunction occurs during the first meiotic division in the production of sperm, this leads to two kinds of sperm cells—those with both the X and Y chromosomes, and those with no sex chromosomes. If an XY sperm fertilizes a normal ovum, an XXY individual will be the result. The XXY individual is a male (Klinefelter's Syndrome), but is usually sterile, lacking functional testes. About 80 per cent of these males develop small breasts and at least 25 per cent are of limited intelligence.

If nondisjunction occurs at the second meiotic division of the pa-

The XYY Syndrome

No.	Population	Status	Height Inches	Intelligence	Traits	XYY	XXYY	XY/XXY	XXY XYY	XYYY XYY	Reference
10,725	Maternity	Newborn				—	1	5	12	—	Maclean, N. et al. Lancet, i: 286–290, 1964.
2,607	Ordinary			Subnormal		—	2	—	—	—	Maclean, N. et al. Lancet, i: 293, 1962.
197	Security	Criminal	73.1	Subnormal		7	1	1	—	—	Jacobs, P. et al. Nature, Vol. 208: 1351, 1352, 1965.
942	Institutional	Criminal		Subnormal		12	7	2	—	—	Casey, M. et al. Nature, Vol. 209: 641, 642, 1966.
50	Institutional Mentally III	Non-criminal				4	—	—	—	—	Casey, M. et al. Lancet, i: 859, 860, 1966.
24	Institutional	Criminal				2	—	—	—	—	Casey, M. et al. Lancet, i: 859, 860, 1966.
315	Security	Criminal	6 over 72	8 Subnormal 1 Schizophrenic		9	—	—	—	—	Price, W. et al. Lancet, i: 565, 566, 1966.
464	Institutional	Delinquent		Subnormal	Aggressive Grand mal	1	—	—	—	—	Welch, J. et al. Nature, Vol. 214: 500, 501, 1967.
19	Detention center	Criminal Sex crimes	74.1	I.Q. 83	Negro Acne	1	—	—	—	—	Telfer, M. et al. Lancet, i: 95, 1968.

No.	Setting	Status	Height/Age	I.Q.	Characteristic						Reference
129	Institutional	Criminal	+72		Psychopathic	5	—	—	7	—	Telfer, M. et al. Science, Vol. 159: 1249, 1250, 1968
34	Prison	Criminal	69–82½	2 Subnormal		3	—	—	—	1	Wiener, S. et al. Lancet, ii: 159, 1968.
1,021	Institutional Boys	Delinquent	Tall	I.Q.s 77, 78, 91	Property offenses	3	—	—	1	—	Hunter, H. Lancet, i: 816, 1968.
200	Institutional	Criminal	+72		Aggressive sex offenders	9	—	—	—	—	Vanasek, F. et al. Atascadero State Hospital, Calif. (in press), 1968.
1	Ordinary	Embezzlement	78	I.Q. 118	Not overtly aggressive Depressed	1	—	—	—	—	Leff, J. and Scott, P. Lancet, ii: 645, 1968.
1	Ordinary	8 yrs. 7 mo.	57	I.Q. 95	Aggressive	1	—	—	—	—	Cowie, J. and Kahn, J. British Medical Journal, Vol. 1: 748, 749, 1968.
1	Ordinary	5 yrs. 6 mo.		I.Q. 85	Undescended testes Simian creases	—	—	—	—	—	Townes, P. Lancet, i: 1041–1043, 1965.
1	Ordinary	44 yrs.	72	Average	Trouble keeping jobs	1	—	—	—	—	Hauschka, T. et al. American Journal of Human Genetics, Vol. 14: 22–30, 1962.
1	Ordinary	12 yrs.		Average	Undescended testes	1	—	—	—	—	Sandberg, A. et al. New England Journal of Medicine, Vol. 268: 585–589, 1963.

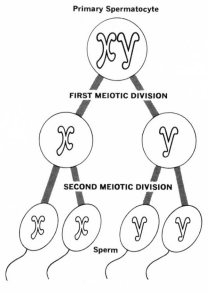

**NORMAL MALE MEIOSIS
(Formation of the sperm)**

ternal germ cells, three types of sperm are produced: XX, YY, and those containing no sex chromosomes. Offspring resulting from fertilization of a normal ovum will be, respectively, XXX, XYY, and XO.

An XYY individual also could be produced if the sex chromosomes fail to separate normally in the early stages of division (mitosis) of a normal, fertilized XY-ovum. However, in such an event, an individual with some type of mosaicism is more likely to occur.

Mosaicism refers to the existence of a different number of sex chromosomes in different tissues or parts of the body. For example, an individual may have only one X chromosome in some of his cells, and three chromosomes (XYY) in other cells. Such a mosaic would be designated XO/XYY. The O refers to the missing X or Y chromosome. If the single X

NONDISJUNCTION OF SEX CHROMOSOMES IN MALE MEIOSIS

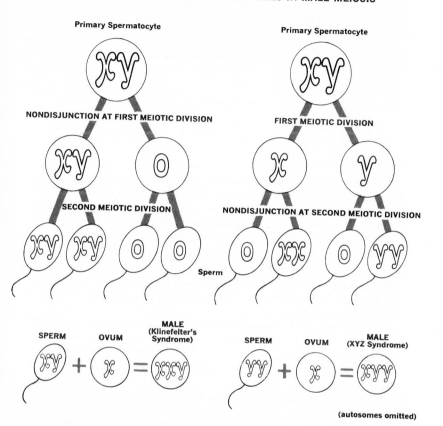

(autosomes omitted)

chromosome is coupled with an isochromosome (I)—a chromosome with two identical arms—then the mosaic would be XI/XYY. Of course, other mosaics such as XY/XYY or XYY/XYYY occur.

Major physical abnormalities do not occur in XYY individuals for the reason that the Y chromosome carries relatively few genes. However, the physical abnormalities that do occur are interesting. As in most cases in which an extra sex chromosome is present, there is a high incidence of abnormal internal and external genitalia. Even in childhood, XYY individuals are usually strikingly tall, and as adults usually exceed six feet in height. Facial acne appears to be frequent in adolescence. Mentally, these individuals are usually rather dull, with I.Q.s between 80 and 95. Abnormal electroencephalographic recordings, and a relatively high incidence of epileptic and epileptiform conditions, suggest a wide spectrum of brain dysfunction. Disorders of the teeth, such as discolored enamel, malocclusion and arrested development, also have been noted.

NORMAL MITOTIC DIVISION

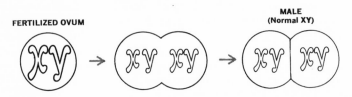

Allowing for the fact that in many cases tall prison inmates were selected for study of the XYY syndrome, and while a number of known XYY individuals fall several inches short of 6 feet, it is nonetheless clear that tallness usually characterizes the XYY individual.

This may be a significant factor in influencing the individual's behavioral development. Among children his own age, an XYY boy may be teased and taunted because of his height, and impelled either to withdrawal or aggression. As a juvenile, adolescent or adult, he may find himself nurtured in environments that encourage physical aggression as a means of adaptation.

This should not be interpreted to mean that all tall men have an XYY constitution. Recently, Richard Goodman and his colleagues at Ohio State University examined the chromosomes of 36 basketball players ranging in height from 5 feet, 11 inches to 6 feet, 10 inches, and found no chromosomal abnormalities.

The resort to brawn rather than brain is not limited to individuals endowed with an extra Y chromosome. Most violent crimes are committed by chromosomally normal individuals. However, the high frequency with which individuals with XYY chromosomes commit crimes of violence leaves little doubt that in some cases the additional Y chromosome exerts a preponderantly powerful influence in the genesis of aggressive behavior.

In a maximum security prison in Melbourne, Australia, Saul Wiener and his colleagues found four XYY-type males in a study of 34 tall prisoners, all between 5 feet 9 inches and 6 feet 10.5 inches in height. A striking frequency of 11.8 per cent! Three of the inmates were XYY, one of whom was charged with attempted murder, the second had committed murder, and the third larceny. The fourth was an XYY/XYYY mosaic, and had committed murder.

An interesting fact is that the tallest of the XYY murderers, 6 feet 10.5 inches tall, had a sister who was even taller. The tallness of the sister indicates that even though the X chromosome is not usually associated with excessive height in families where the males are extremely tall, a trait for tallness may be also carried in the X chromosome.

As a consequence of the discovery of what may be called the XYY syndrome, there now can be very little doubt that genes do influence, to some extent, the development of behavior.

It also appears clear, that, with all other factors constant, genes of the same kind situated at the same locus on the chromosomes of different people may vary greatly both in their penetrance and their expressivity.

Penetrance refers to the regularity with which a gene produces its effect. When a gene regularly produces the same effect, it is said to have complete penetrance. When the trait is not manifested in some cases, the gene is said to have reduced penetrance.

Expressivity refers to the manifestation of a trait produced by a gene. When the manifestation differs from individual to individual, the gene is said to have variable expressivity. For example, the dominant gene for allergy may express itself as asthma, eczema, hay fever, urticarial rash, or angioneurotic edema.

Hence, it would be an error to identify the XYY constitution as *predisposed* to aggressive behavior. Whatever genes are involved, they often fail to produce aggressive behavior, and even more often may be expressed in many different ways. In fact, the XYY phenotype, the product of the joint action of genes and environment, does vary from normal to various degrees of abnormality.

Some individuals, however, seem to be driven to their aggressive behavior as if they are possessed by a demon. The demon, it would seem, lies in the peculiar nature of the double-Y chromosome complement. That the combined power of several Y chromosomes can be so great, in some cases, as to cause a man to become unrestrainedly aggressive is dramatically borne out by a case reported by John Cowie and Jacob Kahn of East Ham Child Clinic, London, in March 1968.

The first-born, wanted child of a mother aged 23 and a father aged 25 was referred at the age of four and a half years to a psychiatrist because he was unmanageable at home, destructive, mischievous and defiant. He would smash his toys, rip the curtains, set fire to the room in his mother's absence, kick the cat and hit his eight-month-old brother. He was over-adventurous and without fear. At two years of age, he began wandering away from home, and was brought back by the police on five occasions. He started school at five years and at once developed an interest in sharp-pointed objects. He would shoot drawing compasses across the schoolroom from an elastic band, and injured several children. In one incident, he rammed a screwdriver into a little girl's stomach.

At the age of eight years, seven months, he was 4 feet 9 inches tall, handsome, athletically proportioned, and of normal appearance. He is of average intelligence, and often considerate and happy. His electroencephalogram is mildly abnormal. Both his parents and his brother have normal chromosomal complements, but the boy is of XYY constitution. His brother is a normally behaving child, and the parents are concerned, loving people.

As illustrated by this case, there is now an increasing amount of evidence that XYY individuals commence their aggressive and social behavior in early prepubertal years. In many cases, the offenses committed are against property rather than against persons. The XYY anomaly,

MITOTIC NONDISJUNCTION

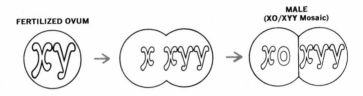

(autosomes omitted)

therefore, should not be associated with one particular behavioral trait, but rather regarded as an aberration characterized by a wide spectrum of behavioral possibilities ranging from totally normal to persistent antisocial behavior. The degree of aggressiveness varies, and is only one component of the highly variable spectrum of behavioral contingencies.

We have shown how the XYY chromosomal aberration can originate in nondisjunction during meiosis or during mitosis. But does an XYY male transmit the abnormality to his offspring? To this question the answer is: probably not. One report on an Oregon XYY man indicates the double-Y chromosome complement may not be transmitted. The man has six sons, and all are of normal XY chromosomal constitution.

On the other hand, T. S. Hauschka of Roswell Park Memorial Institute and the Medical Foundation of Buffalo, and his colleagues, who discovered one of the first XYY individuals in 1961, suggest that there may be a hereditary predisposition to nondisjunction. The XYY individual they identified was a normal male who came to their attention because he had a daughter who suffered from Down's syndrome (mongolism). Since Down's syndrome, in most cases, also arises as a result of nondisjunction, this, coupled with other abnormalities in his offspring, suggested that he might be transmitting a hereditary tendency to nondisjunction.

The fact that the XYY complement is now known to be associated with persistent antisocial behavior in a large number of individuals raises a number of questions that the reasonable society, if not the Great Society, must consider seriously.

A first question, if not a first priority, is whether it would not now be desirable to type chromosomally all infants at birth or shortly after. At least one per cent of all babies born have a chromosomal abnormality of some sort, and about one-quarter of these involve sex chromosome abnormalities. Some of these will be XYY. Forearmed with such information, it might be possible to institute the proper preventive and other measures at an early age. These measures would be designed to help the individuals with the XYY chromosomal constitution to follow a less stormy development than they otherwise might.

A second question is how society should deal with individuals known to be of XYY constitution. Such individuals are genetically abnormal. They are not normal and, therefore, should not be treated as if they were.

If the individal has the misfortune to have been endowed with an extra chromosome Number 21, he would have suffered from Down's syndrome (mongolism). He would not have been expected to behave as a normal individual. And why should the XYY individual be held any more responsible for his behavior than a mongoloid? Mongoloids are usually likeable, unaggressive individuals, and most sociable. The aggressive XYY individual is often the very opposite. Yet the unaggressive behavior of mongoloids is as much due to their genetic constitution as is the aggressive and antisocial behavior of the XYY individual.

Recognizing this fact, it becomes very necessary for us to consider how society and the law should deal with such individuals. We have learned how to identify and treat the hereditary defect of PKU (phenylketonuria), which can result in idiocy if not treated. Cannot we also develop measures to treat the XYY syndrome? Surgical intervention, such as sterilization, is totally inappropriate since it will not "cure" or alleviate the condition, nor will it reduce the frequency of XYY individuals in the general population. The XYY aberration, as far as we know, is not directly inherited, and quite probably arises primarily from nondisjunction of the sex chromosomes in completely normal parents.

Although we are in no position to control the genetic inheritance of an individual, we can do a great deal to change certain environmental conditions that may encourage the XYY individual to commit criminal acts.

A society does not properly acquit itself of its responsibilities if it places the entire burden of caring for abnormal individuals upon the parents. What we are talking about here is not a program of eugenic control, but a program of social therapy. There is every reason to believe that if we can successfully develop effective methods to help the aggressive XYY individual, then we will be moving in the right direction to control those social conditions that drive men to crime—regardless of their genotype.

Schizotaxia, schizotypy, schizophrenia

Paul E. Meehl

INTRODUCTION Schizophrenia is a behavior disorder well known to the psychological and psychiatric community. English and English define it as "a group of psychotic reactions characterized by fundamental disturbances in reality relationships, by a conceptual world determined excessively by feeling, and by marked affective, intellectual, and overt behavior disturbances . . . many varieties are distinguished clinically."*

What causes schizophrenia? We still do not know for sure. However, many studies designed to answer this question have suggested a possible relationship between schizophrenia and certain genetic factors (e.g., Heston, 1970). In the following article Paul E. Meehl of the University of Minnesota reviews some of these studies and reaches some important conclusions about hereditary factors in schizophrenia.

In the course of the last decade, while spending several thousand hours in the practice of intensive psychotherapy, I have treated —sometimes unknowingly except in retrospect—a considerable number of schizoid and schizophrenic patients. Like all clinicians, I have formed some theoretical opinions as a result of these experiences. While I have not until recently begun any systematic research efforts on this baffling disorder, I felt that to share with you some of my thoughts, based though they are upon clinical impressions in the context of selected research by others, might be an acceptable use of this occasion.

Let me begin by putting a question which I find is almost never answered correctly by our clinical students on PhD orals, and the answer to which they seem to dislike when it is offered. Suppose that you were required to write down a procedure for selecting an individual from the

* English, H., & English, A. *A comprehensive dictionary of psychological and psychoanalytical terms.* New York: David McKay, 1958.

Meehl, P. E. Schizotaxia, schizotypy, schizophrenia. *American Psychologist,* 1962, **17,** 827–838. Copyright 1962 by the American Psychological Association, and reproduced by permission.

population who would be diagnosed as schizophrenic by a psychiatric staff: you have to wager $1,000 on being right; you may not include in your selection procedure any behavioral fact, such as a symptom or trait, manifested by the individual. What would you write down? So far as I have been able to ascertain, there is only one thing you could write down that would give you a better than even chance of winning such a bet—namely, "Find an individual X who has a schizophrenic identical twin." Admittedly, there are many other facts which would raise your odds somewhat above the low base rate of schizophrenia. You might, for example, identify X by first finding mothers who have certain unhealthy child-rearing attitudes; you might enter a subpopulation defined jointly by such demographic variables as age, size of community, religion, ethnic background, or social class. But these would leave you with a pretty unfair wager, as would the rule, "Find an X who has a fraternal twin, of the same sex, diagnosed as schizophrenic" (Fuller & Thompson, 1960, pp. 272–283; Stern, 1960, pp. 581–584).

Now the twin studies leave a good deal to be desired methodologically (Rosenthal, in press); but there seems to be a kind of "double standard of methodological morals" in our profession, in that we place a good deal of faith in our knowledge of schizophrenic dynamics, and we make theoretical inferences about social learning factors from the establishment of group trends which may be statistically significant and replicable although of small or moderate size; but when we come to the genetic studies, our standards of rigor suddenly increase. I would argue that the concordance rates in the twin studies need not be accepted uncritically as highly precise parameter estimates in order for us to say that their magnitudes represent the most important piece of etiological information we possess about schizophrenia.

It is worthwhile, I think, to pause here over a question in the sociology of knowledge, namely, why do psychologists exhibit an aversive response to the twin data? I have no wish to argue *ad hominem* here—I raise this question in a constructive and irenic spirit, because I think that a substantive confusion often lies at the bottom of this resistance, and one which can be easily dispelled. Everybody readily assents to such vague dicta as "heredity and environment interact," "there need be no conflict between organic and functional concepts," "we always deal with the total organism," etc. But it almost seems that clinicians do not fully believe these principles in any concrete sense, because they show signs of thinking that *if* a genetic basis were found for schizophrenia, the psychodynamics of the disorder (especially in relation to intrafamilial social learnings) would be somehow negated or, at least, greatly demoted in importance. To what extent, if at all, is this true?

Here we run into some widespread misconceptions as to what is meant by *specific etiology* in nonpsychiatric medicine. By postulating a "specific etiology," one does *not* imply any of the following:

1. The etiological factor always, or even usually, produces clinical illness.
2. If illness occurs, the particular form and content of symptoms is derivable by reference to the specific etiology alone.
3. The course of the illness can be materially influenced only by procedures directed against the specific etiology.
4. All persons who share the specific etiology will have closely similar histories, symptoms, and course.
5. The largest single contributor to symptom variance is the specific etiology.

In medicine, not one of these is part of the concept of specific etiology, yet they are repeatedly invoked as arguments against a genetic interpretation of schizophrenia. I am not trying to impose the causal model of medicine by analogy; I merely wish to emphasize that *if* one postulates a genetic mutation as the specific etiology of schizophrenia, he is not thereby committed to any of the above as implications. Consequently such familiar objections as, "Schizophrenics differ widely from one another" or "Many schizophrenics can be helped by purely psychological methods" should not disturb one who opts for a genetic hypothesis. In medicine, the concept of specific etiology means the *sine qua non*— the causal condition which is necessary, but not sufficient, for the disorder to occur. A genetic theory of schizophrenia would, in this sense, be stronger than that of "one contributor to variance"; but weaker than that of "largest contributor to variance." In analysis of variance terms, it means an interaction effect such that no other variables can exert a main effect when the specific etiology is lacking.

Now it goes without saying that "clinical schizophrenia" as such cannot be inherited, because it has behavioral and phenomenal contents which are learned. As Bleuler says, in order to have a delusion involving Jesuits one must first have learned about Jesuits. It seems inappropriate to apply the geneticist's concept of "penetrance" to the crude statistics of formal diagnosis—if a specific genetic etiology exists, its phenotypic expression in *psychological* categories would be a quantitative aberration in some parameter of a behavioral acquisition function. What could possibly be a genetically determined functional parameter capable of generating such diverse behavioral outcomes, including the preservation of normal function in certain domains?

The theoretical puzzle is exaggerated when we fail to conceptualize at different levels of molarity. For instance, there is a tendency among organically minded theorists to analogize between catatonic phenomena and various neurological or chemically induced states in animals. But Bleuler's masterly *Theory of Schizophrenic Negativism* (1912) shows how the whole range of catatonic behavior, including diametrically opposite modes of relating to the interpersonal environment, can be satisfactorily explained as instrumental acts; thus even a convinced organicist, postulating a biochemical defect as specific etiology, should recognize that the causal linkage between this etiology and catatonia is indirect, requiring for the latter's derivation a lengthy chain of statements which are not even formulable except in molar psychological language.

What kind of behavioral fact about the patient leads us to diagnose schizophrenia? There are a number of traits and symptoms which get a high weight, and the weights differ among clinicians. But thought disorder continues to hold its own in spite of today's greater clinical interest in motivational (especially interpersonal) variables. If you are inclined to doubt this for yourself, consider the following indicators: Patient experiences intense ambivalence, readily reports conscious hatred of family figures, is pananxious, subjects therapist to a long series of testing operations, is withdrawn, and says, "Naturally, I am growing my father's hair."

While all of these are schizophrenic indicators, the last one is the diagnostic bell ringer. In this respect we are still Bleulerians, although we know a lot more about the schizophrenic's psychodynamics than Bleuler did. The significance of thought disorder, associative dyscontrol (or, as I prefer to call it so as to include the very mildest forms it may take, "cognitive slippage"), in schizophrenia has been somewhat deemphasized in recent years. Partly this is due to the greater interest in interpersonal dynamics, but partly also to the realization that much of our earlier psychometric assessment of the thought disorder was mainly reflecting the schizophrenic's tendency to underperform because uninterested, preoccupied, resentful, or frightened. I suggest that this realization has been overgeneralized and led up to swing too far the other way, as if we had shown that there really *is* no cognitive slippage factor present. One rather common assumption seems to be that if one can demonstrate the potentiating effect of a motivational state upon cognitive slippage, light has thereby been shed upon the etiology of schizophrenia. Why are we entitled to think this? Clinically, we see a degree of cognitive slippage not found to a comparable degree among nonschizophrenic persons. Some patients (e.g., pseudoneurotics) are highly anxious and exhibit minimal slippage; others (e.g., burnt-out cases) are minimally anxious with marked slippage. The demonstration that we can intensify a particular patient's cognitive dysfunction by manipulating his affects is not really very illuminating. After all, even ordinary neurological diseases can often be tremendously influenced symptomatically via emotional stimuli; but if a psychologist demonstrates that the spasticity or tremor of a multiple sclerotic is affected by rage or fear, we would not thereby have learned anything about the etiology of multiple sclerosis.

Consequent upon our general assimilation of the insights given us by pschoanalysis, there is today a widespread and largely unquestioned assumption that when we can trace out the motivational forces linked to the content of aberrant behavior, then we understand why the person has fallen ill. There is no compelling reason to assume this, when the evidence is mainly our dynamic understanding of the patient, however valid that may be. The phrase "why the person has fallen ill" may, of course, be legitimately taken to include these things; an account of how and when he falls ill will certainly include them. But they may be quite inadequate to answer the question, "Why does X fall ill and not Y, granted that we can understand both of them?" I like the analogy of a color psychosis, which might be developed by certain individuals in a society entirely oriented around the making of fine color discriminations. Social, sexual, economic signals are color mediated; to misuse a color word is strictly taboo; compulsive mothers are horribly ashamed of a child who is retarded in color development, and so forth. Some color-blind individuals (not all, perhaps not most) develop a color psychosis in this culture; as adults, they are found on the couches of color therapists, where a great deal of *valid* understanding is achieved about color dynamics. Some of them make a social recovery. Nonetheless, if we ask, "What was basically the matter with these patients?" meaning, "What is the specific etiology of the color psychosis?" the answer is that mutated gene on the X chromosome. This is why my own therapeutic experience with schizophrenic patients has not yet convinced me of the schizophrenogenic mother as a specific etiology, even though the picture I get of my patients' mothers is pretty much in accord with the familiar one. There is no question here of accepting the patient's account; my point is that *given* the account, and taking it quite at face value, does not tell me why the patient is a patient and not just a fellow who had a bad mother.

Another theoretical lead is the one given greatest current emphasis, namely, *interpersonal aversiveness*. The schizophrene suffers a degree of social fear, distrust, expectation of rejection, and conviction of his own unlovability which cannot be matched in its depth, pervasity, and resistance to corrective experience by any other diagnostic group.

Then there is a quasi-pathognomonic sign, emphasized by Rado (1956; Rado & Daniels, 1956) but largely ignored in psychologists' diagnostic usage, namely, *anhedonia*—a marked, widespread, and refractory defect in pleasure capacity which, once you learn how to examine for it, is one of the most consistent and dramatic behavioral signs of the disease. Finally, I include *ambivalence* from Bleuler's cardinal four (1950). His other two, "autism" and "dereism," I consider derivative from the combination of slippage, anhedonia, and aversiveness. Crudely put, if a person cannot think straight, gets little pleasure, and is afraid of everyone, he will of course learn to be autistic and dereistic.

If these clinical characterizations are correct, and we combine them with the hypothesis of a genetic specific etiology, do they give us any lead on theoretical possibilities?

Granting its initial vagueness as a construct, requiring to be filled in by neurophysiological research, I believe we should take seriously the old European notion of an "integrative neural defect" as the only direct phenotypic consequence produced by the genic mutation. This is an aberration in some parameter of single cell function, which may or may not be manifested in the functioning of more molar CNS systems, depending upon the organization of the mutual feedback controls and upon the stochastic parameters of the reinforcement regime. This neural integrative defect, which I shall christen *schizotaxia,* is all that can properly be spoken of as inherited. The imposition of a social learning history upon schizotaxic individuals results in a personality organization which I shall call, following Rado, the *schizotype.* The four core behavior traits are obviously not innate; but I postulate that they are universally learned by schizotaxic individuals, given any of the actually existing social reinforcement regimes, from the best to the worst. If the interpersonal regime is favorable, and the schizotaxic person also has the good fortune to inherit a low anxiety readiness, physical vigor, general resistance to stress and the like, he will remain a well-compensated "normal" schizotype, never manifesting symptoms of mental disease. He will be like the gout-prone male whose genes determine him to have an elevated blood uric acid titer, but who never develops clinical gout.

Only a subset of schizotypic personalities decompensate into clinical schizophrenia. It seems likely that the most important causal influence pushing the schizotype toward schizophrenic decompensation is the schizophrenogenic mother.

I hope it is clear that this view does not conflict with what has been established about the mother-child interaction. If this interaction were totally free of maternal ambivalence and aversive inputs to the schizotaxic child, even compensated schizotypy might be avoided; at most, we might expect to find only the faintest signs of cognitive slippage and other minimal neurological aberrations, possibly including body image and other proprioceptive deviations, but not the interpersonal aversiveness which is central to the clinical picture.

Nevertheless, while assuming the etiological importance of mother in determining the course of aversive social learnings, it is worthwhile to speculate about the modification our genetic equations might take on this hypothesis. Many schizophrenogenic mothers are themselves schizotypes in varying degrees of compensation. Their etiological contribution then consists jointly in their passing on the gene *and* in the fact that being schizotypic, they provide the kind of ambivalent regime which potentiates the schizotypy of the child and raises the odds of his decompensating. Hence the incidence of the several parental genotypes among parent pairs of diagnosed proband cases is not calculable from the usual genetic formulas. For example, given a schizophrenic proband, the odds that mother is homozygous (or, if the gene were dominant, that it is mother who carries it) are different from those for father; since we have begun by selection a decompensated case, and formal diagnosis as the phenotype involves a potentiating factor for mother which is psychodynamically greater than that for a schizotypic father. Another important influence would be the likelihood that the lower fertility of schizophrenics is also present, but to an unknown degree, among compensated schizotypes. Clinical experience suggests that in the semicompensated range, this lowering of fertility is greater among males, since many schizotypic women relate to men in an exploited or exploitive sexual way, whereas the male schizotype usually displays a marked deficit in heterosexual aggressiveness. Such a sex difference in fertility among decompensated cases has been reported by Meyers and Goldfarb (1962).

Since the extent of aversive learnings is a critical factor in decompensation, the inherited anxiety readiness is presumably greater among diagnosed cases. Since the more fertile mothers are likely to be compensated, hence themselves to be relatively low anxiety if schizotaxic, a frequent parent pattern should be a compensated schizotypic mother married to a neurotic father, the latter being the source of the proband's high-anxiety genes (plus providing a poor paternal model for identification in male patients, and a weak defender of the child against mother's schizotypic hostility).

These considerations make ordinary family concordance studies, based upon formal diagnoses, impossible to interpret. The most important research need here is development of high-validity indicators for compensated schizotypy. I see some evidence for these conceptions in the report of Lidz and co-workers, who in studying intensively the parents of 15 schizophrenic patients were surprised to find that "minimally, 9 of the 15 patients had at least one parent who could be called schizophrenic, or ambulatory schizophrenic, or clearly paranoid in behavior and attitudes" (Lidz, Cornelison, Terry, & Fleck, 1958, p. 308). As I read the brief personality sketches presented, I would judge that all but two of the probands had a clearly schizotypic parent. These authors, while favoring a "learned irrationality" interpretation of their data, also recognize the alternative genetic interpretation. Such facts do not permit a decision, obviously; my main point is the striking difference between the high incidence of parental schizotypes, mostly quite decompensated (some to the point of diagnosable psychosis), and the zero incidence which a conventional family concordance study would have yielded for this group.

Another line of evidence, based upon a very small sample but exciting because of its uniformity, is McConaghy's report (1959) that among nondiagnosed parent pairs of 10 schizophrenics, subclinical thought disorder was psychometrically detectable in at least one parent of every pair. Rosenthal (in press) reports that he can add five tallies to this parent-pair count, and suggests that such results might indicate that the specific heredity is dominant, and completely penetrant, rather than recessive. The attempt to replicate these findings, and other psychometric efforts to tap subclinical cognitive slippage in the "normal" relatives of schizophrenics, should receive top priority in our research efforts.

Summarizing, I hypothesize that the statistical relation between schizotaxia, schizotypy, and schizophrenia is class inclusion: All schizotaxics become, *on all actually existing social learning regimes,* schizotypic in personality organization; but most of these remain compensated. A minority, disadvantaged by other (largely polygenically determined) constitutional weaknesses, and put on a bad regime by schizophrenogenic mothers (most of whom are themselves schizotypes), are thereby potentiated into clinical schizophrenia. What makes schizotaxic etiologically specific is its role as a *necessary* condition. I postulate that a nonschizotaxic individual, whatever his other genetic makeup and whatever his learning history, would at most develop a character disorder or a psychoneurosis; but he would not become a schizotype and therefore would never manifest its decompensated form, schizophrenia.

What sort of quantitative aberration in the structural or functional parameters of the nervous system can we conceive to be directly determined by a mutated gene, and to so alter initial dispositions that affected individuals will, in the course of their childhood learning history, develop the four schizotypal source traits: cognitive slippage, anhedonia, ambivalence, and interpersonal aversiveness? To me, the most baffling thing about the disorder is the phenotypic heterogeneity of this tetrad. If one sets himself to the task of doing a theoretical Vigotsky job on this list of psychological dispositions, he may manage part of it by invoking a sufficiently vague kind of descriptive unity between ambivalence and interpersonal aversiveness; and perhaps even anhedonia could be somehow subsumed. But the cognitive slippage presents a real roadblock. Since I consider cognitive slippage to be a core element in schizophrenia, any characterization of schizophrenic or schizotypic behavior which purports to abstract its essence but does not include the cognitive slippage must be deemed unsatisfactory. I believe that an adequate theoretical account will necessitate moving downward in the pyramid of the sciences to invoke explanatory constructs not found in social, psychodynamic, or even learning theory language, but instead at the neurophysiological level.

Perhaps we don't know enough about "how the brain works" to theorize profitably at that level; and I daresay that the more a psychologist knows about the latest research on brain function, the more reluctant he would be to engage in etiological speculation. Let me entreat my physiologically expert listeners to be charitable toward this clinician's premature speculations about how the schizotaxic brain might work. I feel partially justified in such speculation because there are some well-attested general truths about mammalian learned behavior which could almost have been set down from the armchair, in the way engineers draw block diagrams indicating what kinds of parts or subsystems a physical system *must* have, and what their interconnections *must* be, in order to function "appropriately." Brain research of the last decade provides a direct neurophysiological substrate for such cardinal behavior requirements as avoidance, escape, reward, drive differentiation, general and specific arousal or activation, and the like (see Delafresnaye, 1961; Ramey & O'Doherty, 1960). The discovery in the limbic system of specific positive reinforcement centers by Olds and Milner in 1954, and of aversive centers in the same year by Delgado, Roberts, and Miller (1954), seems to me to have an importance that can scarcely be exaggerated; and while the ensuing lines of research on the laws of intracranial stimulation as a mode of behavior control present some puzzles and paradoxes, what *has* been shown up to now may already suffice to provide a theoretical framework. As a general kind of brain model let us take a broadly Hebbian conception in combination with the findings on intracranial stimulation.

To avoid repetition I shall list some basic assumptions first but introduce others in context and only implicitly when the implication is obvious. I shall assume that:

When a presynaptic cell participates in firing a postsynaptic cell, the former gains an increment in firing control over the latter. Coactivation of anatomically connected cell assemblies or assembly systems therefore increases their stochastic control linkage, and the frequency of discharges by neurons of a system may be taken as an intensity variable influencing the growth rate of intersystem control linkage as well as the momentary activity level induced in the other systems. (I shall dichotomize acquired cortical systems into "perceptual-cognitive," including central representations of goal objects; and "instrumental," including overarching monitor systems which select and guide specific effector patterns.)

Most learning in mature organisms involves altering control linkages between systems which themselves have been consolidated by previous learnings, sometimes requiring thousands of activations and not necessarily related to the reinforcement operation to the extent that perceptual-to-instrumental linkage growth functions are.

Control linkage increments from coactivation depend heavily, if not entirely, upon a period of reverberatory activity facilitating consolidation.

Feedback from positive limbic centers is facilitative to concurrent perceptual-cognitive or instrumental sequences, whereas negative center feedback exerts an inhibitory influence. (These statements refer to initial features of the direct wiring diagram, not to all long-term results of learning.) Aversive input also has excitatory effects via the arousal system, which maintain activity permitting escape learning to occur because the organism is alerted and keeps doing things. But I postulate that this overall influence is working along with an opposite effect, quite clear from both molar and intracranial experiments, that a major biological function of aversive-center activation is to produce "stoppage" of whatever the organism is currently doing.

Perceptual-cognitive systems and limbic motivational control centers develop two-way mutual control (e.g., discriminative stimuli acquire the reinforcing property; "thoughts" become pleasantly toned; drive-relevant perceptual components are "souped-up").

What kind of heritable parametric aberration could underlie the schizotaxic's readiness to acquire the schizotypic tetrad? It would seem, first of all, that the defect is much more likely to reside in the neurone's synaptic control function than in its storage function. It is hard to conceive of a general defect in storage which would on the one hand permit so many perceptual-cognitive functions, such as tapped by intelligence tests, school learning, or the high order cognitive powers displayed by some schizotypes, and yet have the diffuse motivational and emotional effects found in these same individuals. I am not saying that a storage deficit is clearly excludable, but it hardly seems the best place to look. So we direct our attention to parameters of control.

One possibility is to take the anhedonia as fundamental. What is *phenomenologically* a radical pleasure deficiency may be roughly identified *behaviorally* with a quantitative deficit in the positive reinforcement growth constant, and each of these—the "inner" and "outer" aspects of the organism's appetitive control system—reflect a quantitative deficit in the limbic "positive" centers. The anhedonia would then be a direct consequence of the genetic defect in wiring. Ambivalence and interpersonal aversiveness would be quantitative deviations in the balance of appetitive-aversive controls. Most perceptual-cognitive and instrumental learnings occur under mixed positive and negative schedules, so the normal consequence is a collection of habits and expectancies varying widely in the intensity of their positive and negative components, but mostly "mixed" in character. Crudely put, everybody has *some* ambivalence about almost everything, and everybody has *some* capacity for "social fear." Now if the brain centers which mediate phenomenal pleasure and behavioral reward are numerically sparse or functionally feeble, the aversive centers meanwhile functioning normally, the long-term result would be a general shift toward the aversive end, appearing clinically as ambivalence and exaggerated interpersonal fear. If, as Brady believes, there is a wired-in reciprocal inhibiting relation between positive and negative centers, the long-term aversive drift would be further potentiated (i.e., what we see at the molar level as a sort of "softening" or "soothing" effect of feeding or petting upon anxiety elicitors would be reduced).

Cognitive slippage is not as easy to fit in, but if we assume that normal ego function is acquired by a combination of social reinforcements and the self-reinforcements which become available to the child via identification, then we might say roughly that "everybody has to learn *how* to think straight." Rationality is socially acquired; the secondary process and the reality principle are slowly and imperfectly learned, by even the most clear headed. Insofar as slippage is manifested in the social sphere, such an explanation has some plausibility. An overall aversive drift would account for the paradoxical schizotypic combination of interpersonal distortions and acute perceptiveness of others unconscious, since the latter is really a hypersensitivity to aversive signals rather than an overall superiority in realistically discriminating social cues. On the output side, we might view the cognitive slippage of mildly schizoid speech as originating from poorly consolidated second-order "monitor" assembly systems which function in an editing role, their momentary regnancy constituting the "set to communicate." At this level, selection among competing verbal operants involves slight differences in appropriateness for which a washed-out social reinforcement history provides an insufficiently refined monitor system. However, if one is impressed with the presence of a pervasive and primary slippage, showing up in a diversity of tests (cf. Payne, 1961) and also on occasions when the patient is desperately trying to communicate, an explanation on the basis of deficient positive center activity is not too convincing.

This hypothesis has some other troubles which I shall merely indicate. Schizoid anhedonia is mainly interpersonal, i.e., schizotypes seem to derive adequate pleasure from esthetic and cognitive rewards. Secondly, some successful psychotherapeutic results include what appears to be a genuine normality of hedonic capacity. Thirdly, regressive electroshock sometimes has the same effect, and the animal evidence suggests that shock works by knocking out the aversive control system rather than by souping up appetitive centers. Finally, if the anhedonia is really general in extent, it is hard to conceive of any simple genetic basis for weakening the different positive centers, whose reactivity has been shown by Olds and others to be chemically drive specific.

A second neurological hypothesis takes the slippage factor as primary. Suppose that the immediate consequence of whatever biochemical aberration the gene directly controls were a specific alteration in the neurone's membrane stability, such that the distribution of optional transmission probabilities is more widely dispersed over the synaptic signal space than in normals. That is, presynaptic input signals whose spatio-temporal configuration locates them peripherally in the neurone's signal space yield transmission probabilities which are relatively closer to those at the maximum point, thereby producing a kind of dedifferentiation or flattening of the cell's selectivity. Under suitable parametric assumptions, this synaptic slippage would lead to a corresponding dedifferentiation of competing interassembly controls, because the elements in the less frequently or intensely coactivated control assembly would be accumulating control increments more rapidly than normal. Consider a perceptual-cognitive system whose regnancy is preponderantly associated with positive-center coactivation but sometimes with aversive. The cumulation of control increments will draw these apart; but if synaptic slippage exists, their difference, at least during intermediate stages of control development, will be attenuated. The intensity of aversive-center activation by a given level of perceptual-cognitive system activity will be exaggerated relative to that induced in the positive centers. For a preponderantly aversive control this will be reversed. But now the different algebraic sign of the feedbacks introduces an important asymmetry. Exaggerated negative feedback will tend to lower activity level in the predominantly appetitive case, retarding the growth of the control linkage; whereas exaggerated positive feedback in the predominantly aversive case will tend to heighten activity levels, accelerating the linkage growth. The long-term tendency will be that movement in the negative direction which I call *aversive drift*. In addition to the asymmetry generated by the difference in feedback signs, certain other features in the mixed-regime setup contribute to aversive drift. One factor is the characteristic difference between positive and negative reinforcers in their role as strengtheners. It seems a fairly safe generalization to say that positive centers function only weakly as strengtheners when "on" continuously, and mainly when they are turned on as terminators of a cognitive or instrumental sequence; by contrast, negative centers work mainly as "off" signals, tending to inhibit elements while steadily "on." We may suppose that the former strengthen mainly by facilitating post-activity reverberation (and hence consolidation) in successful systems, the latter mainly by holding down such reverberation in unsuccessful ones. Now a slippage-heightened aversive steady state during predominantly appetitive control sequences reduces their activity level, leaves fewer recently active elements available for a subsequent Olds-plus "on" signal to consolidate. Whereas a slippage-heightened Olds-plus steady state during predominantly aversive-control sequences (*a*) increases their negative control *during* the "on" period and (*b*) leaves relatively more of their elements recently active and hence further consolidated by the negative "off" signal when it occurs. Another factor is exaggerated competition by aversively controlled sequences, whereby the appetitive chains do not continue to the stage of receiving socially mediated positive reinforcement, because avoidant chains (e.g., phobic behavior, withdrawal, intellectualization) are getting in the way. It is worth mentioning that the schizophrenogenic mother's regime is presumably "mixed" not only in the sense of the frequent and unpredictable aversive inputs she provides in response to the child's need signals, but also in her greater tendency to present such aversive inputs *concurrently* with drive reducers—thereby facilitating the "scrambling" of appetitive-and-aversive controls so typical of schizophrenia.

The schizotype's dependency guilt and aversive overreaction to offers of help are here seen as residues of the early knitting together of his cortical representations of appetitive goals with punishment-expectancy assembly systems. Roughly speaking, he has learned that to want anything interpersonally provided is to be endangered.

The cognitive slippage is here conceived as a direct molar consequence of synaptic slippage, potentiated by the disruptive effects of aversive control and inadequate development of interpersonal communication sets. Cognitive and instrumental linkages based upon sufficiently massive and consistent regimes, such as reaching for a seen pencil, will converge to asymptotes hardly distinguishable from the normal. But systems involving closely competing strengths and automatized selection among alternatives, especially when the main basis of acquisition and control is social reward, will exhibit evidences of malfunction.

My third speculative model revives a notion with a long history, namely, that the primary schizotaxic defect is a quantitative deficiency of inhibition. (In the light of Milner's revision of Hebb, in which the inhibitory action of Golgi Type II cells is crucial even for the formation of functionally differentiated cell assemblies, a defective inhibitory parameter could be an alternative basis for a kind of slippage similar in its consequences to the one we have just finished discussing.) There are two things about this somewhat moth-eaten "defective inhibition" idea which I find appealing. First, it is the most direct and uncomplicated neurologizing of the schizoid cognitive slippage. Schizoid cognitive slippage is neither an incapacity to link, nor is it an unhealthy over-capacity to link; rather it seems to be a defective *control* over associations which are also accessible to the healthy (as in dreams, wit, psycho-analytic free association, and certain types of creative work) but are normally "edited out" or "automatically suppressed" by those super-ordinate monitoring assembly systems we lump together under the term "set." Secondly, in working with pseudoneurotic cases one sees a phenomenon to which insufficient theoretical attention has been paid: Namely, these patients cannot turn off painful thoughts. They suffer constantly and intensely from painful thoughts about themselves, about possible adverse outcomes, about the past, about the attitudes and in-tentions of others. The "weak ego" of schizophrenia means a number of things, one of which is failure of defense; the schizophrenic has too ready access to his own id, and is too perceptive of the unconscious of others. It is tempting to read "failure of defense" as "quantitatively deficient inhibitory feedback." As mentioned earlier, aversive signals (whether exteroceptive or internally originated) must exert both an exciting effect via the arousal system and a quick-stoppage effect upon cortical sequences which fail to terminate the ongoing aversive signal, leading the organism to shift to another. Suppose the gene resulted in an insufficient produc-tion (or too rapid inactivation) of the specific inhibitory transmitter substance, rendering all inhibitory neurones quantitatively weaker than normal. When aversively linked cognitive sequences activate negative limbic centers, these in turn soup up the arousal system normally but provide a subnormal inhibitory feedback, thereby permitting their elicitor to persist for a longer time and at higher intensity than normal. This further activates the negative control center, and so on, until an equilibrium level is reached which is above normal in intensity all around, and which meanwhile permits an excessive linkage growth in the aversive chain. (In this respect the semicompensated case would differ from the late-stage deteriorated schizophrenic, whose aversive drift has gradually proliferated so widely that almost any cognitive or instru-mental chain elicits an overlearned defensive "stoppage," whereby even the inner life undergoes a profound and diffuse impoverishment.)

The mammalian brain is so wired that aversive signals tend to produce stoppage of regnant cognitive or instrumental sequences without the aversive signal having been specifically connected to their controlling cues or motivational systems. E.g., lever pressing under thirst or hunger can be inhibited by shock-associated buzzer, even though the latter has not been previously connected with hunger, paired with the discriminative stimulus, nor presented as punishment for the operant. A deficient capacity to inhibit concurrent activity of fringe elements (aversively connected to ambiguous social inputs from ambivalent mother) would accelerate the growth linkages between them and appetitive systems not hitherto punished. Sequential effects are here especially important, and combine with the schizophrenogenic mother's tendency not to provide differential cues of high consistency as predictors of whether aversive or appetitive consequences will follow upon the child's indications of demand.

Consider two cortical systems having shared "fringe" subsystems (e.g., part percepts of mother's face). When exteroceptive inputs are the elicitors, negative feedback from aversive centers cannot usually produce stoppage; in the absence of such overdetermining external controls, the relative activity levels are determined by the balance of facilitative and inhibitory feedbacks. "Fringe" assemblies which have already acquired more aversive control, if they begin to be activated by regnant perceptual-cognitive sequences, will increase inhibitory feedback; and being "fringe" they can thereby be held down. The schizotaxic, whose aversive-feedback stoppage of fringe-element activity is weakened, accumulates excessive intertrial Hebbian increments toward the aversive side, the predominantly aversive fringe elements being more active and becoming more knit into the system than normally. On subsequent exteroceptively controlled trials, whenever the overdetermining stimulus input activates predominantly aversive perceptual-cognitive assembles, their driving of the negative centers will be heightened. The resulting negative feedback may now be strong enough so that, when imposed upon "fringe" assemblies weakly activated and toward the appetitive side, it can produce stoppage. On such occasions the more appetitive fringe elements will be retarded in their linkage growth, receiving fewer Hebbian increments. And those which do get over threshold will become further linked during such trials to the concurrent negative center activity. The result is twofold: a retarded growth of appetitive perceptual-cognitive linkages, and a progressive drawing of fringe elements into the aversive ambit.

"Ambiguous regimes," where the pairing of S+ and S− inputs occurs very unpredictably, will have a larger number of fringe elements. Also, if the external schedule is dependent upon regnant appetitive drive states as manifested in the child's instrumental social acts, so that these are often met with mixed S+ (drive-relevant) and S− (anxiety-eliciting) inputs, the appetitive and aversive assemblies will tend to become linked, and to activate positive and negative centers concurrently. The anhedonia and ambivalence would be consequences of this plus-minus "scrambling," especially if the positive and negative limbic centers are mutually inhibitory but here deficiently so. We would then expect schizotypic anhedonia to be basically interpersonal, and only derivatively present, if at all, in other contexts. This would in part explain the schizotype's preservation of relatively normal function in a large body of instrumental domains. For example, the acquisition of basic motor and cognitive skills would be relatively less geared to a mixed input, since "successful" mastery is both mechanically rewarded (e.g., how to open a door) and also interpersonally rewarded as "school success," etc. The hypercathexis of intellect, often found even among nonbright schizotypes, might arise from the fact that these performances are rewarded rather "impersonally" and make minimal demands on the reinforcing others. Also, the same cognitive and mechanical instrumental acts can often be employed both to turn on positive center feedback and to turn off negative, an equivalence much less true of purely social signals linked to interpersonal needs.

Having briefly sketched three neurological possibilities for the postulated schizotaxic aberration, let me emphasize that while each has sufficient merit to be worth pursuing, they are mainly meant to be illustrative of the vague concept "integrative neural defect." I shall myself not be surprised if all three are refuted, whereas I shall be astounded if future research shows no fundamental aberration in nerve-cell function in the schizotype. Postulating schizotaxia as an open concept seems at first to pose a search problem of needle-in-haystack proportions, but I suggest that the plausible alternatives are really somewhat limited. After all, what does a neuron do to another neuron? It excites, or it inhibits! The schizotypic preservation of relatively normal function in selected domains directs our search toward some minimal deviation in a synaptic control parameter, as opposed to, say, a gross defect in cell distribution or structure, or the kind of biochemical anomaly that yields mental deficiency. Anything which would give rise to defective storage, grossly impaired transmission, or sizable limitations on functional complexity can be pretty well excluded on present evidence. What we are looking for is a quantitative aberration in synaptic control—a deviation in amount or patterning of excitatory or inhibitory action—capable of yielding cumulative departures from normal control linkages under mixed appetitive-aversive regimes; but slight enough to permit convergence to quasi-normal asymptotes under more consistent schedules (or when massive repetition with motive-incentive factors unimportant is the chief basis for consolidation). The defect must generate aversive drift on mixed social reinforcement regimes, and must yield a primary cognitive slippage which, however, may be extremely small in magnitude except as potentiated by the cumulative effects of aversive drift. Taken together these molar constraints limit our degrees of freedom considerably when it comes to filling in the neurophysiology of schizotaxia. Leaving aside the specific nature of schizotaxia, we must now raise the familiar question [of] whether such a basic neurological defect, however subtle and nonstructural it might be, should not have been demonstrated hitherto. In reply to this objection I shall content myself with pointing out that there are several lines of evidence which, while not strongly arguing *for* a neurological theory, are rebuttals of an argument presupposing clear and consistent *negative* findings. For example: Ignoring several early European reports with inadequate controls, the literature contains a half-dozen quantitative studies showing marked vestibular system dysfunction in schizophrenics (Angyal & Blackman, 1940, 1941; Angyal & Sherman, 1942; Colbert & Koegler, 1959; Freeman & Rodnick, 1942; Leach, 1960; Payne & Hewlett, 1960; Pollock & Krieger, 1958). Hoskins (1946) concluded that a neurological defect in the vestibular system was one of the few clear-cut biological findings in the Worcester studies. It is of prime importance to replicate these findings among compensated and pseudoneurotic cases, where the diffuse withdrawal and deactivation factor would not provide the explanation it does in the chronic, burnt-out case (cf. Collins, Crampton, & Posner, 1961). Another line of evidence is in the work of King (1954) on psychomotor deficit, noteworthy for its careful use of task simplicity, asymptote performance, concern for patient cooperation, and inclusion of an outpatient pseudoneurotic sample. King himself regards his data as indicative of a rather basic behavior defect, although he does not hold it to be schizophrenia-specific. Then we have such research as that of Barbara Fish (1961) indicating the occurrence of varying signs of perceptual-motor maldevelopment among infants and children who subsequently manifest clinical schizophrenia. The earlier work of Schilder and Bender along these lines is of course well known, and there has always been a strong minority report in clinical psychiatry that many schizophrenics provide subtle and fluctuating neurological signs of the "soft" variety, if one keeps alert to notice or elicit them. I have myself been struck by the frequent occurrence, even among pseudoneurotic patients, of transitory neurologic-like complaints (e.g., diplopia, localized weakness, one-sided tremor, temperature dyscontrol, dizziness, disorientation) which seem to lack dynamic meaning or secondary gain and whose main effect upon the patient is to produce bafflement and anxiety. I have seen preliminary findings by J. McVicker Hunt and his students in which a rather dramatic quantitative deficiency in spatial cognizing is detectable in schizophrenics of above-normal verbal intelligence. Research by Cleveland (1960; Cleveland, Fisher, Reitman, & Rothaus, 1962) and by Arnhoff and Damianopoulos (in press) on the clinically well-known body-image anomalies in schizophrenia suggests that this domain yields quantitative departures from the norm of such magnitude that with further instrumental and statistical refinement it might be used as a quasi-pathognomonic sign of the disease. It is interesting to note a certain thread of unity running through this evidence, which perhaps lends support to Rado's hypothesis that a kinesthetic integrative defect is even more characteristic of schizotypy than is the radical anhedonia.

All these kinds of data are capable of a psychodynamic interpretation. "Soft" neurological signs are admittedly ambiguous, especially when found in the severely decompensated case. The only point I wish to make here is that *since* they exist and are at present unclear in etiology, an otherwise plausible neurological view cannot be refuted on the ground that there is a *lack* of any sign of neurological dysfuntion in schizophrenia; there is no such lack.

Time forces me to leave detailed research strategy for another place, but the main directions are obvious and may be stated briefly: The clinician's Mental Status ratings on anhedonia, ambivalence, and interpersonal aversiveness should be objectified and preferably replaced by psychometric measures. The research findings on cognitive slippage, psychomotor dyscontrol, vestibular malfunction, body image, and other spatial aberrations should be thoroughly replicated and extended into the pseudoneurotic and semicompensated ranges. If these efforts succeed, it will be possible to set up a multiple sign pattern, using optimal cuts on phenotypically diverse indicators, for identifying compensated schizotypes in the nonclinical population. Statistics used must be appropriate to the theoretical model of a dichotomous latent taxonomy reflecting itself in otherwise independent quantitative indicators. Family concordance studies should then be run relating proband schizophrenia to schizotypy as identified by this multiple indicator pattern. Meanwhile we should carry on an active and varied search for more direct neurological signs of schizotaxia, concentrating our hunches on novel stimulus inputs (e.g., the stabilized retinal image situation) which may provide a better context for basic neural dysfunction to show up instead of being masked by learned compensations or imitated by psychopathology.

In closing, I should like to take this unusual propaganda opportunity to play the prophet. It is my strong personal conviction that such a research strategy will enable psychologists to make a unique contribution in the near future, using psychological techniques to establish that schizophrenia, while its content is learned, is fundamentally a neurological disease of genetic origin.

Paul E. Meehl   223

REFERENCES

ANGYAL, A., & BLACKMAN, N. Vestibular reactivity in schizophrenia. *Arch. Neurol. Psychiat.*, 1940, **44**, 611–620.

ANGYAL, A., & BLACKMAN, N. Paradoxical reactions in schizophrenia under the influence of alcohol, hyperpnea, and CO_2 inhalation. *Amer. J. Psychiat.*, 1941, **97**, 893–903.

ANGYAL, A., & SHERMAN, N. Postural reactions to vestibular stimulation in schizophrenic and normal subjects. *Amer. J. Psychiat.*, 1942, **98**, 857–862.

ARNHOFF, F., & DAMIANOPOULOS, E. Self-body recognition and schizophrenia: An exploratory study. *J. abnorm. soc. Psychol.*, in press.

BLEULER, E. *Theory of schizophrenic negativism.* New York: Nervous and Mental Disease Publishing, 1912.

BLEULER, E. *Dementia praecox.* New York: International Universities Press, 1950.

CLEVELAND, S. E. Judgment of body size in a schizophrenic and a control group. *Psychol. Rep.*, 1960, **7**, 304.

CLEVELAND, S. E., FISHER, S., REITMAN, E. E., & ROTHAUS, P. Perception of body size in schizophrenia. *Arch. gen. Psychiat.*, 1962, **7**, 277–285.

COLBERT, G., & KOEGLER, R. Vestibular dysfunction in childhood schizophrenia. *AMA Arch. gen. Psychiat.*, 1959, **1**, 600–617.

COLLINS, W. E., CRAMPTON, G. H., & POSNER, J. B. The effect of mental set upon vestibular nystagmus and the EEG. *USA Med. Res. Lab. Rep.*, 1961, No. 439.

DELAFRESNAYE, J. F. (Ed.) *Brain mechanisms and learning.* Springfield. Ill.: Charles C Thomas, 1961.

DELGADO, J. M. R., ROBERTS, W. W., & MILLER, N. E. Learning motivated by electrical stimulation of the brain. *Amer. J. Physiol.*, 1954, **179**, 587–593.

FISH, BARBARA. The study of motor development in infancy and its relationship to psychological functioning. *Amer. J. Psychiat.*, 1961, **117**, 1113–1118.

FREEMAN, H., & RODNICK, E. H. Effect of rotation on postural steadiness in normal and schizophrenic subjects. *Arch. Neurol. Psychiat.*, 1942, **48**, 47–53.

FULLER, J. L., & THOMPSON, W. R. *Behavior genetics.* New York: Wiley, 1960. Pp. 272–283.

HOSKINS, R. G. *The biology of schizophrenia.* New York: Norton, 1946.

KING, H. E. *Psychomotor aspects of mental disease.* Cambridge: Harvard Univer. Press, 1954.

LEACH, W. W. Nystagmus: An integrative neural deficit in schizophrenia. *J. abnorm. soc. Psychol.*, 1960, **60**, 305–309.

LIDZ, T., CORNELISON, A., TERRY, D., & FLECK, S. Intrafamilial environment of the schizophrenic patient: VI. The transmission of irrationality. *AMA Arch. Neurol. Psychiat.*, 1958, **79**, 305–316.

MCCONAGHY, N. The use of an object sorting test in elucidating the hereditary factor in schizophrenia. *J. Neurol. Neurosurg. Psychiat.*, 1959, **22**, 243–246.

MEYERS, D., & GOLDFARB, W. Psychiatric appraisals of parents and siblings of schizophrenic children. *Amer. J. Psychiat.*, 1962, **118**, 902–908.

OLDS, J., & MILNER, P. Positive reinforcement produced by electrical stimulation of septal area and other regions of rat brain. *J. comp. physiol. Psychol.,* 1954, 47, 419–427.

PAYNE, R. W. Cognitive abnormalities. In H. J. Eysenck (Ed.), *Handbook of abnormal psychology.* New York: Basic Books, 1961. Pp. 248–250.

PAYNE, R. S., & HEWLETT, J. H. G. Thought disorder in psychotic patients. In H. J. Eysenck (Ed.), *Experiments in personality.* Vol. 2. London: Routledge, Kegan, Paul, 1960. Pp. 3–106.

POLLACK, M., & KRIEGER, H. P. Oculomotor and postural patterns in schizophrenic children. *AMA Arch. Neurol. Psychiat.,* 1958, 79, 720–726.

RADO, S. *Psychoanalysis of behavior.* New York: Grune & Stratton, 1956.

RADO, S., & DANIELS, G. *Changing concepts of psychoanalytic medicine.* New York: Grune & Stratton, 1956.

RAMEY, E. R., & O'DOHERTY, D. S. (Eds.) *Electrical studies on the unanesthetized brain.* New York: Hoeber, 1960.

ROSENTHAL, D. Problems of sampling and diagnosis in the major twin studies of schizophrenia. *J. psychiat. Res.,* in press.

STERN, K. *Principles of human genetics.* San Francisco: Freeman, 1960. Pp. 581–584.

Excerpt from the relation of habitual thought and behavior to language

Benjamin Lee Whorf

INTRODUCTION   It has been said that the fish will be the last organism to discover water. Why? Because, the argument goes, the fish is surrounded by it. So it is with man trying to discover cultural influences on his behavior. It is difficult for an individual, surrounded by his own culture, to be cognizant of its impact on him. Often the only way we can become aware of cultural influences on our behavior is to study the way other people behave in cultures different from our own. Such cross-cultural research allows us to "get outside" our own culture and see it more as an observer than a participant.

One man who used the cross-cultural approach to great advantage was Benjamin Lee Whorf. By examining different cultures he was able to show that the language a person spoke influenced the manner in which he viewed his world. In the following article Whorf shows how our behavior is a function of the language we speak. He does so in an interesting manner: by claiming that the causes of some fires are due not to carelessness or arson but to the linguistic habits of the people who start them! And Whorf should know about such things—his examples are drawn from actual case studies, collected while he was a fire inspector for the Hartford Life Insurance Company.

There will probably be general assent to the proposition that an accepted pattern of using words is often prior to certain lines of thinking and forms of behavior, but he who assents often sees in such a statement nothing more than a platitudinous recognition of the hypnotic power of philosophical and learned terminology on the one hand or of

B. L. Whorf, "The relation of habitual thought and behavior to language," in *Language, Culture and Personality* (essays in memory of Edward Sapir), edited by Leslie Spier. Menasha, Wis.: Sapir Memorial Publication Fund, 1941.

catchwords, slogans, and rallying-cries on the other. To see only thus far is to miss the point of one of the important interconnections which Sapir saw between language, culture, and psychology. . . . It is not so much in these special uses of language as in its constant ways of arranging data and its most ordinary every-day analysis of phenomena that we need to recognize the influence it has on other activities, cultural and personal.

THE NAME OF THE SITUATION AS AFFECTING BEHAVIOR

I came in touch with an aspect of this problem before I had studied under Dr. Sapir, and in a field usually considered remote from linguistics. It was in the course of my professional work for a fire insurance company, in which I undertook the task of analyzing many hundreds of reports of circumstances surrounding the start of fires, and in some cases, of explosions. My analysis was directed toward purely physical conditions, such as defective wiring, presence or lack of air spaces between metal flues and woodwork, etc., and the results were presented in these terms. Indeed it was undertaken with no thought that any other significances would or could be revealed. But in due course it became evident that not only a physical situation *qua* physics, but the meaning of that situation to people, was sometimes a factor, through the behavior of the people, in the start of the fire. And this factor of meaning was clearest when it was a *linguistic meaning*, residing in the name or the linguistic description commonly applied to the situaton. Thus around a storage of what are called "gasoline drums" behavior will tend to a certain type, that is, great care will be exercised; while around a storage of what are called "empty gasoline drums" it will tend to be different—careless, with little repression of smoking or of tossing cigarette stubs about. Yet the "empty" drums are perhaps the more dangerous, since they contain explosive vapor. Physically the situation is hazardous, but the linguistic analysis according to regular analogy must employ the word "empty," which inevitably suggests lack of hazard. The word "empty" is used in two linguistic patterns: (1) as a virtual synonym for "null and void, negative, inert," (2) applied in analysis of physical situations without regard to, e.g., vapor, liquid vestiges, or stray rubbish, in the container. The situation is named in one pattern (2) and the name is then "acted out" or "lived up to" in another (1); this being a general formula for the linguistic conditioning of behavior into hazardous forms.

In a wood distillation plant the metal stills were insulated with a composition prepared from limestone and called at the plant "spun limestone." No attempt was made to protect this covering from excessive heat or the contact of flame. After a period of use the fire below one of the stills spread to the "limestone," which to everyone's great surprise burned vigorously. Exposure to acetic acid fumes from the stills had converted part of the limestone (calcium carbonate) to calcium acetate. This when heated in a fire decomposes, forming inflammable acetone. Behavior that tolerated fire close to the covering was induced by use of the name "limestone," which because it ends in "stone" implies noncombustibility.

A huge iron kettle of boiling varnish was observed to be overheated, nearing the temperature at which it would ignite. The operator moved it off the fire and ran it on its wheels to a distance, but did not cover it. In a minute or so the varnish ignited. Here the linguistic influence is more complex; it is due to the metaphorical objectifying . . . of "cause" as contact or the spatial juxtaposition of "things"—to analyzing the situation as "on" versus "off" the fire. In reality the stage when the external fire was the main factor had passed; the overheating was now an internal process of convection in the varnish from the intensely heated kettle, and still continued when "off" the fire.

An electric glow heater on the wall was little used, and for one workman had the meaning of a convenient coat-hanger. At night a watchman entered and snapped a switch, which action he verbalized as "turning on the light." No light appeared, and this result he verbalized as "light is burned out." He could not see the glow of the heater because of the old coat hung on it. Soon the heater ignited the coat, which set fire to the building.

A tannery discharged waste water containing animal matter into an outdoor settling basin partly roofed with wood and partly open. This situation is one that ordinarily would be verbalized as "pool of water." A workman had occasion to light a blow-torch nearby, and threw his match into the water. But the decomposing waste matter was evolving gas under the wood cover, so that the setup was the reverse of "watery." An instant flare of flame ignited the woodwork, and the fire quickly spread into the adjoining building.

A drying room for hides was arranged with a blower at one end to make a current of air along the room and thence outdoors through a vent at the other end. Fire started at a hot bearing on the blower, which blew the flames directly into the hides and fanned them along the room destroying the entire stock. This hazardous setup followed naturally from the term "blower" with its linguistic equivalence to "that which blows," implying that its function necessarily is to "blow." Also its function is verbalized as "blowing air for drying," overlooking that it can blow other things, e.g., flames and sparks. In reality a blower simply makes a current of air and can exhaust as well as blow. It should have been installed at the vent end to *draw* the air over the hides, then through the hazard (its own casing and bearings) and thence outdoors.

Beside a coal-fired melting pot for lead reclaiming was dumped a pile of "scrap lead"—a misleading verbalization, for it consisted of the lead sheets of old radio condensers, which still had paraffin paper between them. Soon the paraffin blazed up and fired the roof, half of which was burned off.

Such examples, which could be greatly multiplied, will suffice to show how the cue to a certain line of behavior is often given by the analogies of the linguistic formula in which the situation is spoken of, and by which to some degree it is analyzed, classified, and allotted its place in that world which is "to a large extent unconsciously built up on the language habits of the group." And we always assume that the linguistic analysis made by our group reflects reality better than it does.

Cultural differences in the perception of geometric illusions

Marshall Segall, Donald Campbell and Melville Herskovits

INTRODUCTION   Around 440 B.C. there lived a Greek Sophist named Protagoras of Abdera, who had some rather interesting notions about perception. This man rejected the concept of objective truth. Knowledge, he maintained, is whatever people construe it to be. The act of perceiving, according to Protagoras, is a creative form of behavior and depends upon the individual's unique history of experience. Consequently, the character of perception varies from individual to individual.

Such a belief—that each person perceives the world in his own way —is still held by many contemporary scientists and philosophers. In the following article we will see that peoples' perceptions also vary from culture to culture, due to the unique history of experience shared by groups of individuals in different parts of the world.

Stimulus materials based upon geometric illusions were prepared in 1956 for standardized administration under varying field conditions in an effort to encourage the collection of cross-cultural data that might bear on the nativist-empiricist controversy concerning space perception (*1*). Over a 6-year period anthropologists and psychologists administered these tests to 14 non-European samples of children and adults, ranging in size from 46 to 344 in 12 locations in Africa and one in the Philippines, to a sample (*N* = 44) of South Africans of European descent in Johannesburg, to an American undergraduate sample (*N* = 30), and to a house-to-house sample (*N* = 208) in Evanston, Ill. In all, data were

"Cultural Differences in the Perception of Geometric Illusions," Segall, M., et al., *Science*, Vol. 139, pp. 769–771, 22 February 1963. Copyright 1963 by the American Association for the Advancement of Science.

collected from 1878 persons. Analysis of these protocols provides evidence of substantial cross-cultural differences in response to these materials. The nature of these differences constitutes strong support for the empiricistic hypothesis that the perception of space involves, to an important extent, the acquisition of habits of perceptual inference.

The stimulus materials to be considered here consisted of 39 items, each one a variation of one of four figures constructed of straight lines, generally referred to in the psychological literature as perceptual, or geometric, illusions. These were the Müller-Lyer figure (12 items), the Sander Parallelogram (seven), and two forms of the Horizontal-vertical figure (nine and eleven). For each illusion the discrepancy in length of the segments to be compared varied from item to item so as to permit the employment of a version of the psychophysical method of constant stimuli. As each stimulus was shown to a respondent, his task was simply to indicate the longer of two linear segments. To minimize difficulties of communication, the materials were designed so that the linear segments to be compared were not connected to the other lines, and were printed in different colors. Respondents could indicate choice by selecting one of two colors (saying *red* or *black*) in response to the Horizonal-vertical items, and by indicating *right* or *left* for the other illusions. Other steps taken to enhance the validity of response protocols included the administration of a short comprehension test requiring judgments similar to, but more obvious than, those demanded by the stimulus figures. Nonetheless, since no amount of precautionary measures could insure the elimination of all sources of error (for example, communication difficulties, response sets, and so forth) which could result in artifactually produced cross-cultural differences, an internal consistency check was made and all protocols containing gross departures from orderliness were withheld from analysis. (Another analysis was performed with all 1878 cases included, and the results were substantially the same as those obtained in the analysis of consistent cases only.)

The analysis proceeded as follows: Each respondent's four protocols were first examined for evidence of internal consistency. To be considered consistent, a protocol had to contain no more than one Guttman error (2). Each consistent protocol was then assigned a score which was simply the total number of times in that stimulus set that the respondent chose the typically overestimated segment. The mean of these scores was computed for each sample, and differences between pairs of means were evaluated by t-tests with significance levels modified by the Scheffé procedure (3) to compensate for the increase in error rate that accompanies nonindependent, multiple comparisons.

On both the Müller-Lyer and Sander Parallelogram illusions the three "European" samples made significantly more illusion-produced responses than did the non-European samples. (The innumerable t ratios resulting can only be sampled here. For example, on the Müller-Lyer illusion, comparisons of the Evanston sample with the non-European samples resulted in t ratios ranging from 7.96 to 15.39. A value of 3.57 is significant at the $p = .05$ level by the Scheffé test.) On the latter two illusions, the European samples had relatively low scores, with many, but not all, of the non-European samples having significantly larger mean scores. (For these illusions, the largest t ratios, up to 17.41, were found between pairs of non-European groups. Comparisons involving the Evanston sample and five non-European groups resulted in t's ranging from 11.04 to 4.69.) When the samples were ranked according to mean number of illusion responses on each illusion, and the rank order correlations among the five illusions factor-analyzed, two orthogonal factors emerged: the Müller-Lyer and Sander Parallelogram illusions loaded highly on one, and the Horizontal-vertical illusions loaded highly on the other. Thus, the overall pattern of intersample differences indicates not only cross-cultural differences in illusion susceptibility, but in addition a systematic variation in those cross-cultural differences over two classes of illusion figures.

Both to illustrate and substantiate the findings which emerged from the analysis just described, proportions of individuals in each sample choosing the typically overestimated segment were computed for each item, separately for each illusion set. Psychophysical ogives were then constructed from these proportions and points of subjective equality (PSE) determined graphically. Table 1 contains PSE scores and mean number of illusion-responses for all samples on each of the illusions. (The scores shown in Table 1 were computed for internally consistent cases only, and, except where otherwise noted, the groups consisted of children and adults combined. In samples containing both children and adults, children typically had higher means and PSE's. Combining children and adults as in Table 1 tends to attenuate some intersample differences.) Figure 1 contains four sets of ogives which illustrate (i) the lesser susceptibility of the combined non-European samples as compared with the combined European samples to the Müller-Lyer and Sander Parallelogram illusions, and (ii) the greater susceptibility to the two Horizontal-vertical illusions shown by one non-European sample group as compared to one European sample, and the lesser susceptibility of another non-European sample. Examples of the four illusions are also presented in Fig. 1.

Cross-cultural comparisons made over a half-century ago by Rivers (4) also indicated that two non-Western peoples were simultaneously less susceptible to the Müller-Lyer illusion and more susceptible to the Hori-

Table 1—Points of Subjective Equality and Mean Number of Illusion Responses

Group	N	PSE (%)	Mean	Group	N	PSE (%)	Mean
Müller-Lyer illusion				*Horizontal-vertical illusion (⊥)*			
Evanstonians	188	20.3	5.36	Suku	69	21.0	6.55
N. U. students*	27	16.2	5.00	Banyankole	261	22.5	6.54
S. A. Europeans*	36	13.5	4.33	Dahomeans†	57	22.3	6.49
Dahomeans†	40	11.9	4.23	Toro	105	20.0	6.44
Senegalese	125	12.2	4.18	Ijaw School†	46	20.7	6.28
Ijaw School†	54	6.6	3.67	S. A. mineboys*	69	19.3	6.27
Zulu	35	11.2	3.66	Fang	98	19.3	6.18
Toro	86	10.3	3.56	Senegalese	130	22.7	6.11
Banyankole	224	9.3	3.45	Ijaw	86	19.5	6.06
Fang	85	6.2	3.28	Bushmen*	41	19.5	5.93
Ijaw	84	6.5	3.16	Evanstonians	198	18.4	5.81
Songe	89	6.2	3.07	Songe	91	18.2	5.80
Hanunoo	49	7.7	3.00	N. U. students*	29	18.7	5.72
Bete	75	3.2	2.72	Hanunoo	52	15.3	5.46
Suku	61	2.8	2.69	S. A. Europeans*	42	15.0	5.33
Bushmen*	36	1.7	2.28	Zulu	35	9.5	4.80
S. A. mineboys*	60	1.4	2.23	Bete	79	9.8	4.62
Sander-parallelogram illusion				*Horizontal-vertical illusion (⌐)*			
N. U. students*	28	19.9	3.54	Dahomeans†	63	19.2	6.52
Evanstonians	196	19.1	3.27	Toro	98	19.5	6.38
Ijaw School†	53	18.3	3.15	Banyankole	291	17.0	6.15
S. A. Europeans*	42	17.4	2.98	Ijaw School†	57	18.4	6.02
Zulu	67	18.5	2.97	Suku	69	9.0	5.74
Senegalese	198	15.7	2.90	S. A. mineboys*	69	11.5	5.71
Fang	96	17.3	2.86	Songe	95	8.9	5.60
Ijaw	98	16.9	2.74	Ijaw	97	8.9	5.55
Banyankole	262	17.3	2.69	Fang	105	9.1	5.49
Dahomeans†	58	16.0	2.55	Bushmen*	39	8.6	5.15
Hanunoo	52	13.5	2.52	Zulu	74	7.8	5.03
Toro	105	14.3	2.49	Evanstonians	203	7.2	4.90
Songe	97	14.7	2.41	N. U. students*	30	7.2	4.83
Bete	86	12.8	2.37	Hanunoo	53	6.3	4.70
Suku	91	9.7	2.14	S. A. Europeans*	42	5.0	4.67
S. A. mineboys*	71	8.7	2.06	Senegalese	168	6.0	4.45
(Bushmen not administered this set)				Bete	88	2.0	3.81

* Adults only.
† Children only.

zontal-vertical illusion that were a group of English respondents. Since the non-European samples uniformly perform better than Europeans on one type of illusion and generally worse on the others, any explanation based on presumed contrasting characteristics of "primitive" and "civilized" peoples is difficult to maintain. Rather, evidence seems to point to

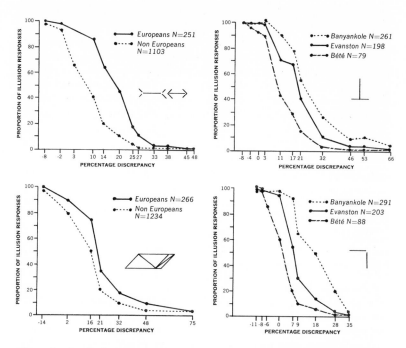

Fig. 1. Psychophysical ogives based on proportions of illusion responses to item of varying percentage discrepancy. (Upper left) Müller-Lyer illusion responses plotted for European (three samples combined) and non-Europeans (all other samples combined). (Lower left) Sander Parallelogram illusion responses plotted for same two combined groups. (Upper right) Horizontal-vertical (⊥) illusion responses by one European and two non-European samples. (Lower right) Horizontal-vertical (⌐) illusion responses by same three samples. These graphs are all based on internally consistent cases only. (Art adapted from Segall *et al.*)

cross-cultural differences in visual inference systems learned in response to different ecological and cultural factors in the visual environment. In a monograph now in preparation which reports the present study in detail (5), Rivers' findings as well as our own are shown to be in accord with an empiricistic, functionalistic interpretation which relates visual response habits to cultural and ecological factors in the visual environment.

An example of a cultural factor which seems relevant is the prevalence of rectangularity in the visual environment, a factor which seems to be related to the tendency to interpret acute and obtuse angles on a two-dimensional surface as representative of rectangular objects in three-dimensional space. This inference habit is much more valid in highly carpentered, urban, European environments, and could enhance, or even produce, the Müller-Lyer and Sander Parallelogram illusions. This interpretation is consistent with traditional explanation of these illusions. Less clearly, the Horizontal-vertical illusion can perhaps be understood as the result of an inference habit of interpreting vertical lines as extensions away from one in the horizontal plane. Such an inference habit would have more validity for those living in open, flat terrain than in rain forests or canyons. An examination of such factors, and thorough examination of alternative explanations of our findings, are contained in the forthcoming monograph. Whether or not the correct environmental features have been isolated, the cross-cultural differences in susceptibility to geometric illusions seem best understood as symptomatic of functional differences in learned visual inference habits.

REFERENCES AND NOTES

(1) M. J. HERSKOVITS, D. T. CAMPBELL, M. H. SEGALL, *Materials for a Cross-Cultural Study of Perception* (Program of African Studies. Northwestern University, Evanston, Ill., 1956).

(2) L. GUTTMAN, "The Cornell technique for scale and intensity analysis," *Educ. Psychol. Measurement* **7**, 247 (1947). In the present study a Guttman error was defined as an illusion-produced response to one item combined with a non-illusion response to an item of lesser percentage-discrepancy. Percentage-discrepancy refers to the percentage by which the segment that is usually underestimated is actually longer than the other comparison segment in a particular illusion drawing. A choice of the usually overestimated segment is termed an illusion-produced response. Thus, a perfectly internally consistent protocol would consist of illusion-produced responses to one or more items, followed by non-illusion responses to all items of greater percentage discrepancy within a figure set.

(3) H. SCHEFFÉ, "A method for judging all contrasts in the analysis of variance." *Biometrika* **40**, 87 (1953). It is generally agreed that the Scheffé procedure is the most conservative of several available techniques for making postmortem, nonindependent comparisons. If our use of this procedure has led to any errors in conclusions other than the usual α-level type 1 error, such errors can only be failures to reject the null hypothesis when it should have been rejected (type 2 errors). We assume the heightened risk of type 2 errors in order that confidence in the obtained significant differences may be enhanced.

(4) W. H. R. RIVERS, "Vision," in *Reports of the Cambridge Anthropological Expedition to the Torres Straits*, A. C. Haddon, Ed. (Cambridge, The University Press, 1901), vol. 2, part 1; *Brit. J. Psychol.* **1**, 321 (1905).

(5) M. H. SEGALL, D. T. CAMPBELL, M. J. HERSKOVITS, "The influence of culture on perception," in preparation. This report includes an examination of age differences as well as total sample differences. Included also is a development of the theoretical arguments suggested here, presented in the context of a review of the literature bearing on the nativist-empiricist controversy, and a discussion of the significance of these data for the anthropological concept of cultural relativism.

part 5:

Behavior control and social welfare

We can no longer afford to ignore developments in the realm of behavior control; the advances are too rapid, the implications too great. The race between scientific progress in behavior control and man's capacity to cope with that progress is quickening; mankind must have the motivation and knowledge to keep pace with its own discoveries. We must always realize that there is a certain irony in behavior control research: as it develops the power to free man's mind from worry (e.g., through therapy) it also gains the means to enslave his thoughts. Like the atom, the science of behavior control is neutral: man determines whether research findings will be used to liberate or subjugate the human spirit; to serve or destroy; to cure or infect.

How will man choose to employ his powerful new behavior control technology? What implications does such a technology have for 20th century American democracy? We have already touched upon these questions in the Andrews and Karlins article in Part 1. In this closing part of the book we return to them once again, hopeful that such a double emphasis will alert the reader to the importance of such inquiries.

Some issues concerning the control of human behavior: a symposium

Carl R. Rogers and B. F. Skinner

INTRODUCTION What happens when a humanistic psychologist like Carl Rogers decides to discuss the topic of human behavior control with a behavioristic psychologist like B. F. Skinner? Plenty —including one of the most memorable and meaningful intellectual exchanges in contemporary behavioral science. Although Rogers and Skinner do not always see eye to eye on behavior control issues, it should be remembered that both men, in their own way, believe they are working to provide contemporary man with a sense of dignity and worth which he will need to remain free and proud.

I [Skinner]

Science is steadily increasing our power to influence, change, mold—in a word, control—human behavior. It has extended our "understanding" (whatever that may be) so that we deal more successfully with people in nonscientific ways, but it has also identified conditions or variables which can be used to predict and control behavior in a new, and increasingly rigorous, technology. The broad disciplines of government and economics offer examples of this, but there is special cogency in those contributions of anthropology, sociology, and psychology which deal with individual behavior. Carl Rogers has listed some of the achievements to date in a recent paper (*1*). Those of his examples which show or imply the control of the single organism are primarily due, as we should expect, to psychology. It is the experimental study of behavior which carries us beyond awkward or inaccessible "principles," "factors," and so on, to variables which can be directly manipulated.

It is also, and for more or less the same reasons, the conception of

"Some Issues Concerning the Control of Human Behavior," Rogers, C. R. and Skinner, B. F., *Science*, Vol. 124, pp. 1057–1066, 30 November 1956.

human behavior emerging from an experimental analysis which most directly challenges traditional views. Psychologists themselves often do not seem to be aware of how far they have moved in this direction. But the change is not passing unnoticed by others. Until only recently it was customary to deny the possibility of a rigorous science of human behavior by arguing, either that a lawful science was impossible because man was a free agent, or that merely statistical predictions would always leave room for personal freedom. But those who used to take this line have become most vociferous in expressing their alarm at the way these obstacles are being surmounted.

Now, the control of human behavior has always been unpopular. Any undisguised effort to control usually arouses emotional reactions. We hesitate to admit, even to ourselves, that we are engaged in control, and we may refuse to control, even when this would be helpful, for fear of criticism. Those who have explicitly avowed an interest in control have been roughly treated by history. Machiavelli is the great prototype. As Macaulay said of him, "Out of his surname they coined an epithet for a knave and out of his Christian name a synonym for the devil." There were obvious reasons. The control that Machiavelli analyzed and recommended, like most political control, used techniques that were aversive to the controllee. The threats and punishments of the bully, like those of the government operating on the same plan, are not designed—whatever their success—to endear themselves to those who are controlled. Even when the techniques themselves are not aversive, control is usually exercised for the selfish purposes of the controller and, hence, has indirectly punishing effects upon others.

Man's natural inclination to revolt against selfish control has been exploited to good purpose in what we call the philosophy and literature of democracy. The doctrine of the rights of man has been effective in arousing individuals to concerted action against governmental and religious tyranny. The literature which has had this effect has greatly extended the number of terms in our language which express reactions to the control of men. But the ubiquity and ease of expression of this attitude spells trouble for any science which may give birth to powerful technology of behavior. Intelligent men and women, dominated by the humanistic philosophy of the past two centuries, cannot view with equanimity what Andrew Hacker has called "the specter of predictable man" (2). Even the statistical or actuarial prediction of human events, such as the number of fatalities to be expected on a holiday weekend, strikes many people as uncanny and evil, while the prediction and control of individual behavior is regarded as little less than the work of the devil. I am not so much concerned here with the political or economic consequences for psychology, although research following certain channels may well suffer harmful effects. We ourselves, as intelligent men and women, and as exponents of Western thought, share these attitudes. They have already interfered with the free exercise of a scientific analysis, and their influence threatens to assume more serious proportions.

Three broad areas of human behavior supply good examples. The first of these—*personal control*—may be taken to include person-to-person relationships in the family, among friends, in social and work groups, and in counseling and psychotherapy. Other fields are *education* and *government*. A few examples from each will show how nonscientific preconceptions are affecting our current thinking about human behavior.

Personal Control

People living together in groups come to control one another with a technique which is not inappropriately called "ethical." When an individual behaves in a fashion acceptable to the group, he receives admiration, approval, affection, and many other reinforcements which increase the likelihood that he will continue to behave in that fashion. When his behavior is not acceptable, he is criticized, censured, blamed, or otherwise punished. In the first case the group calls him "good"; in the second, "bad." This practice is so thoroughly ingrained in our culture that we often fail to see that it is a technique of control. Yet we are almost always engaged in such control, even though the reinforcements and punishments are often subtle.

The practice of admiration is an important part of a culture, because behavior which is otherwise inclined to be weak can be set up and maintained with its help. The individual is especially likely to be praised, admired, or loved when he acts for the group in the face of great danger, for example, or sacrifices himself or his possessions, or submits to prolonged hardship, or suffers martyrdom. These actions are not admirable in any absolute sense, but they require admiration if they are to be strong. Similarly, we admire people who behave in original or exceptional ways, not because such behavior is itself admirable, but because we do not know how to encourage original or exceptional behavior in any other way. The group acclaims independent, unaided behavior in part because it is easier to reinforce than to help.

As long as this technique of control is misunderstood, we cannot judge correctly an environment in which there is less need for heroism, hardship, or independent action. We are likely to argue that such an environment is itself less admirable or produces less admirable people. In the old days, for example, young scholars often lived in undesirable quarters, ate unappetizing or inadequate food, performed unprofitable tasks for a living or to pay for necessary books and materials or publication. Older scholars and other members of the group offered compensating reinforcement in the form of approval and admiration for these sacrifices. When the modern graduate student receives a generous scholarship, enjoys good living conditions, and has his research and publication subsidized, the grounds for evaluation seem to be pulled from under us. Such a student no longer *needs* admiration to carry him over a series of obstacles (no matter how much he may need it for other reasons), and, in missing certain familiar objects of admiration, we are likely to conclude that such *conditions* are less admirable. Obstacles to scholarly work may serve as a useful measure of motivation—and we may go wrong unless some substitute is found—but we can scarcely defend a deliberate harassment of the student for this purpose. The productivity of any set of conditions can be evaluated only when we have freed ourselves of the attitudes which have been generated in us as members of an ethical group.

A similar difficulty arises from our use of punishment in the form of censure or blame. The concept of responsibility and the related concepts of foreknowledge and choice are used to justify techniques of control using punishment. Was So-and-So aware of the probable consequences of his action, and was the action deliberate? If so, we are justified in punishing him. But what does this mean? It appears to be a question concerning the efficacy of the contingent relations between behavior and punishing consequences. We punish behavior because it is objectionable to us or the group, but in a minor refinement of rather recent origin we have come to withhold punishment when it cannot be expected to have any effect. If the objectionable consequences of an act were accidental and not likely to occur again, there is no point in punishing. We say that the individual was not "aware of the consequences of his action" or that the consequences were not "intentional." If the action could not have been avoided—if the individual "had no choice"—punishment is also withheld, as it is if the individual is incapable of being changed by punishment because he is of "unsound mind." In all these cases—different as they are—the individual is held "not responsible" and goes unpunished.

Just as we say that it is "not fair" to punish a man for something he could not help doing, so we call it "unfair" when one is rewarded beyond his due or for something he could not help doing. In other words, we also object to wasting *reinforcers* where they are not needed or will do no good. We make the same point with the words *just* and *right*. Thus we have no right to punish the irresponsible, and a man has no right to reinforcers he does not earn or deserve. But concepts of choice, responsibility, justice, and so on, provide a most inadequate analysis of efficient reinforcing and punishing contingencies because they carry a heavy semantic cargo of a quite different sort, which obscures any attempt to clarify controlling practices or to improve techniques. In particular, they fail to prepare us for techniques based on other than aversive techniques of control. Most people would object to forcing prisoners to serve as subjects of dangerous medical experiments, but few object when they are induced to serve by the offer of return privileges—even when the reinforcing effect of these privileges has been created by forcible deprivation. In the traditional scheme the right to refuse guarantees the individual against coercion or an unfair bargain. But to what extent *can* a prisoner refuse under such circumstances?

We need not go so far afield to make the point. We can observe our own attitude toward personal freedom in the way we resent any interference with what we want to do. Suppose we want to buy a car of a particular sort. Then we may object, for example, if our wife urges us to buy a less expensive model and to put the difference into a new refrigerator. Or we may resent it if our neighbor questions our need for such a car or our ability to pay for it. We would certainly resent it if it were illegal to buy such a car (remember Prohibition); and if we find we cannot actually afford it, we may resent governmental control of the price through tariffs and taxes. We resent it if we discover that we cannot get the car because the manufacturer is holding the model in deliberately short supply in order to push a model we do not want. In all this we assert our democratic right to buy the car of our choice. We are well prepared to do so and to resent any restriction on our freedom.

But why do we not ask *why* it is the car of our choice and resent the forces which made it so? Perhaps our favorite toy as a child was a car, of a very different model, but nevertheless bearing the name of the car we now want. Perhaps our favorite TV program is sponsored by the manufacturer of that car. Perhaps we have seen pictures of many beautiful or prestigeful persons driving it—in pleasant or glamorous places. Perhaps the car has been designed with respect to our motivational patterns: the device on the hood is a phallic symbol; or the horsepower has been stepped up to please our competitive spirit in enabling us to pass other cars swiftly (or, as the advertisements say, "safely"). The concept of freedom that has emerged as part of the cultural practice of our group makes little or no provision for recognizing or dealing with these kinds of control. Concepts like "responsibility" and "rights" are scarcely applicable. We are prepared to deal with coercive measures, but we have no traditional recourse with respect to other measures which in the long run (and especially with the help of science) may be much more powerful and dangerous.

Education

The techniques of education were once frankly aversive. The teacher was usually older and stronger than his pupils and was able to "make them learn." This meant that they were not actually taught but were surrounded by a threatening world from which they could escape only by learning. Usually they were left to their own resources in discovering how to do so. Claude Coleman has published a grimly amusing reminder of these older practices (3). He tells of a schoolteacher who published a careful account of his services during 51 years of teaching, during which he administered: ". . . 911,527 blows with a cane; 124,010 with a rod; 20,989 with a ruler; 136,715 with the hand; 10,295 over the mouth; 7,905 boxes on the ear; [and] 1,115,800 slaps on the head. . . ."

Progressive education was a humanitarian effort to substitute positive reinforcement for such aversive measures, but in the search for useful human values in the classroom it has never fully replaced the variables it abandoned. Viewed as a branch of behavioral technology, education remains relatively inefficient. We supplement it, and rationalize it, by admiring the pupil who learns *for himself;* and we often attribute the learning process, or knowledge itself, to something *inside* the individual. We admire behavior which seems to have inner sources. Thus we admire one who *recites* a poem more than one who simply *reads* it. We admire one who *knows* the answer more than one who *knows where to look it up*. We admire the *writer* rather than the *reader*. We admire the arithmetician who can do a problem in his head rather than with a slide rule or calculating machine, or in "original" ways rather than by a strict application of rules. In general we feel that any aid or "crutch"—except those aids to which we are now thoroughly accustomed—reduces the credit due. In Plato's *Phaedus*, Thamus, the king, attacks the invention of the alphabet on similar grounds! He is afraid "it will produce forgetfulness in the minds of those who learn to use it, because they will not practice their memories. . . ." In other words, he holds it more admirable to remember than to use a memorandum. He also objects that pupils "will read many things without instruction . . . [and] will therefore seem to know many things when they are for the most part ignorant." In the same vein we are today sometimes contemptuous of book learning, but, as educators, we can scarcely afford to adopt this view without reservation.

By admiring the student for knowledge and blaming him for ignorance, we escape some of the responsibility of teaching him. We resist any analysis of the educational process which threatens the notion of inner wisdom or questions the contention that the fault of ignorance lies with the student. More powerful techniques which bring about the same changes in behavior by manipulating *external* variables are decried as brainwashing or thought control. We are quite unprepared to judge *effective* educational measures. As long as only a few pupils learn much of what is taught, we do not worry about uniformity or regimentation. We do not fear the feeble technique; but we should view with dismay a system under which every student learned everything listed in a syllabus

—although such a condition is far from unthinkable. Similarly, we do not fear a system which is so defective that the student must *work* for an education; but we are loath to give credit for anything learned without effort—although this could well be taken as an ideal result—and we flatly refuse to give credit if the student already knows what a school teaches.

A world in which people are wise and good without trying, without "having to be," without "choosing to be," could conceivably be a far better world for everyone. In such a world we should not have to "give anyone credit"—we should not need to admire anyone—for being wise and good. From our present point of view we cannot believe that such a world would be admirable. We do not even permit ourselves to imagine what it would be like.

Government

Government has always been the special field of aversive control. The state is frequently defined in terms of the power to punish, and jurisprudence leans heavily upon the associated notion of personal responsibility. Yet it is becoming increasingly difficult to reconcile current practice and theory with these earlier views. In criminology, for example, there is a strong tendency to drop the notion of responsibility in favor of some such alternative as capacity or controllability. But no matter how strongly the facts, or even practical expedience, support such a change, it is difficult to make the change in a legal system designed on a different plan. When governments resort to other techniques (for example, positive reinforcement), the concept of responsibility is no longer relevant and the theory of government is no longer applicable.

The conflict is illustrated by two decisions of the Supreme Court in the 1930's which dealt with, and disagreed on, the definition of control or coercion (*4*, p. 233). The Agricultural Adjustment Act proposed that the Secretary of Agriculture make "rental or benefit payments" to those farmers who agreed to reduce production. The government agreed that the Act would be unconstitutional if the farmer had been *compelled* to reduce production but was not, since he was merely *invited* to do so. Justice Robert (*4*) expressed the contrary majority view of the court that "The power to confer or withhold unlimited benefits is the power to coerce or destroy." This recognition of positive reinforcement was withdrawn a few years later in another case in which Justice Cardozo (*4*, p. 244) wrote "To hold that motive or temptation is equivalent to coercion is to plunge the law in endless difficulties." We may agree with him, without implying that the proposition is therefore wrong. Sooner or later the law must be prepared to deal with all possible techniques of governmental control.

The uneasiness with which we view government (in the broadest possible sense) when it does not use punishment is shown by the reception of my utopian novel, *Walden Two* (*4a*). This was essentially a proposal to apply a behavioral technology to the construction of a workable, effective, and productive pattern of government. It was greeted with wrathful violence. *Life* magazine called it "a travesty on the good life," and "a menace . . . a triumph of mortmain or the dead hand not envisaged since the days of Sparta . . . a slur upon a name, a corruption of an impulse." Joseph Wood Krutch devoted a substantial part of his book, *The Measure of Man* (*5*), to attacking my views and those of the protagonist, Frazier, in the same vein, and Morris Viteles has recently criticized the book is a similar manner in *Science* (*6*). Perhaps the reaction is best expressed in a quotation from *The Quest for Utopia* by Negley and Patrick (*7*):

"Halfway through this contemporary utopia, the reader may feel sure, as we did, that this is a beautifully ironic satire on what has been called 'behavioral engineering.' The longer one stays in this better world of the psychologist, however, the plainer it becomes that the inspiration is not satiric, but messianic. This is indeed the behaviorally engineered society, and while it was to be expected that sooner or later the principle of psychological conditioning would be made the basis of a serious construction of utopia—Brown anticipated it in *Limanora*—yet not even the effective satire of Huxley is adequate preparation for the shocking horror of the idea when positively presented. Of all the dictatorships espoused by utopists, this is the most profound, and incipient dictators might well find in this utopia a guidebook of political practice."

One would scarcely guess that the authors are talking about a world in which there is food, clothing, and shelter for all, where everyone chooses his own work and works on the average only 4 hours a day, where music and the arts flourish, where personal relationships develop under the most favorable circumstances, where education prepares every child for the social and intellectual life which lies before him, where—in short— people are truly happy, secure, productive, creative, and forward-looking. What is wrong with it? Only one thing: someone "planned it that way." If these critics had come upon a society in some remote corner of the world which boasted similar advantages, they would undoubtedly have hailed it as providing a pattern we all might well follow—provided that it was clearly the result of a natural process of cutural evolution. Any evidence that intelligence had been used in arriving at this version of the good life would, in their eyes, be a serious flaw. No matter if the planner of *Walden Two* diverts none of the proceeds of the community to his own use, no matter if he has no current control or is, indeed, unknown to most of the other members of the community (he planned that, too), somewhere back of it all he occupies the position of prime mover. And this, to the child of the democratic tradition, spoils it all.

The dangers inherent in the control of human behavior are very real. The possibility of the misuse of scientific knowledge must always be faced. We cannot escape by denying the power of a science of behavior or arresting its development. It is no help to cling to familiar philosophies of human behavior simply because they are more reassuring. As I have pointed out elsewhere (8), the new techniques emerging from a science of behavior must be subject to the explicit countercontrol which has already been applied to earlier and cruder forms. Brute force and deception, for example, are now fairly generally suppressed by ethical practices and by explicit governmental and religious agencies. A similar countercontrol of scientific knowledge in the interests of the group is a feasible and promising possibility. Although we cannot say how devious the course of its evolution may be, a cultural pattern of control and countercontrol will presumably emerge which will be most widely supported because it is most widey reinforcing.

If we cannot foresee all the details of this (as we obviously cannot), it is important to remember that this is true of the critics of science as well. The dire consequences of new techniques of control, the hidden menace in original cultural designs—these need some proof. It is only another example of my present point that the need for proof is so often overlooked. Man has got himself into some pretty fixes, and it is easy to believe that he will do so again. But there is a more optimistic possibility. The slow growth of the methods of science, now for the first time being applied to human affairs, *may* mean a new and exciting phase of human life to which historical analogies will not apply and in which earlier political slogans will not be appropriate. If we are to use the knowledge that a science of behavior is now making available with any hope of success, we must look at human nature as it is brought into focus through the methods of science rather than as it has been presented to us in a series of historical accidents.

If the advent of a powerful science of behavior causes trouble, it will not be because science itself is inimical to human welfare but because older conceptions have not yielded easily or gracefully. We expect resistance to new techniques of control from those who have heavy investments in the old, but we have no reason to help them preserve a series of principles that are not ends in themselves but rather outmoded means to an end. What is needed is a new conception of human behavior which is compatible with the implications of a scientific analysis. All men control and are controlled. The question of government in the broadest possible sense is not how freedom is to be preserved but what kinds of control are to be used and to what ends. Control must be analyzed and considered in its proper proportions. No one, I am sure, wishes to develop new master-slave relationships or bend the will of the people to despotic rulers in new ways. These are patterns of control appropriate to a world without science. They may well be the first to go when the experimental analysis of behavior comes into its own in the design of cultural practices.

II [Rogers]

There are, I believe, a number of matters in connection with this important topic on which the authors of this article, and probably a large majority of psychologists, are in agreement. These matters then are not issues as far as we are concerned, and I should like to mention them briefly in order to put them to one side.

Points of Agreement

I am sure we agree that men—as individuals and as societies—have always endeavored to understand, predict, influence, and control human behavior—their own behavior and that of others.

I believe we agree that the behavioral sciences are making and will continue to make increasingly rapid progress in the understanding of behavior, and that as a consequence the capacity to predict and to control behavior is developing with equal rapidity.

I believe we agree that to deny these advances, or to claim that man's behavior cannot be a field of science, is unrealistic. Even though this is not an issue for us, we should recognize that many intelligent men still hold strongly to the view that the actions of men are free in some sense such that scientific knowledge of man's behavior is impossible. Thus Reinhold Niebuhr, the noted theologian, heaps scorn on the concept of psychology as a science of man's behavior and even says, "In any event, no scientific investigation of past behavior can become the basis of predictions of future behavior" (9). So, while this is not an issue for psychologists, we should at least notice in passing that it is an issue for many people.

I believe we are in agreement that the tremendous potential power of a science which permits the prediction and control of behavior may be misused, and that the possibility of such misuse constitutes a serious threat.

Consequently Skinner and I are in agreement that the whole question of the scientific control of human behavior is a matter with which psychologists and the general public should concern themselves. As Robert Oppenheimer told the American Psychological Association last year (10) the problems that psychologists will pose for society by their growing ability to control behavior will be much more grave than the problems posed by the ability of physicists to control the reactions of matter. I am not sure whether psychologists generally recognize this. My impression is that by and large they hold a laissez-faire attitude. Obviously Skinner and I do not hold this laissez-faire view, or we would not have written this article.

Points at Issue

With these several points of basic and important agreement, are there then any issues that remain on which there are differences? I believe there are. They can be stated very briefly: Who will be controlled? Who will exercise control? What type of control will be exercised? Most important of all, toward what end or what purpose, or in the pursuit of what value, will control be exercised?

It is on questions of this sort that there exist ambiguities, misunderstandings, and probably deep differences. These differences exist among psychologists, among members of the general public in this country, and among various world cultures. Without any hope of achieving a final resolution of these questions, we can, I believe, put these issues in clearer form.

Some Meanings

To avoid ambiguity and faulty communication, I would like to clarify the meanings of some of the terms we are using.

Behavioral science is a term that might be defined from several angles but in the context of this discussion it refers primarily to knowledge that the existence of certain describable conditions in the human being and/or in his environment is followed by certain describable consequences in his actions.

Prediction means the prior identification of behaviors which then occur. Because it is important in some things I wish to say later, I would point out that one may predict a highly specific behavior, such as an eye blink, or one may predict a class of behaviors. One might correctly predict "avoidant behavior," for example, without being able to specify whether the individual will run away or simply close his eyes.

The word *control* is a very slippery one, which can be used with any one of several meanings. I would like to specify three that seem most important for our present purposes. *Control* may mean: (i) The setting of conditions by B for A, A having no voice in the matter, such that certain predictable behaviors then occur in A. I refer to this as external control. (ii) The setting of conditions by B for A, A giving some degree of consent to these conditions, such that certain predictable behaviors then occur in A. I refer to this as the influence of B on A. (iii) The setting of conditions by A such that certain predictable behaviors then occur in himself. I refer to this as internal control. It will be noted that

Skinner lumps together the first two meanings, external control and influence, under the concept of control. I find this confusing.

Usual Concept of Control of Human Behavior

With the underbrush thus cleared away (I hope), let us review very briefly the various elements that are involved in the usual concept of the control of human behavior as mediated by the behavioral sciences. I am drawing here on the previous writings of Skinner, on his present statements, on the writings of others who have considered in either friendly or antagonistic fashion the meanings that would be involved in such control. I have not excluded the science fiction writers, as reported recently by Vandenburg (*11*), since they often show an awareness of the issues involved, even though the methods described are as yet fictional. These then are the elements that seem common to these different concepts of the application of science to human behavior.

1) There must first be some sort of decision about goals. Usually desirable goals are assumed, but sometimes, as in George Orwell's book *1984,* the goal that is selected is an aggrandizement of individual power with which most of us would disagree. In a recent paper Skinner suggests that one possible set of goals to be assigned to the behavioral technology is this: "Let men be happy, informed, skillful, well-behaved and productive" (*12*). In the first draft of his part of this article, which he was kind enough to show me, he did not mention such definite goals as these, but desired "improved" educational practices, "wiser" use of knowledge in government, and the like. In the final version of his article he avoids even these value-laden terms, and his implicit goal is the very general one that scientific control of behavior is desirable, because it would perhaps bring "a far better world for everyone."

Thus the first step in thinking about the control of human behavior is the choice of goals, whether specific or general. It is necessary to come to terms in some way with the issue, "For what purpose?"

2) A second element is that, whether the end selected is highly specific or is a very general one such as wanting "a better world," we proceed by the methods of science to discover the means to these ends. We continue through further experimentation and investigation to discover more effective means. The method of science is self-correcting in thus arriving at increasingly effective ways of achieving the purpose we have in mind.

3) The third aspect of such control is that as the conditions or methods are discovered by which to reach the goal, some person or some group establishes these conditions and uses these methods, having in one way or another obtained the power to do so.

4) The fourth element is the exposure of individuals to the pre-

scribed conditions, and this leads, with a high degree of probability, to behavior which is in line with the goals desired. Individuals are now happy, if that has been the goal, or well-behaved, or submissive, or whatever it has been decided to make them.

5) The fifth element is that if the process I have described is put in motion then there is a continuing social organization which will continue to produce the types of behavior that have been valued.

Some Flaws

Are there any flaws in this way of viewing the control of human behavior? I believe there are. In fact the only element in this description with which I find myself in agreement is the second. It seems to me quite incontrovertibly true that the scientific method is an excellent way to discover the means by which to achieve our goals. Beyond that, I feel many sharp differences, which I will try to spell out.

I believe that in Skinner's presentation here and in his previous writings, there is a serious underestimation of the problem of power. To hope that the power which is being made available by the behavioral sciences will be exercised by the scientists, or by a benevolent group, seems to me a hope little supported by either recent or distant history. It seems far more likely that behavioral scientists, holding their present attitudes, will be in the position of the German rocket scientists specializing in guided missiles. First they worked devotedly for Hitler to destroy the U.S.S.R. and the United States. Now, depending on who captured them, they work devotedly for the U.S.S.R. in the interest of destroying the United States, or devotedly for the United States in the interest of destroying the U.S.S.R. If behavioral scientists are concerned solely with advancing their science, it seems most probable that they will serve the purposes of whatever individual or group has the power.

But the major flaw I see in this review of what is involved in the scientific control of human behavior is the denial, misunderstanding, or gross underestimation of the place of ends, goals or values in their relationship to science. This error (as it seems to me) has so many implications that I would like to devote some space to it.

Ends and Values in Relation to Science

In sharp contradiction to some views that have been advanced, I would like to propose a two-pronged thesis: (i) In any scientific endeavor —whether "pure" or applied science—there is a prior subjective choice of the purpose or value which that scientific work is perceived as serving. (ii) This subjective value choice which brings the scientific endeavor into being must always lie outside of that endeavor and can never become a part of the science involved in that endeavor.

Let me illustrate the first point from Skinner himself. It is clear that in his earlier writing (*12*) it is recognized that a prior value choice is necessary, and it is specified as the goal that men are to become happy, well-behaved, productive, and so on. I am pleased that Skinner has retreated from the goals he then chose, because to me they seem to be stultifying values. I can only feel that he was choosing these goals for others, not for himself. I would hate to see Skinner become "well-behaved," as that term would be defined for him by behavioral scientists. His recent article in the *American Psychologist* (*13*) shows that he certainly does not want to be "productive" as that value is defined by most psychologists. And the most awful fate I can imagine for him would be to have him constantly "happy." It is the fact that he is very unhappy about many things which makes me prize him.

In the first draft of his part of this article, he also included such prior value choices, saying for example, "We must decide how we are to use the knowledge which a science of human behavior is now making available." Now he has dropped all mention of such choices, and if I understand him correctly, he believes that science can proceed without them. He has suggested this view in another recent paper, stating that "We must continue to experiment in cultural design . . . testing the consequences as we go. Eventually the practices which make for the greatest biological and psychological strength of the group will presumably survive" (*8*, p. 549).

I would point out, however, that to choose to experiment is a value choice. Even to move in the direction of perfectly random experimention is a value choice. To test the consequences of an experiment is possible only if we have first made a subjective choice of a criterion value. And implicit in his statement is a valuing of biological and psychological strength. So even when trying to avoid such choice, it seems inescapable that a prior subjective value choice is necessary for any scientific endeavor, or for any application of scientific knowledge.

I wish to make it clear that I am not saying that values cannot be included as a subject of science. It is not true that science deals only with certain classes of "facts" and that these classes do not include values. It is a bit more complex than that, as a simple illustration or two may make clear.

If I value knowledge of the "three R's" as a goal of education, the methods of science can give me increasingly accurate information on how this goal may be achieved. If I value problem-solving ability as a goal of education, the scientific method can give me the same kind of help.

Now, if I wish to determine whether problem-solving ability is "better" than knowledge of the three R's, then scientific method can also study those two values but *only*—and this is very important—in terms of some other value which I have subjectively chosen. I may value college success. Then I can determine whether problem-solving ability or knowledge of the three R's is most closely associated with that value. I may value personal integration or vocational success or responsible citizenship. I can determine whether problem-solving ability or knowledge of the three R's is "better" for achieving any one of these values. But the value or purpose that gives meaning to a particular scientific endeavor must always lie outside of that endeavor.

Although our concern in this symposium is largely with applied science, what I have been saying seems equally true of so-called "pure" science. In pure science the usual prior subjective value choice is the discovery of truth. But this is a subjective choice, and science can never say whether it is the best choice, save in the light of some other value. Geneticists in the U.S.S.R., for example, had to make a subjective choice of whether it was better to pursue truth or to discover facts which upheld a governmental dogma. Which choice is "better"? We could make a scientific investigation of those alternatives but only in the light of some other subjectively chosen value. If, for example, we value the survival of a culture, then we could begin to investigate with the methods of science the question of whether pursuit of truth or support of governmental dogma is most closely associated with cultural survival.

My point then is that any endeavor in science, pure or applied, is carried on in the pursuit of a purpose or value that is subjectively chosen by persons. It is important that this choice be made explicit, since the particular value which is being sought can never be tested or evaluated, confirmed or denied, by the scientific endeavor to which it gives birth. The initial purpose or value always and necessarily lies outside the scope of the scientific effort which it sets in motion.

Among other things this means that if we choose some particular goal or series of goals for human beings and then set out on a large scale to control human behavior to the end of achieving those goals, we are locked in the rigidity of our initial choice, because such a scientific endeavor can never transcend itself to select new goals. Only subjective human persons can do that. Thus if we chose as our goal the state of happiness for human beings (a goal deservedly ridiculed by Aldous Huxley in *Brave New World*), and if we involved all of society in a successful scientific program by which people became happy, we would be locked in a colossal rigidity in which no one would be free to question this goal, because our scientific operations could not transcend themselves to question their guiding purposes. And without laboring this point, I would remark that colossal rigidity, whether in dinosaurs or dictatorships, has a very poor record of evolutionary survival.

If, however, a part of our scheme is to set free some "planners" who do not have to be happy, who are not controlled, and who are therefore free to choose other values, this has several meanings. It means that the purpose we have chosen as our goal is not a sufficient and a satisfying one for human beings but must be supplemented. It also means that if it is necessary to set up an elite group which is free, then this shows all too clearly that the great majority are only the slaves—no matter by what high-sounding name we call them—of those who select the goals.

Perhaps, however, the thought is that a continuing scientific endeavor will evolve its own goals; that the initial findings will alter the directions, and subsequent findings will alter them still further, and that science somehow develops its own purpose. Although he does not clearly say so, this appears to be the pattern Skinner has in mind. It is surely a reasonable description, but it overlooks one element in this continuing development, which is that subjective personal choice enters in at every point at which the direction changes. The findings of a science, the results of an experiment, do not and never can tell us what next scientific purpose to pursue. Even in the purest of science, the scientist must decide what the findings mean and must subjectively choose what next step will be most profitable in the pursuit of his purpose. And if we are speaking of the application of scientific knowledge, then it is distressingly clear that the increasing scientific knowledge of the structure of the atom carries with it no necessary choice as to the purpose to which this knowledge will be put. This is a subjective personal choice which must be made by many individuals.

Thus I return to the proposition with which I began this section of my remarks—and which I now repeat in different words. Science has its meaning as the objective pursuit of a purpose which has been subjectively chosen by a person or persons. This purpose or value can never be investigated by the particular scientific experiment or investigation to which it has given birth and meaning. Consequently, any discussion of the control of human beings by the behavioral sciences must first and most deeply concern itself with the subjectively chosen purposes which such an application of science is intended to implement.

Is the Situation Hopeless?

The thoughtful reader may recognize that, although my remarks up to this point have introduced some modifications in the conception of the processes by which human behavior will be controlled, these remarks may have made such control seem, if anything, even more inevitable. We might sum it up this way: Behavioral science is clearly moving forward; the increasing power for control which it gives will be held by someone or some group; such an individual or group will surely choose the values or goals to be achieved; and most of us will then be increasingly controlled by means so subtle that we will not even be aware of them as controls. Thus, whether a council of wise psychologists (if this is not a contradiction in terms), or a Stalin, or a Big Brother has the power, and whether the goal is happiness, or productivity, or resolution of the Oedipus complex, or submission, or love of Big Brother, we will inevitably find ourselves moving toward the chosen goal and probably thinking that we ourselves desire it. Thus, if this line of reasoning is correct, it appears that some form of *Walden Two* or of *1984* (and at a deep philosophic level they seem indistinguishable) is coming. The fact that it would surely arrive piecemeal, rather than all at once, does not greatly change the fundamental issues. In any event, as Skinner has indicated in his writings, we would then look back upon the concepts of human freedom, the capacity for choice, the responsibility for choice, and the worth of the human individual as historical curiosities which once existed by cultural accident as values in a prescientific civilization.

I believe that any person observant of trends must regard something like the foregoing sequence as a real possibility. It is not simply a fantasy. Something of that sort may even be the most likely future. But is it an inevitable future? I want to devote the remainder of my remarks to an alternative possibility.

Alternative Set of Values

Suppose we start with a set of ends, values, purposes, quite different from the type of goals we have been considering. Suppose we do this quite openly, setting them forth as a possible value choice to be accepted or rejected. Suppose we select a set of values that focuses on fluid elements of process rather than static attributes. We might then value: man as a process of becoming, as a process of achieving worth and dignity through the development of his potentialities; the individual human being as a self-actualizing process, moving on to more challenging and enriching experiences; the process by which the individual creatively adapts to an ever-new and changing world; the process by which knowledge transcends itself, as, for example, the theory of relativity transcended Newtonian physics, itself to be transcended in some future day by a new perception.

If we select values such as these we turn to our science and technology of behavior with a very different set of questions. We will want to know such things as these: Can science aid in the discovery of new modes of richly rewarding living? more meaningful and satisfying modes of interpersonal relationships? Can science inform us on how the human race can become a more intelligent participant in its own evolution—its physical, psychological and social evolution? Can science inform us on ways of releasing the creative capacity of individuals, which seem so necessary if we are to survive in this fantastically expanding atomic age? Oppenheimer has pointed out (*14*) that knowledge, which used to double in millenia or centuries, now doubles in a generation or a decade. It appears that we must discover the utmost in release of creativity if we are to be able to adapt effectively. In short, can science discover the methods by which man can most readily become a continually developing and self-transcending process, in his behavior, his thinking, his knowledge? Can science predict and release an essentially "unpredictable" freedom?

It is one of the virtues of science as a method that it is as able to advance and implement goals and purposes of this sort as it is to serve static values, such as states of being well-informed, happy, obedient. Indeed we have some evidence of this.

Small Example

I will perhaps be forgiven if I document some of the possibilities along this line by turning to psychotherapy, the field I know best.

Psychotherapy, as Meerloo (*15*) and others have pointed out, can be one of the most subtle tools for the control of A by B. The therapist can subtly mold individuals in imitation of himself. He can cause an individual to become a submissive and conforming being. When certain therapeutic principles are used in extreme fashion, we call it brainwashing, an instance of the disintegration of the personality and a reformulation of the person along lines desired by the controlling individual. So the principles of therapy can be used as an effective means of external control of human personality and behavior. Can psychotherapy be anything else?

Here I find the developments going on in client-centered psychotherapy (*16*) an exciting hint of what a behavioral science can do in achieving the kinds of values I have stated. Quite aside from being a somewhat new orientation in psychotherapy, this development has important implications regarding the relation of a behavioral science to the control of human behavior. Let me describe our experience as it relates to the issues of this discussion.

In client-centered therapy, we are deeply engaged in the prediction and influencing of behavior, or even the control of behavior. As therapists, we institute certain attitudinal conditions, and the client has relatively little voice in the establishment of these conditions. We predict that if these conditions are instituted, certain behavioral consequences will ensue in the client. Up to this point this is largely external control, no different from what Skinner has described, and no different from what I have discussed in the preceding sections of this article. But here any similarity ceases.

The conditions we have chosen to establish predict such behavioral consequences as these: that the client will become self-directing, less rigid, more open to the evidence of his senses, better organized and integrated, more similar to the ideal which he has chosen for himself. In other words, we have established by external control conditions which we predict will be followed by internal control by the individual, in pursuit of internally chosen goals. We have set the conditions which predict various classes of behaviors—self-directing behaviors, sensitivity to realities within and without, flexible adaptiveness—which are by their very nature unpredictable in their specifics. Our recent research (*17*) indicates that our predictions are to a significant degree corroborated, and our commitment to the scientific method causes us to believe that more effective means of achieving these goals may be realized.

Research exists in other fields—industry, education, group dynamics —which seems to support our own findings. I believe it may be conservatively stated that scientific progress has been made in identifying those conditions in an interpersonal relationship which, if they exist in *B*, are followed in *A* by greater maturity in behavior, less dependence on others, an increase in expressiveness as a person, an increase in variability, flexibility and effectiveness of adaptation, an increase in self-responsibility and self-direction. And, quite in contrast to the concern expressed by some, we do not find that the creatively adaptive behavior which results from such self-directed variability of expression is a "happy accident" which occurs in "chaos." Rather, the individual who is open to his experience, and self-directing, is harmonious not chaotic, ingenious rather than random, as he orders his responses imaginatively toward the achievement of his own purposes. His creative actions are no more a "happy accident" than was Einstein's development of the theory of relativity.

Thus we find ourselves in fundamental agreement with John Dewey's statement: "Science has made its way by releasing, not by suppressing, the elements of variation, of invention and innovation, of novel creation in individuals" (*18*). Progress in personal life and in group living is, we believe, made in the same way.

Possible Concept of the Control of Human Behavior

It is quite clear that the point of view I am expressing is in sharp contrast to the usual conception of the relationship of the behavioral sciences to the control of human behavior. In order to make this contrast even more blunt, I will state this possibility in paragraphs parallel to those used before.

1) It is possible for us to choose to value man as a self-actualizing process of becoming; to value creativity, and the process by which knowledge becomes self-transcending.

2) We can proceed by the methods of science, to discover the conditions which necessarily precede these processes and, through continuing experimentation, to discover better means of achieving these purposes.

3) It is possible for individuals or groups to set these conditions, with a minimum of power or control. According to present knowledge, the only authority necessary is the authority to establish certain qualities of interpersonal relationship.

4) Exposed to these conditions, present knowledge suggests that individuals become more self-responsible, make progress in self-actualization, become more flexible, and become more creatively adaptive.

5) Thus such an initial choice would inaugurate the beginnings of a social system or subsystem in which values, knowledge, adaptive skills, and even the concept of science would be continually changing and self-transcending. The emphasis would be upon man as a process of becoming.

I believe it is clear that such a view as I have been describing does not lead to any definable utopia. It would be impossible to predict its final outcome. It involves a step-by-step development, based on a continuing subjective choice of purposes, which are implemented by the behavioral sciences. It is in the direction of the "open society," as that term has been defined by Popper (*19*), where individuals carry responsibility for personal decisions. It is at the opposite pole from his concept of the closed society, of which *Walden Two* would be an example.

I trust it is also evident that the whole emphasis is on process, not on end-states of being. I am suggesting that it is by choosing to value certain qualitative elements of the process of becoming that we can find a pathway toward the open society.

The Choice

It is my hope that we have helped to clarify the range of choice which will lie before us and our children in regard to the behavioral sciences. We can choose to use our growing knowledge to enslave people in ways never dreamed of before, depersonalizing them, controlling them by means so carefully selected that they will perhaps never be aware of their loss of personhood. We can choose to utilize our scientific knowledge to make men happy, well-behaved, and productive, as Skinner earlier suggested. Or we can insure that each person learns all the syllabus which we select and set before him, as Skinner now suggests. Or at the other end of the spectrum of choice we can choose to use the behavioral sciences in ways which will free, not control; which will bring about constructive variability, not conformity; which will develop creativity, not contentment; which will facilitate each person in his self-directed process of becoming; which will aid individuals, groups, and even the concept of science to become self-transcending in freshly adaptive ways of meeting life and its problems. The choice is up to us, and, the human race being what it is, we are likely to stumble about, making at times some nearly disastrous value choices and at other times highly constructive ones.

I am aware that to some, this setting forth of a choice is unrealistic, because a choice of values is regarded as not possible. Skinner has stated: "Man's vaunted creative powers . . . his capacity to choose and our right to hold him responsible for his choice—none of these is conspicuous in this new self-portrait (provided by science). Man, we once believed, was free to express himself in art, music, and literature, to inquire into nature, to seek salvation in his own way. He could initiate action and make spontaneous and capricious changes of course. . . . But science insists that action is initiated by forces impinging upon the individual, and that caprice is only another name for behavior for which we have not yet found a cause" (*12*, pp. 52–53).

I can understand this point of view, but I believe that it avoids looking at the great paradox of behavioral science. Behavior, when it is examined scientifically, is surely best understood as determined by prior causation. This is one great fact of science. But responsible personal choice, which is the most essential element in being a person, which is the core experience in psychotherapy, which exists prior to any scientific endeavor, is an equally prominent fact in our lives. To deny the experience of responsible choice is, to me, as restricted a view as to deny the possibility of a behavioral science. That these two important elements of our experience appear to be in contradiction has perhaps the same significance as the contradiction between the wave theory and the corpuscular theory of light, both of which can be shown to be true, even though incompatible. We cannot profitably deny our subjective life, any more than we can deny the objective description of that life.

In conclusion then, it is my contention that science cannot come into being without a personal choice of the values we wish to achieve. And these values we choose to implement will forever lie outside of the science which implements them; the goals we select, the purposes we wish to follow, must always be outside of the science which achieves them. To me this has the encouraging meaning that the human person, with his capacity of subjective choice, can and will always exist, separate from and prior to any of his scientific undertakings. Unless as individuals and groups we choose to relinquish our capacity of subjective choice, we will always remain persons, not simply pawns of a self-created science.

III [*Skinner*]

I cannot quite agree that the practice of science *requires* a prior decision about goals or a prior choice of values. The metallurgist can study

the properties of steel and the engineer can design a bridge without raising the question of whether a bridge is to be built. But such questions
are certainly frequently raised and tentatively answered. Rogers wants to
call the answers "subjective choices of values." To me, such an expression
suggests that we have had to abandon more rigorous scientific practices
in order to talk about our own behavior. In the experimental analysis of
other organisms I would use other terms, and I shall try to do so here.
Any list of values is a list of reinforcers—conditioned or otherwise. We are
so constituted that under certain circumstances food, water, sexual contact, and so on, will make any behavior which produces them more likely
to occur again. Other things may acquire this power. We do not need to
say that an organism chooses to eat rather than to starve. If you answer
that it is a very different thing when a man chooses to starve, I am only
too happy to agree. If it were not so, we should have cleared up the
question of choice long ago. An organism can be reinforced by—can be
made to "choose"—almost any given state of affairs.

Rogers is concerned with choices that involve multiple and usually
conflicting consequences. I have dealt with some of these elsewhere (*20*)
in an analysis of self-control. Shall I eat these delicious strawberries today
if I will then suffer an annoying rash tomorrow? The decision I am to
make used to be assigned to the province of ethics. But we are now studying similar combinations of positive and negative consequences, as well
as collateral conditions which affect the result, in the laboratory. Even
a pigeon can be taught some measure of self-control! And this work helps
us to understand the operation of certain formulas—among them value
judgments—which folk-wisdom, religion, and psychotherapy have advanced in the interests of self-discipline. The observable effect of any statement of value is to alter the relative effectiveness of reinforcers. We may
no longer enjoy the strawberries for thinking about the rash. If rashes
are made sufficiently shameful, illegal, sinful, maladjusted, or unwise,
we may glow with satisfaction as we push the strawberries aside in a
grandiose avoidance response which would bring a smile to the lips of
Murray Sidman.

People behave in ways which, as we say, conform to ethical, governmental, or religious patterns because they are reinforced for doing so.
The resulting behavior may have far-reaching consequences for the survival of the pattern to which it conforms. And whether we like it or not,
survival is the ultimate criterion. This is where, it seems to me, science
can help—not in choosing a goal, but in enabling us to predict the survival value of cultural practices. Man has too long tried to get the kind
of world he wants by glorifying some brand of immediate reinforcement.
As science points up more and more of the remoter consequences, he may
begin to work to strengthen behavior, not in a slavish devotion to a

chosen value, but with respect to the ultimate survival of mankind. Do not ask me why I want mankind to survive. I can tell you why only in the sense in which the physiologist can tell you why I want to breathe. Once the relation between a given step and the survival of my group has been pointed out, I will take that step. And it is the business of science to point out just such relations.

The values I have occasionally recommended (and Rogers has not led me to recant) are transitional. Other things being equal, I am betting on the group whose practices make for healthy, happy, secure, productive, and creative people. And I insist that the values recommended by Rogers are transitional, too, for I can ask him the same kind of question. Man as a process of becoming—*what?* Self-actualization—for what? Inner control is no more a goal than external.

What Rogers seems to me to be proposing, both here and elsewhere (*1*), is this: Let us use our increasing power of control to create individuals who will not need and perhaps will no longer respond to control. Let us solve the problem of our power by renouncing it. At first blush this seems as implausible as a benevolent despot. Yet power has occasionally been foresworn. A nation has burned its Reichstag, rich men have given away their wealth, beautiful women have become ugly hermits in the desert, and psychotherapists have become nondirective. When this happens, I look to other possible reinforcements for a plausible explanation. A people relinquish democratic power when a tyrant promises them the earth. Rich men give away wealth to escape the accusing finger of their fellowmen. A woman destroys her beauty in the hope of salvation. And a psychotherapist relinquishes control because he can thus help his client more effectively.

The solution that Rogers is suggesting is thus understandable. But is he correctly interpreting the result? What evidence is there that a client ever truly becomes truly *self*-directing? What evidence is there that he ever makes a truly *inner* choice of ideal or goal? Even though the therapist does not do the choosing, even though he encourages "self-actualization"—he is not out of control as long as he holds himself ready to step in when occasion demands—when, for example, the client chooses the goal of becoming a more accomplished liar or murdering his boss. But supposing the therapist does withdraw completely or is no longer necessary —what about all the other forces acting upon the client? Is the self-chosen goal independent of his early ethical and religious training? of the folk-wisdom of his group? of the opinions and attitudes of others who are important to him? Surely not. The therapeutic situation is only a small part of the world of the client. From the therapist's point of view it may appear to be possible to relinquish control. But the control passes, not to a "self," but to forces in other parts of the client's world. The solution of the therapist's problem of power cannot be *our* solution, for we must consider *all* the forces acting upon the individual.

The child who must be prodded and nagged is something less than a fully developed human being. We want to see him hurrying to his appointment, not because each step is taken in response to verbal reminders from his mother, but because certain temporal contingencies, in which dawdling has been punished and hurrying reinforced, have worked a change in his behavior. Call this a state of better organization, a greater sensitivity to reality, or what you will. The plain fact is that the child passes from a temporary verbal control exercised by his parents to control by certain inexorable features of the environment. I should suppose that something of the same sort happens in successful psychotherapy. Rogers seems to me to be saying this: Let us put an end, as quickly as possible, to any pattern of master-and-slave, to any direct obedience to command, to the submissive following of suggestion. Let the individual be free to adjust himself to more rewarding features of the world about him. In the end, let his teachers and counselors "wither away," like the Marxist state. I not only agree with this as a useful ideal, I have constructed a fanciful world to demonstrate its advantages. It saddens me to hear Rogers say that "at a deep philosophic level" *Walden Two* and George Orwell's *1984* "seem indistinguishable." They could scarcely be more unlike—at any level. The book *1984* is a picture of immediate aversive control for vicious selfish purposes. The founder of *Walden Two,* on the other hand, has built a community in which neither he nor any other person exerts any *current* control. His achievement lay in his original *plan,* and when he boasts of this ("It is enough to satisfy the thirstiest tyrant") we do not fear him but only pity him for his weakness.

Another critic of *Walden Two,* Andrew Hacker (*21*), has discussed this point in considering the bearing of mass conditioning upon the liberal notion of autonomous man. In drawing certain parallels between the Grand Inquisition passage in Dostoevsky's *Brothers Karamazov,* Huxley's *Brave New World,* and *WaldenTwo,* he attempts to set up a distinction to be drawn in any society between conditioners and conditioned. He assumes that "the conditioner can be said to be autonomous in the traditional liberal sense." But then he notes: "Of course the conditioner has been conditioned. But he has not been conditioned by the conscious manipulation of another *person.*" But how does this affect the resulting behavior? Can we not soon forget the origins of the "artificial" diamond which is identical with the real thing? Whether it is an "accidental" cultural pattern, such as is said to have produced the founder of *Walden Two,* or the engineered environment which is about to produce his successors, we are dealing with sets of conditions generating human behavior which will ultimately be measured by their contribution to the strength of the group. We look to the future, not the past, for the test of "goodness" or acceptability.

If we are worthy of our democratic heritage we shall, of course, be ready to resist any tyrannical use of science for immediate or selfish purposes. But if we value the achievements and goals of democracy we must not refuse to apply science to the design and construction of cultural patterns, even though we may then find ourselves in some sense in the position of controllers. Fear of control, generalized beyond any warrant, has led to a misinterpretation of valid practices and the blind rejection of intelligent planning for a better way of life. In terms which I trust Rogers will approve, in conquering this fear we shall become more mature and better organized and shall, thus, more fully actualize ourselves as human beings.

REFERENCES AND NOTES

(1) C. R. ROGERS, *Teachers College Record* **57**, 316 (1956).

(2) A. HACKER, *Antioch Rev.* **14**, 195 (1954).

(3) C. COLEMAN, *Bull. Am. Assoc. Univ. Professors* **39**, 457 (1953).

(4) P. A. FREUND et al., *Constitutional Law: Cases and Other Problems*, vol. 1 (Little, Brown, Boston, 1954).

(4a) B. F. SKINNER, *Walden Two* (Macmillan, New York, 1948).

(5) J. W. KRUTCH, *The Measure of Man* (Bobbs-Merrill, Indianapolis, 1953).

(6) M. VITELES, *Science* **122**, 1167 (1955).

(7) G. NEGLEY & J. M. PATRICK, *The Quest for Utopia* (Schuman, New York, 1952).

(8) B. F. SKINNER, *Trans. N.Y. Acad. Sci.* **17**, 547 (1955).

(9) R. NIEBUHR, *The Self and the Dramas of History* (Scribner, New York, 1955), p. 47.

(10) R. OPPENHEIMER, *Am. Psychol.* **11**, 127 (1956).

(11) S. G. VANDENBERG, *ibid.* **11**, 339 (1956).

(12) B. F. SKINNER, *Am. Scholar*, **25**, 47 (1955–56).

(13) ———, *Am. Psychol.* **11**, 221 (1956).

(14) R. OPPENHEIMER, *Roosevelt University Occasional Papers* **2** (1956).

(15) J. A. M. MEERLOO, *J. Nervous Mental Disease* **122**, 353 (1955).

(16) C. R. ROGERS, *Client-Centered Therapy* (Houghton-Mifflin, Boston, 1951).

(17) ——— & R. DYMOND, Eds., *Psychotherapy and Personality Change* (Univ. of Chicago Press, Chicago, 1954).

(18) J. RATNER, Ed., *Intelligence in the Modern World: John Dewey's Philosophy* (Modern Library, New York, 1939), p. 359.

(19) K. R. POPPER, *The Open Society and Its Enemies* (Rutledge and Kegan Paul, London, 1945).

(20) B. F. SKINNER, *Science and Human Behavior* (Macmillan, New York, 1953).

(21) A. HACKER, *J. Politics* **17**, 590 (1955).

Behavior control and
social responsibility

Leonard Krasner

INTRODUCTION   *Leonard Krasner is an expert on behavior control. He has studied it in his laboratory and discussed it in his writings (e.g., Krasner & Ullmann, 1965). Krasner believes we need socially responsible scientists, men who are concerned with the social ramifications of their work and are willing to work for the humane utilization of behavior control procedures. In the article you will be reading, he expresses this belief decisively in a message to psychologists: "Behavior control represents a relatively new, important, and very useful development in psychological research. It also may be horribly misused unless the psychologist is constantly alert to what is taking place in society and unless he is active in investigating and controlling the social uses of behavior control."*

In recent years, research in psychotherapy has increasingly focused on investigations which could be interpreted as being part of a broad psychology of behavior control (Bandura, 1961; Frank, 1961; Kanfer, 1961; Krasner, 1958, 1961; Salzinger, 1959; Skinner, 1953). The essential element of behavior control studies is the influence, persuasion, and manipulation of human behavior. Two broad categories of controlling techniques have been utilized. The first can be termed the "social reinforcement" process, namely, those techniques which utilize the behavior of the examiner and structure of the interview situation as a means of influencing behavior. These include studies of psychotherapy, hypnosis, operant conditioning, attitude influence, placebos, and brainwashing. A second category of influence techniques involves the use of physical devices or drugs, such as tranquillizers, brain stimulation, sensory deprivation, or teaching machines. Both categories of investigation have in com-

Krasner, L. Behavior control and social responsibility. *American Psychologist,* 1964, **17,** 199–204. Copyright 1964 by the American Psychological Association, and reproduced by permission.

mon the development of techniques for enhancing the effectiveness of the control or manipulation of individual behavior. Many investigators in this field have been influenced by Skinnerian behaviorism with its emphasis on environmental control and shaping of behavior (Skinner, 1953). Although there is as yet no direct evidence on this point, it is hypothesized that the social reinforcement type of influence is more effective than physical devices because the subject is less likely to be aware of them and thus is more likely to respond to them.

* * *

It is in the field of psychotherapy that the issues of the *moral* and *ethical implications* of behavior control first arose as a relevant problem. Psychotherapy involves the direct application of the findings of behavior control (Krasner, 1961). A professionally trained individual uses a variety of techniques to change, modify, or direct the behavior of another person. It differs from brainwashing in the implied assent given by the patient to this manipulation. This view of the therapist as a manipulator of behavior is one that arouses considerable opposition from many therapists who deny that they are actively involved in controlling behavior. This is perhaps best expressed by Rogers, both in his debate with Skinner (Rogers & Skinner, 1956) and in his article on "Persons or Science" (1955). In this latter paper, he goes into the dangers of control and deplores the tendency toward social control implicit in the results of the kinds of studies discussed in this paper. His attitude is that therapy is a process which is "intensely personal, highly subjective in its inwardness, and dependent entirely on the relationship of two individuals, each of whom is an experiencing media." Rogers contends that:

> Therapists recognize—usually intuitively—that any advance in therapy, any fresh knowledge of it, any significant new hypothesis in regard to it, must come from the experience of the therapists and clients, and can never come from science.

He feels that there is a danger in science which may lead toward manipulation of people, and cites as examples of this the attempts to apply laws of learning to control people through advertisements and propaganda. Skinner's *Walden Two* (1948) is cited as a psychologist's picture of paradise:

> A paradise of manipulation in which the extent to which one can be a person is greatly reduced unless one can be a member of the ruling council.

This point of view can be best summarized as Rogers does, as follows:

> What I will do with the knowledge gained through scientific method
> —whether I will use it to understand, enhance, enrich, or use it to
> control, manipulate, and destroy—is a matter of subjective choices
> depending upon the values which have personal meaning for me.

Yet in another paper (Rogers & Skinner, 1956) even Rogers is willing to
concede that:

> In client-centered therapy, we are deeply engaged in the prediction
> and influencing of behavior, or even the control of behavior. As
> therapists, we institute certain attitudinal conditions, and the client
> has relatively little voice in the establishment of these conditions.
> We predict that if these conditions are instituted, certain behavioral
> consequences will ensue in the client.

The "anti-control" view is also well presented in a series of papers
by Jourard (1959, 1961). He contends that manipulation will have harmful effects both on the patient and on the therapist. Jourard (1959) contends that:

> "Behavioristic" approaches to counseling and psychotherapy, while
> rightly acknowledging a man's susceptibility to manipulation by an-
> other, ignore the possibly deleterious impact of such manipulation
> on the whole man and, moreover, on the would-be manipulator him-
> self—whereas the essential factor in the psychotherapeutic situation
> is a loving, honest and spontaneous relationship between the ther-
> apist and the patient.

In contrast, a "behavioristic" viewpoint might argue that apparent
spontaneity on the therapist's part may very well be the most effective
means of manipulating behavior. The therapist is an individual pro-
gramed by his training into a fairly effective behavior control machine.
Most likely the machine is most effective when it least appears like a
machine.

Despite the views of Rogers and of other therapists, the evidence
seems quite strong that psychotherapy as a social reinforcement process
is part of a broader psychology of behavior control in which the therapist is actively influencing the behavior, attitudinal and value system of
the patient (Krasner, 1961). Further, recent research has begun to put
the therapist back into the therapy situation insofar as studying his personality and other personal attributes, including his value system. Mar-

mor (1961) points out that psychoanalysis, as well as other types of psychotherapy, involves the communication of the therapist's implicit values and behavioral characteristics. Marmor's conviction is that:

> Whether or not the analyst is *consciously* "tempted to act as a teacher, model, and ideal" to his patients, he *inevitably* does so to a greater or lesser extent; and this is a central aspect of the psychoanalytic process.

One of the reasons for denial on the part of therapists that they control behavior, or that they even desire to do so, is that such control would raise many moral, ethical, and legal problems, which the therapist is not prepared to handle. Thus, therapists are put in the paradoxical position of saying to the patient, "we will change your behavior, but we do not really want to change your behavior." Generally, science fiction is more willing to come to grips with some of the basic issues involved than is the professional therapist (Vandenberg, 1956).

*   *   *

Yet, we cannot avoid facing the issue of values. In fact, psychology is in the process of having a strong revival of interest in values. Recognition of the need for concern with the *ethics* or *moral values* of the therapist is implicit in an increasing number of articles (May, 1953; Papanek, 1958; Patterson, 1958; Rotter, 1961; Watson, 1958; Whitehorn, 1959). For example, May (1953) points out that the progress of psychoanalysis in the last decade can be judged by the increasing recognition that it is an illusion for the analyst to suppose that he can avoid value judgments. He feels that this recognition is explicit in the writings of Fromm and Horney and implicit in the works of Fromm-Reichman, Kubie, Alexander, and French. May cites a statement of J. McV. Hunt, who says ". . . I have reluctantly come to the conclusion that the scientist cannot avoid the value assumptions merely by deciding to do so." Hunt concludes, and May agrees, that values do belong to the subject material of science and must be taken into account in devising measuring instruments of behavioral or situational change. The study of Rosenthal (1955) on changes in "moral values" following psychotherapy is an illustration. Patients who are rated as "improved" changed significantly in their performance on a value test in the direction of values held by their therapists in sex, aggression, and authority, whereas unimproved patients tended to become less like their therapists in these values.

Lowe (1959) points out some of the ethical dilemmas involved insofar as the therapist is concerned, with possible conflicts over four sets of values. After reviewing value systems in four different categories, called naturalism, culturism, humanism, theism, Lowe concludes that "there is no single professional standard to which the psychologist's values can conform." The dilemma for the psychologist, as he sees it, is that if *one* set of values is to become absolute, psychology would cease to be a science and would become a social movement. However, he feels that psychologists cannot, on the other hand, do research without intending it to serve a particular value orientation. His suggestion is that value orientations be dealt with as objectively as possible, and that each area in psychology become more fully aware of the implications of its efforts. Further, since value orientations are in such conflict that at this point they are unresolvable, each therapist must understand his own values and those of others.

There have been infrequent attempts to measure attitudes of therapists, but most of these have been in terms of attitudes to therapy rather than attitudes to the broader implications of their social role (Shaffer, 1953). There have certainly been investigations of personality variables of the therapist, or psychologist, or psychiatrist (Holt & Luborsky, 1958; Kelley & Fiske, 1951), but these have been generally oriented towards traditional personality variables rather than value attitudes. Shaffer (1953), for example, found in his analysis of objective versus intuitive psychologists, that the differences are not in terms of personality but in terms of attitudes toward role. Skinner (Rogers & Skinner, 1956), who was among the first to call attention to the ethical problems inherent in a psychology of behavior control, has pointed out that an important reinforcement for the therapist himself is his success in manipulating human behavior.

While the issue of behavior control first arose in regard to psychotherapy, it is now far broader and covers other areas such as operant conditioning, teaching machines, hypnosis, sensory deprivation, subliminal stimulation, and similar studies. There is considerable public interest, concern, and misunderstanding about the range and power of psychological findings.

*   *   *

How does a "psychology of behavior control" differ from the science of psychology? The differences are subtle, but important. A science of psychology seeks to determine the lawful relationships in behavior. The orientation of a "psychology of behavior control" is that these lawful relationships are to be used to deliberately influence, control, or change behavior. This implies a manipulator or controller, and with it an ethical and value system of the controller. As we learn more about human behavior, it is increasingly obvious that it is controllable by various techniques. Does this mean that we, as psychologists, researchers, or even therapists, *at this point* could modify somebody's behavior in any way we wanted? The answer is no, primarily because research into the techniques of control thus far is at the elementary stage. Science moves at a very rapid pace, however, and now is the time to concern ourselves with this problem before basic knowledge about the techniques overwhelms us.

The obvious analogy is with the atomic physicists, who have been very concerned about the application of their scientific findings. Of course, many of the comments from the physical scientists have come *since* the dropping of the first atom bomb. The concern of the psychologist must come before the techniques of behavior control are fully developed. *Public* concern is more readily discernible at this point as shown by popular articles (Brecher & Brecher, 1961) and the cries of indignation some years back when subliminal stimulation was a going fad.

Carl Rogers has recently been quoted as saying that:

> To hope that the power which is being made available by the behavioral sciences will be exercised by the scientists, or by a benevolent group, seems to me to be a hope little supported by either recent or distant history. It seems far more likely that behavioral scientists, holding their present attitudes, will be in the position of the German rocket scientists specializing in guided missiles. . . . If behavioral scientists are concerned solely with advancing their science, it seems most probable that they will serve the purpose of whatever group has the power [Brecher & Brecher, 1961].

This rather pessimistic quotation is from a popular article in a recent issue of *Harper's* magazine. The authors cite this and other research, particularly the work of Olds on brain stimulation, as evidence for deep concern about the role of the behavioral scientist. In what is perhaps an overdramatization of the situation, yet one which may legitimately express lay concern, they conclude that:

> New methods of controlling behavior now emerging from the laboratory may soon add an awe-inspiring power to enslave us all with our own engineered consent.

Oppenheimer (1956), in comparing the responsibility of the physicist with that of the psychologist, makes the cogent point that:

> The psychologist can hardly do anything without realizing that for him the acquisition of knowledge opens up the most terrifying pros-

pects of controlling what people do and how they think and how they behave and how they feel.

We can approach the problem of social responsibility by asking three basic questions:

1. Is human behavior controllable? Overwhelming experimental evidence in fields of motivation, conditioning, and personality development indicates that this is true.

2. If so, is it desirable or wise for psychologists to continue research in these fields? Psychologists have no choice but to continue their research. The findings can be used just as meaningfully to help man as to hinder him. Further, methods of counter control can be developed. The danger is *not* in the research findings but in their potential misuse.

3. What safeguards can be incorporated into this type of research? The answer to this is the crux of the psychologist's dilemma. First, a code of ethics such as that of the APA is a good first step, but certainly not enough. An ethical code merely says that the psychologist will not deliberately misuse his findings. It does not go into the more basic question of the psychologist or behavior controller's value system. If we see him as one who is in a position to change or modify other's behavior, this implies a value decision as to what is "good behavior," what is "mental health," and what is desirable adjustment. To deny control is to do a disservice and, in effect, to hide one's head in the sand like the proverbial ostrich. The fact that the behavior controllers are professional individuals is no guarantee that behavior control will not be misused. We have only to turn to the role of German physicians in medical atrocities as evidence of misuse by a supposedly professional group.

Berg (1954) goes into one aspect of the ethical and value problem in discussing principles that should guide the use of human subjects in psychological research. His concern with the problem is an outgrowth of the "barbarous medical experiments" performed on human subjects by Nazi physicians in the name of science. These German physicians were not mere tools, but were leaders in their profession. Berg suggests that future researchers using human subjects adhere to the principles of "consent," "confidence," and "standard procedure." He cites the basic principles governing permissible government experiments laid down at the Nuremberg trials. These are relevant for future discussion of the kinds of behavior permissible, or not permissible, to behavior controllers.

Basically, they are similar to the principles that Roe (1959) pointed out, namely, that *awareness* is a major ingredient in defense against manipulation. Roe makes pertinent comments in stressing the need for man to be aware of himself and the world around him:

Awareness of our own needs and attitudes is our most effective instrument for maintaining our own integrity and control over our own reactions.

Roe contends that the psychologist's role in changing society should be an active one. She cites a talk by Halpern who reported a survey which showed that an overwhelming number of our young psychologists were interested only in the practice of therapy. Halpern is quoted as follows:

> It seems to me that there is something a bit amiss with a group of scientists who are so overwhelmingly service oriented and who, recognizing that life adjustment has been increasingly complex and difficult, offer to cure the ills resulting from the present state of affairs, but do little or nothing to help society learn how best to meet their interpersonal, emotional and social problems so that the present seemingly all-pervasive disturbances may be avoided.

A somewhat similar view is expressed by Cattell (1948), who also calls for research into ethical values and feels that moral laws can be derived from psychological and physiological investigation of living matter. He does not accept the viewpoint, which he attibutes to a majority of psychologists and most laymen, that ethical values lie outside the realm of science. Creegan (1958) also concerns himself with the need for scientific investigation of ethical problems. In comparing the responsibility of the psychologist with that of the atomic physicist he points out that:

> Psychology does not produce nuclear warheads, nor does it produce the apocalyptic birds which may take them to a selected target, but psychology is concerned with human decisions. . . . The greatest power in the world is the power of rational decision. Atomic physics deals with the release of great forces, but answers to ethical questions may be the decisive ones for the future of humanity.

Creegan further goes into questions of whether force and hidden persuasion ought to be used for a good cause. Once we have committed ourselves on economic, social, and religious problems, how should we go about implementing our ideals? How does the psychologist define "the good life"? Does the psychologist constitute an ethical elite? Creegan points out that at present it is the physicist who communicates with the public about moral problems, rather than the psychologist. Muller (1958) also feels that values are a legitimate source of scientific investigation. He disagrees with those who say that man's values are determined by a higher authority outside of himself or those who say that values are a private matter. But Muller is a biologist, not a psychologist.

The attacks on psychological investigators of behavior control are often quite unfair. For example, Krutch (1954) is highly critical of the implications of Skinner's *Walden Two* because of a fear that social control will pass into the hands of experimentalists who are not concerned with moral issues. Yet it is often these experimenters who are most concerned with value problems and who are in a position to approach on an objective basis the whole question of moral and value issues.

* * *

We would suggeest two major steps be taken at this point. The first is to develop techniques of approaching experimentally the basic problem of social and ethical issues involved in behavior control. One initial approach would be to investigate the attitudes and fantasies of experimenters and therapists toward their own role as behavior controllers in studies in which the effectiveness of their influence can be readily tested. As an example, in our laboratory we are presently devising ways of measuring attitudes toward mental health, "the good life," and applications of science. Fantasy behavior will be elicited in response to special stimuli and reports of role perception and role reaction will be obtained from therapists and from experimenters in psychotherapy, verbal conditioning, and other behavior controlling experiments. The attitude measures will be associated with behavioral ratings of these "controllers" and subject responsivity to them. These studies are undertaken within a framework of investigating the variables that go into resisting influence situations.

A second major step in dealing with this problem is communication between the general public and the research investigators. In this field, particularly, researchers must keep in contact with each other. Any kind of research which is kept secret, such as work in sensory deprivation, is to be deplored. Furthermore, it is the psychologist-researcher who should undertake the task of contact with the public rather than leaving it to sensationalists and popularizers.

In summary, behavior control represents a relatively new, important, and very useful development in psychological research. It also may be horribly misused unless the psychologist is constantly alert to what is taking place in society and unless he is active in investigating and controlling the social uses of behavior control.

REFERENCES

BANDURA, A. Psychotherapy as a learning process. *Psychol. Bull.*, 1961, **58**, 143–159.

BERG, I. A. The use of human subjects in psychological research. *Amer. Psychologist*, 1954, **9**, 108–111.

BRECHER, RUTH, & BRECHER, E. The happiest creatures on earth? *Harper's*, 1961, **222**, 85–90.

CATTELL, R. B. Ethics and the social sciences. *Amer. Psychologist*, 1948, **3**, 193–198.

CREEGAN, R. F. Concerning professional ethics. *Amer. Psychologist*, 1958, **13**, 272–275.

FRANK, J. D. *Persuasion and healing: a comparative study of psychotherapy.* Baltimore: Johns Hopkins Press, 1961.

HOLT, R. R., & LUBORSKY, L. *Personality patterns of psychiatrists.* New York: Basic Books, 1958.

JOURARD, S. I-thou relationship versus manipulation in counseling and psychotherapy. *J. indiv. Psychol.*, 1959, **15**, 174–179.

JOURARD, S. On the problem of reinforcement by the psychotherapist of healthy behavior in the patient. In F. J. Shaw (Ed.), *Behavioristic approaches to counseling and psychotherapy: A Southeastern Psychological Association symposium.* University: Univer. Alabama Press, 1961.

KANFER, F. H. Comments on learning in psychotherapy. *Psychol. Rep.*, 1961, **9**, 681–699.

KELLY, E. L., & FISKE, D. W. *The prediction of performance in clinical psychology.* Ann Arbor: Univer. Michigan Press, 1951.

KRASNER, L. Studies of the conditioning of verbal behavior. *Psychol. Bull.*, 1958, **55**, 148–170.

KRASNER, L. The therapist as a social reinforcement machine. Paper presented to second Conference on Research in Psychotherapy, Chapel Hill, University of North Carolina, May 1961.

KRUTCH, J. W. *The measure of man.* New York: Bobbs-Merrill, 1954.

LOWE, C. M. Value orientations: An ethical dilemma. *Amer. Psychologist*, 1959, **14**, 687–693.

MARMOR, J. Psychoanalytic therapy as an educational process: Common denominators in the therapeutic approaches of different psychoanalytic "schools." Paper presented to the Academy of Psychoanalysis, Chicago, May 1961.

MAY, R. Historical and philosophical presuppositions for understanding therapy. In O. H. Mowrer (Ed.) *Psychotherapy theory and research.* New York: Ronald, 1953.

MULLER, H. J. Human values in relation to evolution. *Science*, 1958, **127**, 625–629.

OPPENHEIMER, J. R. Analogy in science. *Amer. Psychologist*, 1956, **11**, 127–135.

PAPANEK, H. Ethical values in psychotherapy. *J. indiv. Psychol.*, 1958, **14**, 160–166.

PATTERSON, C. H. The place of values in counseling and psychotherapy. *J. counsel. Psychol.*, 1958, **5**, 216–223.

ROE, ANNE. Man's forgotten weapon. *Amer. Psychologist*, 1959, **14**, 261–266.

ROGERS, C. R. Persons or science: A philosophical question. *Amer. Psychologist,* 1955, **10**, 267–278.

ROGERS, C. R., & SKINNER, B. F. Some issues concerning the control of human behavior: A symposium. *Science,* 1956, **124**, 1057–1066.

ROSENTHAL, D. Changes in some moral values following psychotherapy. *J. consult. Psychol.,* 1955, **19**, 431–436.

ROTTER, J. B. Psychotherapy. *Annu. Rev. Psychol.,* 1961, **11**, 318–414.

SALZINGER, K. Experimental manipulation of verbal behavior: A review. *J. gen. Psychol.,* 1959, **61**, 65–94.

SHAFFER, L. F. Of whose reality I cannot doubt. *Amer. Psychologist,* 1953, **8**, 608–623.

SKINNER, B. F. *Walden two.* New York: Macmillan, 1948.

SKINNER, B. F. *Science and human behavior.* New York: Macmillan, 1953.

VANDENBERG, S. G. Great expectations or the future of psychology (as seen in science fiction). *Amer. Psychologist,* 1956, **11**, 339–342.

WATSON, G. Moral issues in psychotherapy. *Amer. Psychologist,* 1958, **13**, 574–576.

WHITEHORN, J. C. Goals of psychotherapy. In E. A. Rubinstein & M. B. Parloff (Eds.) *Research in psychotherapy.* Washington, D. C.: American Psychological Association, 1959.

Further readings

General references on behavior control

ANDREWS, L., & KARLINS, M. *Requiem for democracy?* New York: Holt, Rinehart & Winston, 1971 (see Chapter 1).

FARBER, S., & WILSON, R. (Eds.). *The control of the mind.* New York: McGraw-Hill, 1961.

KARLINS, M., & ABELSON, H. *Persuasion.* New York: Springer, 1970.

LONDON, P. *Behavior control.* New York: Harper & Row, 1969.

QUARTON, G. Deliberate efforts to control human behavior and modify personality. *Daedalus,* 1967, **96,** 837–853.

ULRICH, R., STACHNIK, T., & MABRY, J. (Eds.). *Control of human behavior.* Glenview, Ill.: Scott, Foresman, 1966.

Behavior modification

BRAWLEY, E., HARRIS, F., ALLEN, K., FLEMING, R., & PETERSON, R. Behavior modification of an autistic child. *Behavioral Science,* 1969, **14,** 87–97.

GOORNEY, A. Treatment of a compulsive horse race gambler by aversion therapy. *British Journal of Psychiatry,* 1968, **114,** 329–333.

HAMBLIN, R., BUCKHOLDT, D., BUSHELL, D., ELLIS, E., & FERRITOR, D. Changing the game from "get the teacher" to "learn." *Transaction,* January 1969, 20–31.

KRASNER, L., & ULLMANN, L. (Eds.). *Research in behavior modification.* New York: Holt, Rinehart & Winston, 1965.

LENT, J. Mimosa cottage: Experiment in hope. *Psychology Today,* 1968, **2,** 51–58.

Brain stimulation

DELGADO, J. *Physical control of the mind.* New York: Harper & Row, 1969.

HEATH, R. Electrical self-stimulation of the brain in man. *American Journal of Psychiatry,* 1963, **120,** 571–577.

OLDS, J., & MILNER, P. Positive reinforcement produced by electrical stimulation of septal area and other regions of rat brain. *Journal of Comparative and Physiological Psychology,* 1954, **47,** 419–427.

PENFIELD, W. The interpretive cortex. *Science,* 1959, **129,** 1719–1725.

Genetic engineering

LEDERBERG, J. Experimental genetics and human evolution. *Bulletin of the Atomic Scientists,* 1966, **22,** 4–11.

ROSLANSKY, J. (Ed.). *Genetics and the future of man.* New York: Appleton-Century-Crofts, 1966.

SONNEBORN, T. (Ed.). *Control of human heredity and evolution.* New York: Macmillan, 1965.

Drugs

HIMWICH, H. The new psychiatric drugs. *Scientific American,* 1955, **193,** 80–86.
JACKSON, B. White-collar pill party. *Atlantic Monthly,* August, 1966, 35–40.
JARVIK, M. The psychopharmacological revolution. *Psychology Today,* 1967, **1,** 51–59.
TART, C. (Ed.). *States of altered consciousness.* New York: Wiley, 1969. (For the reader who seeks additional information on LSD, an excellent bibliography on the drug is provided on pp. 480–483.)

Advertising

MCGINNIS, J. *The selling of the president.* New York: Trident, 1968.

Environmental design

SOMMER, R. *Personal space: the behavioral basis of design.* Englewood Cliffs, N.J.: Prentice-Hall, 1969.
STUDER, R., & STEA, D. Architectural programming, environmental design, and human behavior. *Journal of Social Issues,* 1966, **22,** 127–136.

Brainwashing

LYNN, R. Brainwashing techniques in leadership and childrearing. *British Journal of Social and Clinical Psychology,* 1966, **5,** 270–273.
SARGANT, W. *Battle of the mind.* London: Heinemann, 1957.

Hypnosis

BROWN, J. A. *Techniques of persuasion.* Baltimore: Penguin, 1963.
STACHOWIAK, J., & MOSS, C. Hypnotic alteration of social attitudes. *Journal of Personality and Social Psychology,* 1965, **2,** 77–83.

Truth serums

FREEDMAN, L. "Truth" drugs. *Scientific American,* 1960, **202,** 145–154.

Behavior control via interpersonal relations

ASCH, S. Studies of independence and conformity: I. A minority of one against a uanimous majority. *Psychological Monographs,* 1965, **70** (416), #9.
BRYAN, J., & TEST, M. Models and helping: Naturalistic studies in aiding behavior. *Journal of Personality and Social Psychology,* 1967, **6,** 400–407.
COLEMAN, J., KATZ, E., & MENZEL, H. The diffusion of an innovation among physicians. *Sociometry,* 1957, **20,** 253–270.
DORNBUSCH, S. The military academy as an assimilating institution. *Social Forces,* 1955, **33,** 316–321.
FESTINGER, L., SCHACHTER, S., & BACK, K. *Social pressures in informal groups: A study of human factors in housing.* New York: Harper, 1950.
FREED, A., CHANDLER, P., MOUTON, J., & BLAKE, R. Stimulus and background factors in sign violation. *Journal of Personality,* 1955, **23,** 499 (abstract).
HASTORF, A., & CANTRIL, H. They saw a game: A case study. *Journal of Abnormal and Social Psychology,* 1954, **49,** 129–134.

HOMANS, G. The Western Electric researches. In Hoslett (Ed.), *Human factors in management*. New York: Harper & Brothers, 1951.

KELLEY, H. Salience of membership and resistance to change of group-anchored attitudes. *Human Relations*, 1955, **8**, 275–289.

KIMBRELL, D., & BLAKE, R. Motivational factors in the violation of a prohibition. *Journal of Abnormal and Social Psychology*, 1958, **56**, 132–133.

KOSLIN, B., HAARLOW, R., KARLINS, M., & PARGAMENT, R. Predicting group status from members' cognitions. *Sociometry*, 1968, **31**, 64–75.

LAMBERT, W., LIBMAN, E., & POSER, E. The effect of increased salience of a membership group on pain tolerance. *Journal of Personality*, 1960, **28**, 350–357.

MILGRAM, S. Behavioral study of obedience. *Journal of Abnormal and Social Psychology*, 1963, **67**, 371–378.

ROY, D. Quota restriction and goldbricking in a machine shop. *American Journal of Sociology*, 1952, **57**, 427–442.

SHERIF, M. Social factors in perception. In Swanson, Newcomb & Hartley (Eds.), *Readings in social psychology*. New York: Holt, 1952.

TRIPLETT, N. The dynamogenic factors in pacemaking and competition. *American Journal of Psychology*, 1897, **9**, 507–533.

WHYTE, W. The outgoing life. *Fortune*, July 1953.

Dispositional and cultural factors in behavior control

ALLPORT, G., & PETTIGREW, T. Cultural influence on the perception of movement: The trapezoidal illusion among Zulus. *Journal of Abnormal and Social Psychology*, 1957, **55**, 104–113.

HALL, E. *The silent language*. Garden City, N.Y.: Doubleday, 1959.

HALL, E. *The hidden dimension*. New York: Doubleday, 1966.

HESTON, L. The genetics of schizophrenia and schizoid disease. *Science*, 1970, **167**, 249–256.

KLINE, N., & TENNEY, A. Constitutional factors in the prognosis of schizophrenia. *American Journal of Psychiatry*, 1950, **107**, 432–441.

LINDZEY, A. Morphology and behavior. In G. Lindzey & C. Hall (Eds.), *Theories of personality: Primary sources and research*. New York: Wiley, 1965.

SEGALL, M., CAMPBELL, D., & HERSKOVITS, M. *The influence of culture on visual perception*. New York: Bobbs-Merrill, 1966.

WHORF, B. Blazing icicles. *The Hartford Agent*, 1941, **32**, 173–176.

Behavior control and social welfare

ANDREWS, L., & KARLINS, M. *Requiem for democracy?* New York: Holt, Rinehart & Winston, 1971.

SKINNER, B. *Science and human behavior*. New York: Macmillan, 1953.

SKINNER, B. Freedom and the control of men. *The American Scholar*, 1955–1956. **25**, 47–65.

Karlins

Man controlled

DATE DUE